Enjoy Spanish

Juan Kattán-Ibarra
Revised by Bruno Paul

Enjoy Spanish

Juan Kattán-Ibarra

Revised by
Bruno Paul

First published in Great Britain in 2014 by Hodder and Stoughton. An Hachette UK company.

British Library Cataloguing in Publication Data: a catalogue record for this title is available from the British Library.

Library of Congress Catalog Card Number: on file.

9781473603028

10 9 8 7 6 5 4 3 2 1

Cover image © Ruth Tomlinson/Robert Harding

Typeset by Integra Software Services Pvt. Ltd, Pondicherry, India.

Printed and bound in Great Britain by CPI Group (UK) Ltd., Croydon, CRO 4YY

John Murray Learning policy is to use papers that are natural, renewable and recyclable products and made from wood grown in sustainable forests. The logging and manufacturing processes are expected to conform to the environmental regulations of the country of origin.

John Murray Learning

338 Euston Road

London NW1 3BH

www.hodder.co.uk

Acknowledgements

The author and publishers would like to acknowledge the following for use of their material in this volume: revistas Cambio 16, Tiempo, Buena Salud, Quo (de divulgación científica), Guía del Ocio; diarios Ya, El Mundo, Diario 16, El Mercurio (Chile), Excelsior (México); radios San Cristóbal, El Conquistador, Clásica (Chile), La Romántica (México); Universidad de Málaga, RENFE, OMIC.

Contents

Meet the author

I am an experienced teacher of Spanish and the author of a number of best-selling Spanish courses. I began my career teaching Spanish in the United Kingdom in 1975, at Ealing College in London, and also acted as an external examiner in Spanish for various London examinations boards.

My first Spanish course was published in London in 1978, in a writing career which continues to this day. I have written or co-written courses in the Teach Yourself series including *Complete Spanish*, *Get Started in Latin American Spanish*, *Complete Latin American Spanish*, *Get Talking Spanish*, *Keep Talking Spanish* and *Essential Spanish Grammar*. Some of my books in the Teach Yourself series have been successfully adapted for use in other countries, among them France, Germany and Italy. I have also written books for other publishers, including the BBC, Routledge and McGraw-Hill. I am now a full-time author and very much look forward to being your guide for your continuing journey into the Spanish language. **¡Vamos!**

Juan Kattán-Ibarra

Introduction

Welcome to *Enjoy Spanish*. If you have already completed a foundation course in Spanish or have learnt the language through contact with Spanish speakers, and you are looking to build on what you know and advance your communication skills, then *Enjoy Spanish* is the right course for you. Perhaps you also wish to revise some of the forms and constructions you learnt some time ago, or explore areas of the language that you are less familiar with. This course offers you ample opportunity to do this in a systematic way, covering a number of key points, with language and usage always going hand in hand.

Although the course has been designed especially for people studying on their own, the material and exercises will also lend themselves to classroom use. Students who are taking evening classes in Spanish, or who are preparing for examinations where the emphasis is on communicative skills, will find that this course can help them achieve their objectives. By the end of *Enjoy Spanish* you will have increased your capacity to understand the spoken and written language, and furthered your ability to communicate with Spanish speakers, orally or in writing.

How the book works

The course consists of a book and audio component, organized in:

▶ 12 thematic units, each with a self-assessment test at the end

▶ a reference section at the back of the book.

THE UNITS

The units are your language building blocks and are organized as follows:

Statement of aims

Tells you what you can expect to learn, in terms of what you will be able to do in Spanish by the end of the unit.

Conversations

The language focus in each unit is derived from two or more conversations which are included on the audio and also printed in the book with a preview of vocabulary. The language in the conversations covers all the basic structures and verb tenses, including more advanced forms such as the subjunctive. Each conversation is followed by one or two comprehension exercises focusing on the content of the dialogue.

New expressions

All new phrases and expressions with their English translation are listed thematically in this section.

Language discovery

In the Language discovery section you learn about the forms of the language, thus enabling you to review structures you may already know a well as learn new ones.

Practice

In the Practice section you will have ample opportunity to use the language that has been presented and to work specifically on your speaking, reading and writing skills. This section also includes **¡A escuchar!**, listening comprehension exercises which are designed to increase your capacity to understand spoken Spanish. Transcripts of these exercises are at the back of the book. A Key to the exercises will also be found at the back of the book.

Test yourself

A Test yourself section at the end of each unit will help you to assess what you have learnt, and allow you to judge whether you have successfully improved your language and communication skills. The answers to these self-assessment tests will be found in the Key to the exercises.

Tips

At different stages throughout the unit you will find tip boxes with further information related to the Spanish language and culture. There are also useful tips for dealing with new language.

REFERENCE

At the end of the book there are sections which you can use for reference:

▶ a key to all the activities in the units, including Test yourself

▶ transcripts of the listening comprehension **¡A escuchar!** exercises

▶ a list of common irregular verbs

▶ Spanish–English vocabulary

▶ English–Spanish vocabulary

▶ a Grammar index.

How to use *Enjoy Spanish*

Make sure at the beginning of each unit that you are clear about what you can expect to learn.

First listen to the conversations on the audio. Try to get the gist of what is being said before you look at the printed text. Then go over the key vocabulary in order to study the conversations in more detail. If you want an explanation of new language points at this stage, study the relevant paragraphs in the **Language discovery** section.

You must try to make the most of the audio material by listening to the conversations at every opportunity – sitting on the train or bus, waiting at the dentist's or stuck in a traffic jam, using what would otherwise be 'dead' time. After you have listened to the conversations, go through the comprehension questions and check that you understood what was said. The answers to these are in the **Key to the exercises**.

Move on next to the **New expressions**. Try covering up the English translations and producing the English equivalents of the Spanish. If you find that relatively easy, go on to cover the Spanish sentences and produce the Spanish equivalents of the English. You will probably find this more difficult. Trying to recall the context in which words and phrases were used may help you learn them better.

You can then study the explanations in the **Language discovery** section in a systematic way. We have tried to make these as user-friendly as possible, since we recognize that many people find grammar daunting. But in the end, it is up to you just how much time you spend on studying and sorting out the grammar points. Some people find that they can do better by getting an ear for what sounds right. Others need to know in detail how the language is put together.

You will then be ready to move on to the **Practice** section and work through the activities alone, with a study partner, or in a group. Most of the activities are communicative in nature, focusing on the aims outlined at the start of the unit. You are the main actor here, so carry out the instructions given for each exercise, which may involve understanding and acting on what a Spanish speaker has said, playing a role, writing a letter, helping a travelling companion who doesn't know any Spanish, and so on.

Some of the activities are listen-only exercises. The temptation may be to go straight to the transcriptions at the back of the book, but try not to do this. The whole point of listening exercises is to improve your listening skills. You will not do this by reading first. The transcriptions are there merely to help you if you get stuck.

Each unit contains, within the **¡A escuchar!** section, longer, authentic reading passages designed to help you increase your passive vocabulary and comprehension of authentic Spanish. Most of these deal with important cultural points related to either Spain or Latin America. Read them through and answer the questions which either precede or follow them. You don't need to understand every single word here, but don't hesitate to use your dictionary if you want to study the passage in more depth.

As you work your way through the activities, check your answers carefully in the **Key to the exercises** at the back of the book. It is easy to overlook your own mistakes. If you have a study buddy, it's a good idea to check each other's work. Most of the exercises have fixed answers, but a few are more open-ended. Most of these come with a model answer which you can adapt for your own purposes.

Before you move on to a new unit, go through the **Test yourself** section, which will allow you to assess what you have learnt in the unit. You can check your answers in the **Key to the exercises** section. If you did well in the test, move on to the next unit; if your performance was not satisfactory, study the relevant information in the **Language discovery** again until you feel confident that you have learnt it.

Abbreviations

m = masculine gender of noun

f = feminine gender of noun

pl = plural form

V = **verdadero** *true*

F = **falso** *false*

sing = singular

Symbols

Throughout the pages of *Enjoy Spanish*, you will find a system of icons to identify the purpose of a section or activity. They are:

 Play the audio track

 Figure something out for yourself

 Learn key words and expressions

 Exercises coming up!

 Write and make notes

 Read for gist and detail

 Speak Spanish out loud (even if you're alone)

 Check your Spanish ability (no cheating)

Learn to learn

The Discovery method

There are lots of philosophies and approaches to language learning, some practical, some quite unconventional, and far too many to list here. Perhaps you know of a few, or even have some techniques of your own. In this book we have incorporated the **Discovery method** of learning, a sort of DIY approach to language learning. What this means is that you will be encouraged throughout the course to engage your mind and figure out the language for yourself, through identifying patterns, understanding grammar concepts, noticing words that are similar to English, and more. This method promotes language awareness, a critical skill in acquiring a new language. As a result of your own efforts, you will be able to better retain what you have learnt, use it with confidence, and, even better, apply those same skills to continuing to learn the language (or, indeed, another one) on your own after you've finished this course.

Everyone can succeed in learning a language – the key is to know how to learn it. Learning is more than just reading or memorizing grammar and vocabulary. It's about being an active learner, learning in real contexts, and, most importantly, using what you've learnt in different situations. Simply put, if you **figure something out for yourself**, you're more likely to understand it. And when you use what you've learnt, you're more likely to remember it.

And because many of the essential but (let's admit it!) challenging details, such as grammar rules, are introduced through the **Discovery method**, you'll have more fun while learning. Soon, the language will start to make sense and you'll be relying on your own intuition to construct original sentences independently, not just listening and repeating.

Enjoy yourself!

Become a successful language learner

1 MAKE A HABIT OUT OF LEARNING

Study a little every day, between 20 and 30 minutes is ideal. Give yourself **short-term goals**, e.g. work out how long you'll spend on a particular unit and work within this time limit; **create a study habit**. Try to **create an environment conducive to learning** which is calm and quiet and free from distractions. As you study, do not worry about your mistakes or the things you can't remember or understand. Languages settle gradually in the brain. Just **give yourself enough time** and you will succeed.

2 MAXIMIZE YOUR EXPOSURE TO THE LANGUAGE

As well as using this course, you can listen to radio, watch television or read online articles and blogs. Do you have a personal passion or hobby? Does a news story interest you? Try to access Spanish information about them. It's entertaining and you'll become used to a range of writing and speaking styles.

3 VOCABULARY

Group new words under **generic categories**, e.g. *computers, phone phrases*, **situations** in which they occur, e.g. under *weather* you can write **soleado** *sunny*, **despejado** *clear*, **nuboso** *cloudy*, and **functions**, e.g. *indicating frequency, expressing hope, how to sound surprised, making complaints*.

▶ Write the words over and over again. Keep lists on your smartphone or tablet, but remember to switch the keyboard language so you can include all accents and special characters.

▶ Listen to the audio several times and say the words out loud as you hear or read them.

▶ Cover up the English side of the vocabulary list and see if you can remember the meaning of words. Do the same for the Spanish. Work your way up to phrases and whole sentences.

▶ Create mind maps.

▶ Flip the language settings of your browser to Spanish and navigate as is your custom.

▶ **Experiment with words**. Look for patterns in words, e.g. try to learn words in families, e.g. **pueblo, poblado, población, despoblado**, etc.

4 GRAMMAR

Experiment with grammar rules. Sit back and reflect on how the rules of Spanish compare with your own language or other languages you may already speak.

▶ Use known vocabulary to practise new grammar structures.

▶ When you learn a new verb form, write the conjugation of several different verbs you know that follow the same form.

5 PRONUNCIATION

▶ Study individual sounds, then full words. Make a list of those words that give you trouble and practise them.

▶ Repeat the conversations line by line and try to mimic what you hear.

▶ Record yourself if you can.

6 LISTENING AND READING

The conversations in this course include questions to help guide you in your understanding. But you can do more:

▶ **Imagine the situation**. Think about where a scene is taking place and make educated guesses, e.g. a conversation in a snack bar is likely to be about food.

▶ **Guess the meaning of key words before you look them up**. When there are key words you don't understand, try to guess what they mean from the context. If you're listening to a Spanish speaker and cannot get the gist of a whole passage because of one word or phrase, try to repeat that word with a questioning tone; the speaker will probably paraphrase it.

7 SPEAKING

Practice makes perfect. The most successful language learners know how to overcome their inhibitions and keep going.

▶ When you conduct simple transactions in your daily life, pretend that you have to do it in Spanish, e.g. *getting a doctor's appointment, changing your hotel reservations, calling for repairs on your house or your car*, and so on.

▶ Rehearse the dialogues out loud, then try to replace sentences with ones that are true for you.

8 LEARN FROM YOUR ERRORS

▶ Making errors is part of any learning process, so don't be so worried about making mistakes that you won't say anything unless you are sure it is correct. This leads to a vicious circle: the less you say, the less practice you get and the more mistakes you make.

▶ Note the seriousness of errors. Many errors are not serious as they do not affect the meaning.

9 LEARN TO COPE WITH UNCERTAINTY

▶ Don't give up if you don't understand everything. Keep following the conversation for a while. The speaker might repeat or paraphrase what you didn't understand and the conversation can carry on.

▶ **Keep talking.** The best way to improve your fluency in Spanish is to seize every opportunity to speak. If you get stuck for a particular word, don't let the conversation stop; paraphrase or use the words you do know, even if you have to simplify what you want to say.

▶ **Don't over-use your dictionary.** Resist the temptation to look up every word you don't know. Read the same passage several times, concentrating on trying to get the gist of it. If after the third time some words still prevent you from making sense of the passage, look them up in the dictionary.

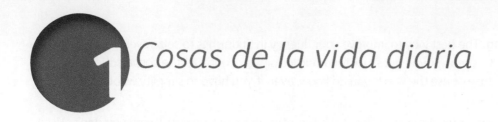

1 Cosas de la vida diaria

In this unit you will learn how to:
▶ *talk about daily activities and habits.*
▶ *say how often you do something.*
▶ *relate a sequence of events.*

CEFR: *Can understand in detail a wide range of texts likely to be encountered in social life (B2); can fluently sustain straightforward descriptions, including a linear sequence of points (B1).*

Conversations

1 ¿QUÉ SUELES HACER? *WHAT DO YOU USUALLY DO?*

Carlos Salinas, escritor, es entrevistado por una periodista de una revista española. En una parte de la entrevista, Carlos comenta acerca de su vida diaria.

1 01.01 **First, look at the vocabulary, then try to answer this question as you listen: Is Carlos generally satisfied with his freelance life?**

vida diaria (f)	*daily living*
¿qué sueles hacer?	*what do you usually do?*
cumplir un horario (m)	*to keep to a timetable*
vérselas con (uno)	*to deal with (someone)*
gruñón/a	*grumbling*
de un lado a otro	*from one end to the other*
en cuanto a	*as regards*
imponer	*to impose*
darse una ducha (f)	*to take a shower*
ser aficionado/a	*to be fond of, to like*

Periodista	Carlos, a veces la gente se pregunta cómo es la vida diaria de un escritor, que no tiene que salir de su casa ni cumplir un horario o vérselas con un jefe autoritario y gruñón.
Carlos	Pues mira, es verdad que trabajar en casa tiene sus grandes ventajas, no tienes que perder el tiempo yendo de un lado a otro de la ciudad en el coche, el metro o lo que sea. Ahora, en cuanto a lo del horario, es cierto que a mí nadie me impone un horario de trabajo determinado como suele ocurrirle a casi todo el mundo. Pero el horario me lo impongo yo mismo. Soy una persona bastante disciplinada. Suelo levantarme sobre las siete de la mañana, me

doy una ducha y luego bebo un café. No acostumbro (a) comer mucho por la mañana. A veces, unas tostadas o algunas pastas. A las ocho me siento frente al ordenador y no paro hasta el mediodía . . .

Periodista ¿Te molesta que interrumpan tu trabajo?

Carlos Sí, pero, vamos, no suele ocurrir. Mi familia y mis amistades conocen muy bien mis hábitos y nunca me llaman por la mañana, a no ser que sea para algo importante. Por la tarde, trabajo menos intensamente.

Periodista ¿Qué sueles hacer por la noche?

Carlos Bueno, yo soy un gran aficionado a la música, principalmente al jazz. A menudo, vienen amigos a casa por la noche, escuchamos música, tomamos unas copas, charlamos . . . A veces, vamos al cine o a cenar fuera . . .

Periodista ¿Cambiarías tu vida por la de una persona normal?

Carlos No, definitivamente no, prefiero seguir haciendo lo que hago.

2 Answer the following questions in Spanish.

   a ¿Qué ventajas ve Carlos en trabajar en casa?

   b ¿Cómo se describe Carlos?

   c ¿Qué hace a las ocho de la mañana?

   d ¿Por qué nadie suele interrumpir su trabajo?

   e ¿Qué hace normalmente por la noche?

> **LANGUAGE TIP**
> **Sí, pero vamos, no suele ocurrir.** In this context **pero vamos** is a filler, used to buy thinking time in the conversation, just as *you know* in English.

3 Match these expressions with their meaning:

   a ¿Te molesta que interrumpan?   **1** whatever it may be

   b o lo que sea   **2** unless it is . . .

   c a no ser que sea . . .   **3** Does it bother you to be interrupted?

> **LANGUAGE TIP**
> Note the use of the present subjunctive in these phrases. In all three cases the subjunctive verb refers to something which is neither a reality nor a fact.

4 01.02 **Role play – Practise talking about your daily activities. Follow the prompts to take part in the conversation. (Answers are given following the pauses on the audio.)**

2 UN DÍA NORMAL *AN ORDINARY DAY*

Alicia Álvarez, ejecutiva de una empresa textil, habla sobre su vida diaria.

1 01.03 **First, look at the vocabulary. Then, as you listen, focus on understanding how long Alicia's typical work day is.**

estar sujeto/a a	*to be tied down*
cubrir	*to cover*
planear	*to programme*
¡qué va!	*certainly not!* (Sometimes used to mean *nonsense!*)
mantenerse en forma	*to keep fit*
relajarse	*to relax*

Periodista	Alicia, ¿cómo es un día normal para una ejecutiva de una gran empresa ?
Alicia	Bueno, difícilmente puedo hablar sobre lo que es un día normal para mí, ya que mis actividades son muchas y muy variadas. Pero, naturalmente, como casi toda la gente que trabaja, estoy sujeta a una cierta rutina que, quiéralo o no, tengo que cumplir. Vivo bastante lejos de la fábrica y por lo general salgo de casa a eso de las ocho, pues si lo hago más tarde el tráfico es fatal. Normalmente, llego a la fábrica sobre las nueve de la mañana. Primero consulto mi agenda para ver qué actividades tendré que cubrir y seguidamente planeo el día con mi secretaria. Hay días de mayor actividad que otros, pero casi siempre estoy muy ocupada.
Periodista	¿Vuelves a casa a comer?
Alicia	No, ¡qué va! Sería imposible, ya que tardaría mucho tiempo. Suelo comer en el restaurante de la empresa que no está nada mal.
Periodista	¿A qué hora vuelves a casa normalmente?
Alicia	Pues, nunca antes de las nueve o las diez de la noche. Lo que pasa es que después de dejar la fábrica hago mis compras o voy a tomar una copa con algún amigo y, de vez en cuando, visito a mis padres.
Periodista	¿Tienes alguna otra actividad, aparte de tu trabajo y tu vida social?
Alicia	Bueno sí, dos veces por semana voy a un gimnasio para mantenerme en forma y relajarme. En verano suelo ir a la piscina los fines de semana.

 2 What phrases have been used in the dialogue to express the following?
   a I can hardly speak . . .
   b Since (or given that) . . .
   c About or around (eight/nine o'clock)
   d It would take me a long time.
   e It's not bad at all.
   f What happens is that . . .
   g To have a drink
   h From time to time

 3 Like o lo que sea in Conversation 1, here are more phrases which use the subjunctive. Can you work out their meaning?

a	quieran o no quieran	*whether they _____ it or not*
b	sea cuando sea	*_____ it may be*
c	diga lo que diga	*whatever he/she _____ say*
d	quiéralo o no	*if I like it or _____*

Note how, in Spanish, repeating the verb has the same effect as saying *when, what* or *if ever* in English.

4

3 ¿QUÉ HACE USTED? *WHAT DO YOU DO?*

Teresa González habla acerca de su vida diaria.

1 01.04 **Look at the vocabulary to spot the words you may not know, then listen. Is Teresa in employment or is she ama de casa (*housewife*)?**

arreglarse	*to get dressed*
rato (m)	*while, moment*
lavar la ropa (f)	*to do the washing*
planchar	*to iron*
coser	*to sew*

Periodista	Teresa, ¿qué hace Vd. en un día normal ?
Teresa	Pues, me levanto a eso de las siete y media para preparar el desayuno para mi marido y mis hijos. Mi marido se va al trabajo a las ocho y media y los chicos salen para el colegio sobre las nueve menos cuarto. Después, me arreglo y salgo a hacer la compra del día. Voy al mercado que está a diez minutos de aquí, a la panadería, dos o tres veces por semana voy al supermercado, vamos, depende de lo que haga falta. Nunca es igual. Luego vuelvo a casa para preparar la comida.
Periodista	¿Sus hijos y su marido vienen a casa a comer?
Teresa	Mis hijos sí, pero mi marido no.
Periodista	¿Y por la tarde, qué hace?
Teresa	Pues, veo un rato la tele, a veces echo una siesta, pero vamos, normalmente no. Siempre hay algo que hacer en casa, lavar la ropa, planchar, coser . . .

2 **Compare Depende de lo que haga falta *It depends on what(ever) we may need* with Hace falta más arroz *We need more rice*. These sentences contain two different forms of the verb hacer. What is the difference in meaning between them?**

> **LANGUAGE TIP**
> Note the use of **para** in: **para preparar el desayuno para mi marido . . ., los chicos salen para el colegio . . .**

3 **Study the conversation once more and then complete the missing information about Teresa's routine. Use your own words if you can.**

a Se levanta a eso de la siete y media para . . .

b Sus chicos salen para . . .

c Después se arregla y sale a . . .

d Luego, vuelve a casa para . . .

e Mira un rato la tele, a veces . . ., pero vamos, normalmente no.

f Siempre hay algo que hacer en casa . . .

NEW EXPRESSIONS

 Look at the Spanish expressions and work out the missing English equivalents. Then mask either column and test your memory.

Talking about daily activities and habits

Suelo levantarme sobre las siete.	*I usually get up at about seven.*
Me doy una ducha.	*I take a shower.*
Bebo un café.	*I have _____*
No acostumbro (a) comer mucho.	*I don't usually _____*
Echo una siesta.	*I have a nap.*

Saying how often you do something

A veces (como) unas tostadas.	*Sometimes I eat some toast.*
Nunca me llaman por la mañana.	*They never call me _____*
A menudo vienen amigos a casa.	*Friends often come to (our) home.*
por lo general	*generally*
de vez en cuando	*from time to time*
generalmente	*_____*
siempre	*always*
normalmente	*_____*
una vez, dos veces por semana	*once, twice a week*
usualmente	*_____*

Relating a sequence of events

Me doy una ducha y luego bebo un café.	*I take a shower and then I drink coffee.*
Primero consulto mi agenda ... seguidamente planeo el día con mi secretaria.	*First I look up in my diary ... then I plan the day with my secretary.*
Después me arreglo.	*Then I get dressed.*
en primer lugar	*in the first place*
primeramente	*firstly, first*
antes que nada	*first of all*
a continuación	*next, immediately after*
finalmente	*_____*
por último	*lastly*

Language discovery

 You have seen this language in action. Now can you work out the rules?

1 Do these two sentences have similar or different meanings?

   a Suele comer en casa con los niños.

   b Acostumbra comer en casa con los niños.

2 Why is the form of the verb tener different in these two sentences?

   a Tengo tiempo para hacer la compra.

   b No creo que tenga tiempo para hacer la compra.

3 How might you translate these sentences?
   a Cuando pueda te llamaré por teléfono.
   b Cuando puedo te llamo por téléfono.

1 TALKING ABOUT ACTIONS YOU DO REGULARLY

a Using the present tense indicative

There are many examples of the use of the present tense in this unit which will help you to revise it. The examples include different types of verbs: **ir**, irregular; **salir**, irregular in the first person singular (**salgo**); **venir**, irregular in the first person singular (**vengo**), and also a stem-changing verb (**e** > **ie**), like **soler** (**o** > **ue**); and **sentarse**, reflexive and stem-changing (**e** > **ie**). Refer to your grammar book if you feel you need to revise non-regular and stem-changing forms.

Vamos **al cine.**	*We go to the cinema.*
Salgo **de casa a eso de las 8.00.**	*I leave the house at about 8.00.*
A menudo *vienen* **amigos a casa.**	*Friends often come to our house.*
Me *siento* **frente al ordenador.**	*I sit in front of the computer.*

b Using soler (o > ue) + infinitive

¿Qué *sueles hacer* **por la noche?**	*What do you usually do in the evening?*
Suelo ir **al cine o a cenar fuera.**	*I usually go to the cinema or to eat out.*

c Acostumbrar (a) + infinitive

Acostumbra (a) trabajar **mucho.**	*He/she usually works a lot.*
No *acostumbro (a) salir* **en verano.**	*I don't usually go away in the summer.*

Acostumbrar is used with the preposition **a** by some speakers, especially in Latin America.

2 THE SUBJUNCTIVE

There are a few examples of the subjunctive in Conversations 1–3, so a general look at its uses and at the forms of the present subjunctive in particular seems appropriate at this stage.

The subjunctive is not a tense but one of three forms or moods of the verb with tenses of its own (present, imperfect, perfect, pluperfect). The other two are the indicative mood (present, preterite, imperfect indicative, etc.) and the imperative mood (used in commands and instructions). The subjunctive is generally used to refer to actions or states which are unreal or which have not yet taken place. If there is certainty, then you must use the indicative mood. Compare the following sentences:

Se alegran cuando *viene* **su abuela.**   *They are glad when their grandmother comes.*
This is a fact, therefore the verb is in the indicative.

Se alegrarán cuando *venga* **su abuela.**   *They'll be glad when their grandmother comes.*
This is not yet a fact, therefore the verb is in the subjunctive.

The subjunctive often occurs in a construction with a main verb, for example **quiero** *I want*, followed by another clause (the subordinate clause) introduced by **que** and a verb in the subjunctive.

No *quiero que* me *interrumpas*.   *I don't want you to interrupt me.*

In this type of construction the subjunctive is dependent on the main verb, which may express a wish (as in the previous example) or uncertainty, hope, need, possibility, permission, prohibition, some kind of emotion, etc. More examples are given with the present subjunctive.

3 THE PRESENT SUBJUNCTIVE

To form the present subjunctive, remove the **-o** of the first person singular of the present indicative and add the appropriate endings: **-e** for **-ar** verbs and **-a** for verbs in **-er** and **-ir** (**hablo > hable, como > coma, vivo > viva, vuelvo > vuelva, tengo > tenga, digo > diga**, etc.)

	hablar	comer	vivir
yo	hable	coma	viva
tú	hables	comas	vivas
él/ella/usted	hable	coma	viva
nosotros	hablemos	comamos	vivamos
vosotros	habléis	comáis	viváis
ellos/ellas/ustedes	hablen	coman	vivan

No quiero que *hables* con ella.   *I don't want you to speak to her.* (wish)

Espero que te lo *comas* todo.   *I hope you eat it all.* (hope)

No creo que *viva* mucho tiempo.   *I don't think he/she'll live long.* (uncertainty)

In positive statements **creer** is followed by an indicative verb:

Creo que *vivirá* muchos años.   *I think he/she'll live for many years.*

A few verbs form the present subjunctive in a different way:

dar *to give*	**dé, des, dé, demos, deis, den**
estar *to be*	**esté, estés, esté, estemos, estéis, estén**
haber *to have*	**haya, hayas, haya, hayamos, hayáis, hayan**
ir *to go*	**vaya, vayas, vaya, vayamos, vayáis, vayan**
saber *to know*	**sepa, sepas, sepa, sepamos, sepáis, sepan**
ser *to be*	**sea, seas, sea, seamos, seáis, sean**

Puede que *estén* en casa.   *They may be at home.* (possibility)

Es posible que ya lo *sepan*.   *It's possible that they may already know.* (possibility)

No me permitirán que *vaya*.   *They won't allow me to go.* (permission)

Me alegra que *seas* sincero.   *I'm glad you're sincere.* (emotion)

4 FURTHER USES OF THE SUBJUNCTIVE

The subjunctive is also used after phrases indicating hope, purpose, concession, condition and time:

Ojalá (que) me *den* un aumento.	*Let's hope they give me an increase.* (hope)
Lo traeré para que lo *veas*.	*I'll bring it so that you can see it.* (purpose)
Iremos aunque *llueva*.	*We'll go even if it rains.* (concession)
Te lo presto siempre que lo *cuides*.	*I'll lend it to you as long as you take care of it.* (condition)
Cuando *lleguen* serviré café.	*When they arrive I'll serve coffee.* (time)

The subjunctive is used with expressions of time only when these refer to the future, otherwise you need the indicative. Compare the last example with the following one:

Cuando *llegan* siempre les sirvo café. *When they arrive I always serve them coffee.*

The above are some of the basic rules governing the use of the subjunctive. The subjunctive is important in Spanish and you may wish to expand on what you have learnt, in which case you would do well to refer to a grammar book, especially one with exercises for you to practise on your own.

Practice

1 Complete this passage with the correct form of the verb in the present tense.

Me llamo Ricardo Aguirre, soy ingeniero y vivo en Bilbao. Trabajo en una fábrica de artículos electrodomésticos. Mis actividades habituales son las siguientes: Normalmente, _____ (despertarse) a las 6.30 de la mañana, luego _____ (levantarse) y _____ (ducharse) y sobre las 7.30 _____ (desayunar) con mi mujer y mis tres hijos. A las 8.30 _____ (salir) de casa para ir a la fábrica. Por lo general _____ (ir) en el coche, pero a veces _____ (coger) el autobús. Al mediodía no _____ (volver) a casa a comer, ya que normalmente yo _____ (almorzar) con unos colegas en un restaurante cerca de la empresa. A las 7.00 _____ (marcharse) a casa, pero de vez en cuando _____ (ir) a un club deportivo donde _____ (jugar) al tenis con algún amigo. Por la noche, después de cenar, a veces _____ (dar) un paseo con mi mujer. Nunca _____ (acostarse) antes de las 12.00.

2 Now relate Ricardo's daily routine as described in the previous passage.

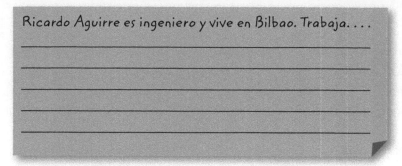

Ricardo Aguirre es ingeniero y vive en Bilbao. Trabaja. . . .

_____

_____

_____

_____

3 Match each word on the left with one of similar meaning on the right.

a normalmente		**1** finalmente
b de vez en cuando		**2** frecuentemente
c antes que nada		**3** a veces
d por último		**4** a continuación
e después		**5** primero
f a menudo		**6** por lo general

4 Imagine a dialogue similar to the ones you have just studied between the same journalist and Carmen Olmo, a secretary. First, you'll need to prepare the questions. Use the familiar form.

a Ask her what time she leaves the house.

b Ask how she goes to work.

c Ask what time she arrives in the office.

d Ask what she does in the morning.

e Ask what time and where she normally has lunch.

f Ask what time she leaves the office.

g Ask what she normally does in the evening.

Now, the following information will help you with the answers.

> Nombre: Carmen Olmo García
>
> Profesión: Secretaria
>
> Actividades diarias:
>
> 1 8.30, salida de casa en dirección a la estación de metro más cercana para ir a la oficina.
>
> 2 8.50–9.00, llegada a la oficina.
>
> 3 Lo que suele hacer en el trabajo: abrir la correspondencia, leerla y clasificarla; escribir las cartas que le dicta su jefe; revisar el correo electrónico; recibir a los clientes de la empresa y fijar citas con el gerente; contestar el teléfono; asistir a reuniones.
>
> 4 1.30, almuerzo con algunos compañeros de trabajo en el bar de la esquina.
>
> 5 7.00, salida de la oficina.
>
> 6 Lo que acostumbra (a) hacer por la noche: cenar, ver la televisión, escuchar música, dar un paseo con su novio.

Check the notes in the **New expressions** and **Language discovery** sections and try using some of the words and constructions you've learnt. In the **Key to the exercises** you will find a basic model dialogue which you may want to look up once you have prepared your own version.

¡A escuchar!

Here is a conversation between Pilar Araya, a teacher from Peru, and her friend Antonio.

5 01.05 **Look at the vocabulary and read the statements before you listen.**

reunión (f)	meeting
acompañar	to accompany
regalo (m)	present
cumpleaños (m)	birthday
¡chao! (esp. Latin America)	bye bye! (familiar)

Now check your understanding. Read each statement, then decide if it is verdadero o falso (*true or false*).

  a Pilar trabaja como profesora.
  b Trabaja seis horas diarias.
  c Empieza a trabajar a las 7.15.
  d Por la tarde no hace nada.
  e Los sábados no trabaja.

> **LEARNING TIP**
> Always preview the vocabulary first. Then try listening to the entire conversation before accessing the script in the **¡A escuchar!** section. Train yourself to only use the text for reading comprehension when you have doubts.

6 01.06 **Role play – You meet Isabel, from Cadiz, at a party in London. Follow the prompts and take part in a conversation with her. Then listen to check and practise your answers out loud.**

You	**(a)** *Ask her what she does.*
Isabel	Soy estudiante. Estudio inglés en un instituto pero solamente por la mañana.
You	**(b)** *Ask her if she comes back home for lunch.*
Isabel	Pues, normalmente no. Suelo comer en un pub, cerca del instituto con mis amigas.
You	**(c)** *Ask her what she usually does in the afternoons.*
Isabel	A veces voy a algún museo o al cine, o simplemente me quedo en casa para ver la televisión o leer. La televisión inglesa es muy buena.
You	**(d)** *Say you also watch television at night but only for a while. There is always something to do at home.*

7 Read the passage about the daily activities of a Spanish swimmer, then answer the questions.

polideportivo (m)	sports centre
entrenar	to train
empresariales (f pl)	business studies
ligero/a	light
bañador (m)	swimming costume

Cristóbal es un gran aficionado a la natación. Cristóbal acostumbra a levantarse todos los días a las seis y media de la mañana. Se ducha, toma un café y sale de su casa para ir a la piscina de un polideportivo donde entrena hasta las ocho y media de la mañana. Normalmente vuelve a casa sobre las nueve, toma una ducha nuevamente y desayuna algo frugal, como fruta y yogur.

Hacia las diez de la mañana se va a la universidad donde estudia empresariales. A la una acostumbra a consumir un almuerzo ligero y sobre las tres suele volver otra vez a casa para descansar. Casi siempre duerme la siesta durante media hora, luego se pone de nuevo el bañador y regresa a la piscina para seguir entrenando. A las seis y media está una vez más de vuelta en casa. Dedica un par de horas a sus estudios, cena algo frugal y luego lee o quizá ve un rato la televisión. Suele acostarse sobre las once. Los fines de semana a lo mejor queda con algún amigo, pero su rutina y disciplina nunca cambian demasiado. Sus padres le han dado todo su apoyo y esperan que algún día Cristóbal consiga su sueño y sea un gran nadador.

   a How many training sessions does Cristóbal have each day?
   b Why does he go home in the middle of the day?
   c How much time does he dedicate to studying in the evenings?

8 Words in context – Read the text again and find:
   a two words meaning *about*, with reference to time.
   b four expressions meaning *again*.
   c three expressions meaning *perhaps*.
   d two expressions meaning *to shower*.
   e two opposites of **abundante** in relation to food.
   f the phrases meaning *he has a nap*, *to continue training*, and *back at home*.
   g three expressions indicating how often something is done.
   h two verbs in the subjunctive. What are their infinitives?

9 Put the verbs in brackets in the appropriate form: the present indicative or the present subjunctive.
   a Me quedaré aquí hasta que ellos _____ (llegar).
   b Cuando Luisa _____ (salir) de la oficina se va directamente a casa.
   c Cuando Antonio _____ (regresar), tomaremos una copa.
   d A mi abuela le molesta que la gente la _____ (llamar) por teléfono.
   e Nos encanta que Ana nos _____ (invitar) a su casa. ¡Es preciosa!
   f Julia y su marido _____ (levantarse) muy temprano cada mañana.
   g Traeré a mi novio para que tú le _____ (conocer).
   h Creo que mi padre _____ (estar) cenando.
   i No quiero que tú se lo _____ (decir) a nadie.
   j Carlos siempre _____ (trabajar) hasta muy tarde por la noche.

Test yourself

1 How would you express the following in English?
   a No acostumbro (a) comer mucho por la noche a menos que tenga que salir.
   b A Julia le molesta que la interrumpan, pero eso no suele ocurrir muy a menudo.
   c Estamos sujetos a una cierta rutina que, querámoslo o no, tenemos que cumplir.
   d Vamos al supermercado una o dos veces por semana, dependiendo de lo que haga falta.
   e No quiero que me llames, a no ser que sea absolutamente necesario.
   f Sería imposible volver a casa a comer, ya que perdería mucho tiempo yendo en el coche, el autobús o lo que sea.

2 Choose the correct form of the verb in the following sentences.
   a Espero que (estás/estés) bien.
   b Hace mucho tiempo que no (sé/sepa) nada de ti.
   c (Yo) todavía (recuerdo/recuerda) nuestras vacaciones en Estambul y quiero que me (envías/envíes) algunas de las fotos de nuestro viaje.
   d No creo que (yo) (puedo/pueda) ir a España este verano. Ojalá (es/sea) posible hacerlo para las Navidades.
   e ¿Cuándo (vienes/vengas) tú por aquí? Sabes que puedes venir a mi casa cuando (quieres/quieras).
   f Te envío mi nuevo email para que me (escribes/escribas) y me (das/des) noticias tuyas.

Check your answers to the Test yourself activities in the Key to the exercises.
If you did well, go on to Unit 2, otherwise go back to the unit and revise all the relevant points.

SELF CHECK	
I CAN . . .	
●	. . . talk about daily activities and habits.
●	. . . say how often I do something.
●	. . . relate a sequence of events.

Tiempo de ocio

In this unit you will learn how to:
▶ *make invitations.*
▶ *make suggestions.*
▶ *state preferences.*
▶ *express likes and dislikes.*

CEFR: *Can understand clear, detailed text on subjects of interest, e.g. cinema (B2); can easily follow interactions between third parties in group discussions and debates (C1); can understand broadcast language spoken at native speed (C1).*

Conversations

1 ¿QUÉ TE PARECE? *WHAT DO YOU THINK?*

Pablo Dávila y Ana Ramírez se han conocido durante las vacaciones. En el bar del hotel hablan de cine.

 1 02.01 **First, look at the vocabulary, then try to answer this question as you listen: Do Pablo and Ana agree to go to the cinema today or tomorrow?**

poner	*to show (a film)*
¿qué te parece si . . . ?	*what about . . .?*
debe de haber una sesión (f)	*there must be a show*
sierra (f)	*mountain*

Pablo	¿Has visto la última película de Almodóvar?
Ana	No, aún no la he visto. Me han dicho que es muy buena. Me gustaría verla. ¿Tú la has visto?
Pablo	No, tampoco. La ponen en el cine Real, en Málaga. ¿Qué te parece si vamos a verla esta noche? Podemos regresar aquí en el último tren.
Ana	Mira, la verdad es que hoy estoy muy cansada. Prefiero ir mañana. ¿Qué te parece?
Pablo	De acuerdo. Debe de haber una sesión a las seis y media o siete. Lo miraré en el periódico.
Ana	¿Te gusta mucho el cine?
Pablo	Bueno, sí, bastante. Suelo ir casi todas las semanas.
Ana	A mí también me gusta, pero no voy muy a menudo. Los fines de semana prefiero salir fuera de Madrid.
Pablo	¿Adónde vas?

Ana	Normalmente a la sierra. Mis padres tienen una casa en San Rafael, pero no van mucho por allí. Yo sí. Suelo irme en el coche el viernes por la tarde y no regreso hasta el domingo por la noche. Es un lugar muy bonito y muy tranquilo y la casa tiene una vista espectacular. Tendrás que venir a verme algún día.
Pablo	Gracias. Me gustaría mucho.
Ana	¡Qué calor hace!
Pablo	Sí, mucho. Yo voy a bajar a la playa. ¿Quieres venir conmigo?
Ana	Vale, vamos.

LANGUAGE TIP

Visto (*seen*) and **dicho** (*told, said*) are the irregular past participles of **ver** (*to see*) and **decir** (*to tell, say*).
¿Has visto la última película?   *Have you seen the latest film?*
Me han dicho que es muy buena.   *I've been told it's very good.*
For more on the perfect tense, see Unit 8.

---

2 **The following sentences contain wrong information. Read or listen to the conversation again and try to correct them.**

a Ana ha visto la última película de Almodóvar y le gustaría verla otra vez.

b Ana acostumbra a ir al cine todos los fines de semana.

c Ana se va a la sierra el domingo por la noche y no regresa hasta el viernes por la tarde.

d Como hace mucho calor, Pablo invita a Ana a bajar al centro para tomar un refresco.

CULTURE TIP
Pedro Almodóvar is a well-known Spanish film director. Among his films are *Matador*, *Mujeres al borde de un ataque de nervios*, *Todo sobre mi madre*, *Hable con ella*, *Volver* and *La piel que habito*.

3 02.02 **Role play – Follow the prompts and take part in the conversation. Then listen to check and practise your answers out loud.**

At a party you are introduced to Victor, a Spanish speaker. He's very keen on el teatro, English theatre, and he's come to London to see some plays.

You	*Ask him if he likes theatre.*
Victor	Sí, me encanta el teatro, ¿y a ti, te gusta?
You	*Yes, you like it but you prefer cinema. Ask him if he likes London.*
Victor	Sí, Londres me gusta muchísimo, es una ciudad muy bonita. ¿Y tú, conoces España?
You	*Yes, you know Madrid and Barcelona.*
Victor	¿Y cuál te gusta más?
You	*You prefer Barcelona, it's a much nicer city.*

2 TIEMPO DE OCIO *LEISURE TIME*

En unas entrevistas realizadas por una radio española, tres personas hablan sobre su tiempo libre. El primer entrevistado, José, es un sudamericano que vive en España.

1 02.03 **First, look at the vocabulary. Then, as you listen, focus on the activities that the three panellists enjoy in their free time. One of them doesn't mention a single physical activity. Who is that person?**

ratos de ocio (m pl)	*leisure time*
polideportivo (m)	*sports centre*
disponer de tiempo (m)	*to have time*
paseo (m)	*drive, ride (in a car)*
allí se está muy bien	*it does us good to be there*
no tiene nada que ver con . . .	*it has nothing to do with . . .*
ser aficionado/a a . . .	*to be fond of, to be a fan of*
no dejar de hacer algo	*to never miss doing something*
por haber venido	*for coming* (lit. *for having come*)

Presentador	Buenas tardes. En nuestro programa de hoy nos referiremos al tema del ocio. ¿Qué hacen y cómo pasan su tiempo libre algunos de los habitantes de nuestra ciudad? En un mundo dominado por la televisión y por la imagen en general, hay quienes dedican sus ratos de ocio a otras actividades. Nuestro primer entrevistado es José Ibáñez, de 23 años. José, ¿qué haces en tus ratos de ocio?
José	Pues, normalmente practico deportes, principalmente fútbol, aunque también me gusta la natación. Tengo la suerte de vivir en un barrio donde hay un excelente polideportivo y eso ha incentivado mucho la práctica de los deportes. Antes de que se construyera el polideportivo solo teníamos el campo de fútbol y, si quería ir a la piscina, tenía que ir a otro barrio. Tardaba por lo menos media hora en ir allí, por lo que no lo hacía muy a menudo. Ahora sí, practico con regularidad.
Presentador	Gracias, José. Y ahora tenemos con nosotros a Antonia Rodríguez, de 35 años. Antonia, ¿a qué te dedicas en tu tiempo libre?
Antonia	Pues, tiempo libre tengo poquísimo, pues trabajo y además estoy casada y tengo dos hijos muy pequeños, pero, vamos, cuando disponemos de algún tiempo, mi marido y yo cogemos el coche y nos vamos con los chicos de paseo, pero eso no suele ocurrir muy a menudo. En verano sí, lo hacemos con más frecuencia. A veces nos vamos de camping. Hay un lugar muy bonito a pocos kilómetros de aquí que nos gusta mucho. Allí se está muy bien.
Presentador	Antonia, muchas gracias por estar con nosotros. Nuestro próximo invitado es Manuel Araya, de 55 años. Manuel, ¿qué prefiere hacer usted en sus ratos de ocio?
Manuel	Pues, yo soy un gran aficionado a la pintura, aunque mi trabajo habitual no tiene nada que ver con esto. Pero es una actividad que siempre me ha gustado y que he venido desarrollando desde que era muy joven. Cuando hay alguna exposición importante, nunca dejo de ir. Desgraciadamente, aquí la vida cultural es muy limitada y es poco lo que se puede aprender. Pero cuando voy a Madrid, voy siempre a algún museo. Prefiero el Museo del Prado, es el que más me gusta.
Presentador	Muchas gracias, Manuel, por haber venido.

> **LANGUAGE TIP**
>
> Notice the use of the imperfect tense in:
> **Si quería ir a la piscina . . .**   *If I wanted to go to the swimming pool . . .*
> **Tenía que ir a otro barrio . . .**   *I had to go to another district . . .*
> **Tardaba por lo menos . . .**   *It used to take me at least . . .*
> **No lo hacía muy a menudo.**   *I didn't do it very often.*
> For the formation and other uses of the imperfect tense, see Unit 5.

2 Answer the following questions in Spanish.

   a José Ibáñez nadaba menos antes que ahora. ¿Por qué?

   b ¿Por qué no dispone de mucho tiempo libre Antonia Rodríguez?

   c ¿Qué hacen ella y su marido cuando están libres?

   d ¿Qué le gusta hacer a Manuel Araya en sus ratos de ocio?

NEW EXPRESSIONS

Focus on understanding the degree of formality in the Spanish expressions and making them your own. For instance, in what circumstances would you say Vale or Me encantaría in response to an invitation? Then mask either column and test your memory.

Making invitations and responding to an invitation

Tendrás que venir a verme algún día. (informal)   *You'll have to come and see me some day.*
Gracias. Me gustaría mucho. (formal/informal)   *Thank you. I'd like to very much.*
¿Quieres venir conmigo? (very informal)   *Do you want to come with me?*
Vale. (very informal)   *OK.*
¿Por qué no viene/vienes a verme algún día?   *Why don't you come and see me*
   (formal/informal)   *some day?*
Ven/venga a verme algún día. (informal/formal)   *Come and see me some day.*
Me gustaría invitarlo/a a . . . (very formal)   *I'd like to invite you to . . .*

Making suggestions

¿Qué te parece si vamos a verla . . . ? (informal)   *How about going to see it . . .?*
Podemos regresar aquí . . .   *We can come back here . . .*
¿Qué le/te parece si . . . ? (formal/informal)   *How/What about . . .?*
¿Por qué no . . . ? (formal/informal)   *Why don't you/we . . .?*
Le/te sugiero que vaya/s (formal/informal)   *I suggest you (go)*

Stating preferences

¿Qué prefiere hacer Vd.?   *What do you prefer to do?*
Prefiero ir mañana.   *I prefer to go tomorrow.*
Prefiero el Museo del Prado.   *I prefer the Prado Museum.*

Expressing likes and dislikes

¿Te gusta el cine?   *Do you like going to the cinema?*
A mí también me gusta.   *I like it too.*
Lo que más me gusta es nadar.   *What I like most is swimming.*
No me gusta.   *I don't like it.*

Language discovery

You have seen this language in action. Now can you work out the rules?

1 How would you say informally: *Do you like Almodovar's films?* And *I've seen his latest film, but I'd love to see it again*?

2 Rank these verbs according to their intensity, from weakest to strongest: **fascinar, gustar, encantar.**

3 Do these three sentences have similar or different meanings?

   a ¿Le gusta cenar fuera?

   b ¿Qué le parece si cenamos fuera?

   c ¿Por qué no salimos a cenar?

4 Find the expressions in Conversation 2 which are used instead of regularmente *regularly* and frecuentemente *more frequently*.

1 GUSTAR *TO LIKE*

Remember that **gustar** is normally used in the third person singular or plural, and it may be followed by a noun (e.g. **el museo** *the museum*) or an infinitive (e.g. **ir al cine** *to go to the cinema*). In this construction, **gustar** is preceded by an indirect object pronoun:

me	gusta(n)	*I like it (them)*
te	gusta(n)	*you like it (them)* (familiar)
le	gusta(n)	*he or she likes it (them); you like it (them)*
nos	gusta(n)	*we like it (them)*
os	gusta(n)	*you like it (them)* (familiar)
les	gusta(n)	*they or you like it (them)*

For emphasis or to avoid ambiguity, as in **le gusta** (*he* or *she likes it* or *you like it*), use the following set of pronouns preceded by the preposition **a**:

a mí, a ti, a él, a ella, a usted, a nosotros/as, a vosotros/as, a ellos/as, a ustedes.

Examples:

A *él* le gusta el cine.	*He likes going to the cinema.*
A *mí* también me gusta.	*I like it too.*
¿A *Vd.* le gusta?	*Do you like it?*
A *mí* no.	*I don't (like it).*

Negative sentences are formed by placing **no** before the indirect object pronoun.

***No* me gustan.**	*I don't like them.*
A ella *no* le gustan.	*She doesn't like them.*

Encantar and **fascinar**, meaning *to love*, express stronger liking and are used in the same way as **gustar**.

Me encanta la música española.	*I love Spanish music.*
Me fascina viajar.	*I love travelling.*

2 PARECER TO SEEM, THINK

Parecer is normally used in a construction similar to that of **gustar**.

¿Qué te parece si . . .?	*What do you think if . . .?*
Me parece bien.	*It seems all right (to me).*

3 ADVERBS AND ADVERBIAL PHRASES

Words such as **rápidamente** *quickly*, **inmediatamente** *immediately* and **fácilmente** *easily* are known as adverbs. Excessive use of words ending in **-mente** is considered clumsy in Spanish, so these are sometimes replaced by adverbial phrases like the following: **de manera rápida** literally, *in a quick way*, **de forma inmediata** *immediately*, **de manera fácil** *in an easy way*. Words like **rápido**, **inmediato** and **fácil** are adjectives and the use of the feminine forms **rápida** and **inmediata** is due to the fact that **manera** and **forma** are feminine words. Some nouns can be used as adverbial phrases preceded by **con** *with*, e.g. **con rapidez** *quickly*, **con facilidad** *easily*, a construction which is less common and more restricted in use (see **con regularidad** and **con más frecuencia** in Conversation 2).

Practice

1 **Complete the sentences with a single word, using the informal form where appropriate.**

  a ¿Qué _____ en tu tiempo libre, Carmen?

  b _____ gusta ver la televisión.

  c ¿Qué tipos de programas te _____ ?

  d _____ los programas deportivos, aunque también me _____ ver películas. ¿Y a _____, qué te gusta hacer?

  e Me _____ los deportes, la televisión _____ me gusta nada.

  f ¿Qué deportes _____?

  g La natación, es lo que _____ me gusta.

  h _____ mí también. ¿Qué _____ parece si vamos a la piscina esta tarde?

  i _____ parece una excelente idea.

2 **Study this conversation between two friends. The word sesión (f) refers to showing times.**

José	¿Qué te parece si vamos al cine?
Elena	Vale, vamos. ¿Qué película te gustaría ver?
José	Podemos ver *El secreto de sus ojos*. ¿Qué te parece?
Elena	Bueno, la verdad es que ese tipo de película no me gusta nada. Yo prefiero ver *El laberinto del fauno*. ¿Te parece bien?
José	De acuerdo. ¿Dónde la ponen?
Elena	En el cine Biógrafo. ¿A qué sesión prefieres ir? Hay una a las 7.00 y otra a las 9.00.
José	Prefiero ir a la de las 9.00.

Now make up a similar conversation using the acclaimed Spanish language films in this advertisement.

CINE REAL

DOLBY STEREO   SPECTRAL RECORDING SR

Pla. Isabel II, (Metro Opera) Tfno. 547 45 77

AHORA EN V.O. Y EN PANTALLA GRANDE

Blancanieves (España)
de Pablo Berger

16:10 – 19:00 – 21:50

Mar adentro (España)
de Alejandro Amenábar

17:00 – 18:50 – 20:55

Diarios de motocicleta (EEUU)
de Walter Salles

16:45 – 18:40 – 20:40

El crimen del padre Amaro (México)
de Carlos Carrera

17:10 – 19:15 – 21:20

Bombón: el perro (Argentina)
de Carlos Sorin

15:30 – 17: 45 – 19:50

3 **Imagine that you are being interviewed on Spanish television. The presenter wants to know about your leisure activities. Look at the prompts and rehearse your answers before speaking them out loud.**

Presentador ¿A qué se dedica usted en su tiempo libre?

Entrevistado(a) *Say you have very little time. You work in an office from 9.00 to 5.00 and you are married and have three children. But when you can, you like to work in the garden and you also like to read. Now you are reading a novel by García Márquez, which you like very much. Ah, you are also studying Spanish, of course. You like Spanish a lot.*

Presentador ¿Y en sus vacaciones viene Vd. normalmente a España?

Entrevistado(a) *Not always. Although you like Spain very much, it is expensive to travel abroad, so you prefer to spend your holidays closer to home.*

Presentador Bueno, nuestro programa tiene una invitación especial para usted. Dos semanas de vacaciones para dos personas en el hotel y lugar de su elección.

Entrevistado(a) *Wonderful! Thank you very much.*

4 You and your travelling companion decide to stay in your hotel room and watch television. Your friend is busy at the moment, so can you tell him/her:

    a what sort of films are on?

    b what they are about?

antecedentes (m pl)	background
suceso (m)	event
cinta (f)	film
en torno a	about
maestro/a	teacher
ribetes (m pl)	elements

LA VIEJA MEMORIA
***

Documental. 2h. 45m

Director: Jaime Camino.

Un eficaz documental en donde, a través de entrevistas y una buena labor de montaje, el director Jaime Camino profundiza en los antecedentes de la Guerra Civil española y en los sucesos ocurridos en Cataluña durante la República. Pese a resultar excesivamente larga, la película se sigue bastante bien. Una lección de historia a no olvidar.

A MÍ NO ME MIRE USTED
***

Comedia. 1h. 19m.

Director: J. L. Sáenz de Heredia.

Intérpretes: Valeriano León, Manuel Arbó y Rosita Yarza.

Una de las cintas más atípicas de Sáenz de Heredia en torno a un maestro rural que utiliza sus poderes hipnóticos para imponer orden en su clase. Una comedia con ribetes casi surrealistas.

---

5 A Spanish-speaking friend has sent you an email announcing that he/she will be passing through your home town. Write an email inviting your friend to stay with you for a few days.

alegrarse de que (+ subjunctive)	to be glad (that . . .)
estar seguro/a	to be sure
confirmar	to confirm
llegada (f)	arrival

    a Say you have received his/her email and that you are glad he/she is coming to your home town.

    b Say you are sure he/she will like it very much.

    c Invite him/her to stay at your house for a few days. You would like that.

    d Suggest he/she phones you to confirm his/her arrival.

¡A escuchar!

You will hear a commentary about an exhibition of Latin American art in Madrid, then an announcement about a forthcoming cultural event.

6 02.04 **Look at the vocabulary before you listen to the broadcast, then answer the questions.**

asistencia (f)	*attendance*
exposición (f)	*exhibition*
asistentes (m/f pl)	*public*
obra (f)	*work*
connotado/a	*famous*
pintores (m pl)	*painters*
iberoamericano/a	*Latin American*
proveniente	*from*

  a How many works will the public be able to see?
  b Where is the exhibition being held?
  c Which are some of the countries represented?
  d What expressions are used in the text to say: *It is taking place, They will be able to see, It was opened by . . .*?

7 02.05 **Listen to an announcement about a festival taking place in Madrid. Look at the vocabulary first, then answer the questions. You will find the transcript in the ¡A escuchar! section.**

coloquio (m)	*talk*
campo (m)	*field, area*
acontecimiento (m)	*event*
espectáculo (m)	*show*
escenario (m)	*stage*

  a What is the name of the festival being announced?
  b What activities will it include?
  c Which countries will be specially represented?

8 **Leisure activities and sports can sometimes be a nuisance to others, as the person who wrote this email to a Spanish newspaper seems to think. What does she complain about? Read it through and then say whether the statements which follow the text are true or false.**

merecer	*to deserve*
esfuerzo (m)	*effort*
relajarse	*to relax*
estridente	*loud*
quejarse por cualquier cosa (f)	*to complain about everything/anything*
disparate (m)	*outrage*
atentar contra	*to threaten*
ayuntamiento (m)	*town hall*

recuperar	to recover
recurrir a	to turn to
adquirir	to acquire, obtain

NO ME MEREZCO ESTO

Hace unos meses, y con mucho esfuerzo, compré un apartamento en el barrio de San Miguel. Buscaba la tranquilidad de un barrio alejado del centro de la ciudad, donde pudiera descansar y relajarme junto a mi familia después de una intensa semana de trabajo.

Creí que por fin había conseguido lo que tanto quería. Pero un buen día, en lo que antes era una tranquila esquina, justo enfrente de mi apartamento, se abrió una discoteca que no nos deja dormir por la noche. La música estridente y el constante ruido de quienes entran y salen empieza hacia la medianoche y no termina hasta el amanecer.

Yo no soy de las personas a las que les gusta quejarse por cualquier cosa, pero me parece que la autorización para la instalación de una discoteca en una zona netamente residencial es un disparate y atenta contra la salud mental de las personas.

Nuestras quejas al Ayuntamiento no han dado resultado. Las autoridades locales nos han ignorado, como suele ocurrir.

¿Qué podemos hacer para recuperar nuestra tranquilidad? ¿A quién podemos recurrir, que nos escuche y nos entienda? ¿O debemos irnos de aquí y dejar este lugar que tanto esfuerzo y dinero nos costó adquirir? ¡Ayúdennos, por favor!

Carmen Martínez
Sevilla

Now check your understanding. Read each statement and decide: ¿Verdadero o falso?

    a Carmen quería un apartamento cerca del centro de la ciudad.

    b Enfrente del apartamento que compró había una discoteca.

    c A Carmen le molesta el ruido de la discoteca.

    d La música y el ruido continúan hasta la medianoche.

    e Carmen no suele quejarse.

    f El Ayuntamiento va a cerrar la discoteca.

⑦ Test yourself

1 How would you express the following in Spanish?
  a He likes theatre but she doesn't.
  b What we like most about this place is the people.
  c You like him? Well, I don't. I prefer Pablo. (informal)
  d What about going for a drink, Silvia? (informal)
  e It's all right with me. (use **parecer**)
  f They love watching this programme. Well, I don't like it at all.

2 Replace each of the adverbs ending in **-mente** in the following sentences with an adverbial phrase, using the words in brackets.
  a El trabajo avanza, pero muy lentamente. (de manera muy . . .)
  b Mis amigos ingleses vienen a España frecuentemente. (con . . .)
  c Carlos se comportó muy descortésmente. (de forma muy . . .)
  d Sus padres nos recibieron muy amablemente. (con mucha . . .)
  e Le expliqué claramente la situación a mi jefe. (de manera . . .)
  f Te prestaré mi ordenador, pero tienes que tratarlo cuidadosamente. (con . . .)

Although gustar, parecer, etc., in Test 1 constitute revision, the construction in which they occur is often a problem for English speakers. Check your answers in the Key to the exercises and see whether you got them right, otherwise go back to the Language discovery notes and practise writing your own examples. The importance of Test 2 is that it focuses on phrases which are commonly used in the spoken and written language. If your answers were right, go on to Unit 3.

SELF CHECK

I CAN . . .
● . . . make invitations.
● . . . make suggestions.
● . . . state preferences.
● . . . express likes and dislikes.

3 ¡A trabajar!

In this unit you will learn how to:

▶ *describe your job.*

▶ *discuss working conditions.*

▶ *say what you like or dislike about your job.*

▶ *refer to events which began in the past and which are still in progress.*

CEFR: *Can pass on detailed information reliably, e.g. take and give messages; can write personal and business letters describing experiences and impressions (B2); can read specialized articles, e.g. business columns (C1).*

Conversations

1 HABLANDO DE TRABAJO *TALKING ABOUT WORK*

En un vuelo hacia un país de habla española, dos extraños hablan sobre su trabajo.

1 03.01 **First, look at the vocabulary, then try to answer this question as you listen: Which of the two passengers flies more often, the man or the woman?**

voy por negocios (m pl)	*I am going on business*
maquinaria agrícola (f)	*agricultural machinery*
artesanía (f)	*handicrafts*
suponer	*to suppose*
socio/a	*partner*
esta vez (f)	*this time*
tocar	*to be one's turn*

Señor	¿Adónde va usted?
Señora	Voy a Lima. ¿Y usted?
Señor	Yo voy a Santiago de Chile.
Señora	¿Va de vacaciones?
Señor	No, voy por negocios. Soy representante de una empresa de maquinaria agrícola. ¿Y usted va de vacaciones?
Señora	No, yo también voy por razones de trabajo, aunque también me tomaré unos días de vacaciones. Pero, principalmente voy de compras. Tengo una tienda de artesanía y en Perú compramos muchos de los artículos que vendemos. También en México. Tienen una artesanía maravillosa.
Señor	Vd. es peruana, ¿verdad?
Señora	Sí, soy peruana, pero vivo en España desde hace muchos años. ¿Y usted ha estado antes en Sudamérica?

Señor	Solamente en Venezuela y en Colombia. Conozco muy bien Venezuela. Trabajé dos años allí en una empresa de petróleo . . .
Señora	Le gusta viajar, supongo.
Señor	Bueno sí, es una de las cosas que más me gusta de mi trabajo. Viajo constantemente.
Señora	A mí me encanta viajar, pero no lo hago muy a menudo. Esta es una excepción. Normalmente las compras las hace mi socio, pero esta vez me ha tocado a mí. Además, necesitaba un descanso.
Señor	¿Cuánto tiempo va a quedarse en Perú?
Señora	Dos semanas solamente. Dedicaré una semana a mis compras y luego me iré por una semana a Arequipa a visitar a mis padres.

LANGUAGE TIP

Note the word order in: **Normalmente las compras las hace mi socio** *The buying is normally done by my partner*. The emphasis in this sentence is on **mi socio**. Word order can be used to shift the focus to another part of the message.

2 **Which of the following information is not expressed in the conversation?**
   a Represento a una empresa de maquinaria agrícola.
   b Vendo artesanía en una tienda que tengo en España.
   c No llevo mucho tiempo viviendo en España.
   d Estuve un par de años trabajando en Venezuela.
   e Detesto viajar, aunque no es algo que haga con frecuencia.
   f Normalmente me toca a mí hacer las compras fuera de España.

3 **Notice the indirect object pronouns me, te, le, nos in these expressions, then match them with their meaning:**
   a Me toca a mí, otra vez.   1 Whose turn is it?
   b Esta vez, te ha tocado a ti.   2 It is our turn, for once.
   c ¿A quién le toca?   3 It is my turn, once again.
   d Nos toca a nosotros, por una vez. 4 This time it's your turn.

4 **Complete the sentences with a suitable preposition.**
   a ¿Viaja usted _____ vacaciones o _____ negocios?
   b Soy representante _____ una empresa _____ productos agrícolas.
   c Voy _____ compras _____ dos semanas solamente.
   d Ellos viven _____ Madrid _____ hace mucho tiempo.
   e Me iré _____ unos días al campo _____ visitar a mi familia.
   f Mi padre tiene una tienda _____ artículos eléctricos.

2 ¿EN QUÉ TRABAJAS? *WHAT WORK DO YOU DO?*

Mercedes y Paloma acaban de conocerse en casa de un amigo común. Las dos chicas hablan sobre sus actividades.

1 03.02 **Preview the vocabulary and focus on this question as you listen: Which particular drawbacks do Mercedes and Paloma mention about their respective jobs?**

aburrido/a	*bored*
quejarse	*to complain*
al principio (m)	*in the beginning*
darse cuenta	*to realize*
trato (m)	*relationship*
cosas por el estilo	*things like that*
extranjero/a	*foreigner*
¡que tengas suerte!	*I hope you are lucky!*

Mercedes	¿En qué trabajas tú?
Paloma	Trabajo en la oficina de turismo.
Mercedes	¡Qué bien! Es un trabajo interesante, ¿no?
Paloma	Pues sí, lo que pasa es que llevo mucho tiempo allí y estoy un poco aburrida. Pero, vamos, tampoco me puedo quejar. El sueldo no está nada mal y tengo un mes de vacaciones al año.
Mercedes	¿Cuánto tiempo hace que trabajas allí?
Paloma	Casi cinco años. Al principio me gustaba mucho, especialmente el contacto con el público. Eso era lo que más me gustaba, pero luego te das cuenta de que el trato es más bien impersonal y estás repitiendo casi siempre lo mismo . . ., que dónde está esto, dónde está lo otro, que si tiene usted un mapa, y cosas por el estilo . . . Bueno, ¿y tú qué haces?
Mercedes	Soy profesora. Enseño español a extranjeros en un instituto de idiomas.
Paloma	¿Y qué tal? ¿Te gusta?
Mercedes	Pues, enseñar sí me gusta, lo que no me gusta es el sueldo. Nos pagan muy poco.
Paloma	¿Por qué no pides un aumento?
Mercedes	¡Vamos, que la cosa no es tan fácil!
Paloma	¿Cuánto tiempo llevas trabajando allí?
Mercedes	Un año solamente, pero espero cambiarme pronto.
Paloma	Bueno, ¡que tengas suerte!
Mercedes	Gracias, tú también.

2 Answer the following questions in Spanish.

   a ¿Qué dice Paloma sobre su sueldo?
   b ¿Cuánto tiempo hace que trabaja en el mismo lugar?
   c ¿Qué es lo que más le gustaba cuando empezó a trabajar?
   d ¿A qué se dedica Mercedes?
   e ¿Le gusta su trabajo?

> **LANGUAGE TIP**
>
> **Lo que** can mean *what* or *the thing that* . . . : **lo que pasa es que** . . . *what happens is that* . . . , **lo que más me gustaba** . . . *what I liked most* . . . , **lo que no me gusta** . . . *the thing that I don't like* . . .

3 Give the English for the following sentences from the conversation.

   a Tampoco me puedo quejar.

   b El sueldo no está nada mal.

   c Al principio me gustaba mucho.

   d El trato es más bien impersonal.

   e Enseñar sí me gusta.

   f ¡Vamos, que la cosa no es tan fácil!

4 03.03 **Role play – A Spanish man and a Peruvian woman are talking about work. Listen closely then, following the prompts on the audio, act the part of the woman.**

NEW EXPRESSIONS

Describing your job

Tengo una tienda de artesanía.	*I have/own a handicraft shop.*
Soy profesora.	*I am a teacher.*
Trabajo en la oficina de turismo.	*I work in the tourist office.*

Discussing working conditions

El sueldo no está nada mal.	*The salary is not bad at all.*
Tengo un mes de vacaciones al año.	*I have a month's holiday a year.*

Saying what you like or dislike about your job

Es una de las cosas que más me gusta de mi trabajo.	*It is one of the things I like most about my job.*
Me gusta enseñar.	*I like teaching.*

Referring to events which began in the past and which are still in progress

¿Cuánto tiempo llevas trabajando allí?	*How long have you been working there?*
¿Cuánto tiempo hace que trabajas allí?	*How long have you worked there?*
Llevo mucho tiempo allí.	*I have been there for a long time.*

Using what you know and some intuition, how would you translate these sentences?

Lo que menos me agrada de mi puesto es el sueldo.

(Ella) trabaja como conductora de una compañía de autobuses.

Language discovery

You have seen this language in action. Now can you work out the rules?

1 Which question does not have the same meaning as the other two?

   a ¿Cuánto tiempo llevan buscando un piso?

   b ¿Hace cuánto tiempo que buscan un piso?

   c ¿Cuánto tiempo van a estar buscando un piso?

2 What questions correspond to these answers?

   a Hace cuatro días que no llueve.

   b Llevo casi doce años jugando al ajedrez.

3 What is the difference in focus in these two sentences?

   a Miguel pasea el perro cuando no puedo.

   b Cuando no puedo, el perro lo pasea Miguel.

1 LLEVAR FOLLOWED BY GERUND

This construction is used to refer to events which began at some point in the past but which are still now in progress. Consider again the sentences in Conversation 2 and these further examples.

¿Cuánto tiempo *llevas viviendo* en este piso?	*How long have you been living in this flat?*
***Llevo* dos años *viviendo* aquí.**	*I have been living here for two years.*
¿*Lleváis* mucho tiempo *trabajando* juntos?	*Have you been working together for a long time?*
***Llevamos* seis meses *trabajando* juntos.**	*We have been working together for six months.*

If the context makes it clear, as with **vivir** and **trabajar**, the gerund **viviendo**, **trabajando** may be omitted. For example:

¿Cuánto tiempo *llevas* en Barcelona?	*How long have you been (living) in Barcelona?*
Él *lleva* cinco años en esta empresa.	*He has been (working) in this company for five years.*

Llevar may also be used in the imperfect tense to refer to an action which began in the past and which continued until some point in the past. For example:

María *llevaba* diez años (*trabajando*) en esa empresa cuando cerró.	*Maria had been (working) in that firm for ten years when it closed.*

To form the gerund, add **-ando** to the stem of **-ar** verbs and **-iendo** to that of **-er and -ir** verbs, e.g. **trabajar**, **trabajando**, **vivir**, **viviendo**.

2 HACE + TIME PHRASE FOLLOWED BY QUE + PRESENT TENSE

An alternative to the construction above is this one with **hace** in the third person. Consider again the example in Conversation 2 and then these further examples:

¿Cuánto tiempo *hace* que vives en España?	*How long have you been living in Spain?*
***Hace* un año que *vivo* en España.**	*I have been living in Spain for a year.*

or

***Vivo* en España *desde hace* un año.**	*I have been living in Spain for a year.*

Notice also the use of **hacer** in the imperfect tense:

***Hacía* tres años que yo no la *veía*.**	*I hadn't seen her for three years.*

Compare this sentence with:

Hace tres años que yo no la veo.   *I have not seen her for three years.*

3 WORD ORDER

Word order within sentences is much more flexible in Spanish than in English. In statements focusing on more than one element, the part of the sentence you want to highlight may be placed in final position.

La compra la hace María.   *It is María who does the shopping.*
El problema lo solucionó José.   *It was José who solved the problem.*

The subject of the sentence, María in the first example, José in the second, has been placed in final position. This deviates from the normal word order pattern, which is subject + verb:

María hace la compra.   *María does the shopping.*
José solucionó el problema.   *José solved the problem.*

In short sentences, the tendency is to place the verb before the subject.

Salió el avión.   *The plane left.*
Llamó Andrés.   *Andrés phoned.*

Within a clause, the verb is normally placed before the subject.

Lo que quiere mi madre es que no la dejemos sola.   *What my mother wants is not to be left alone.*

 Practice

1 **How would you ask Antonio how long he has been doing each of the following and how would he reply? Use the construction with llevar with an appropriate verb from the box:**

> jugar   hacer yoga   estudiar   tocar   vivir   trabajar

a

Tres años

b

Dos años y medio

c

Cinco años

d

Cuatro años

e

Seis meses

f

Tres semanas

2 Can you now say how long Antonio has been doing each of these activities? This time, use the alternative construction with hace + time phrase.

3 Complete the passage with the appropriate words.

Me llamo Martín Iglesias, _____ hace cuatro años trabajo _____ administrativo en una agencia _____ empleos. Es mi primer _____ y estoy bastante contento con _____, ya que tengo la _____ de relacionarme con mucha gente _____, especialmente gente joven que _____ trabajo por primera vez. Eso es _____ que más me gusta.

Mi _____ de trabajo no está mal, pues _____ a las 9.00 de _____ mañana y termino a las 6.00. Los sábados _____ tengo libres. Mis vacaciones _____ de tres semanas.

Mi _____ no es muy bueno, ya que ahora solo _____ 1.200 euros al mes, pero _____ que a comienzos del año que _____ me den un aumento.

Lo único que no me _____ de mi trabajo es que tengo que viajar mucho, pues _____ bastante lejos del barrio _____ vivo, pero en el futuro espero _____ a un lugar más cercano.

4 You will be spending six months at a language school in Spain and you wish to do some part-time work to earn some money and have contact with Spanish people. Two job advertisements in a newspaper attract your attention.

First, look at the vocabulary, then read the adverts and try to guess the nature of the jobs.

superables (m/f pl)	*and more (on target earnings)*
formación a nuestro cargo	*training to be provided by us*
mensuales (m/f pl)	*per month*

PERSONA MAYOR

DE 23 AÑOS

90 EUROS DIARIOS

SUPERABLES

Llamar de 9.00 a 14.00 horas y de 16.00 a 19.30 horas.

TELS.: 91 471 14 00 y

91 462 79 00

PREGUNTAR POR LA SRTA. TOÑI

¡¡OPORTUNIDAD ÚNICA!!

PERSONAS MAYORES

DE 23 AÑOS

Empresa líder Ofrece:

TRABAJO 3 HORAS DIARIAS

– Formación a nuestro cargo

– 1,700 euros mensuales

TELEF.: 91 361 25 88

You decide to telephone to get more information on the jobs. Rehearse your answers and try speaking them as you would on the telephone.

anuncio (m)	*advertisement*
no cuelgue	*don't hang up*
le pongo con . . .	*I'll put you through to . . .*
vendedor/a a domicilio	*door-to-door salesman/woman*
estar dispuesto/a a	*to be willing to*
entrenamiento (m)	*training*
está comunicando	*it is engaged*
página web (f)	*web page; company website*
formulario de solicitud (f)	*job application form*
en línea	*online*

Telefonista	Hispánica, buenos días. ¿Dígame?
Tú	*Good morning. Say you are calling about the advertisement in the newspaper and that you would like to speak to señorita Toñi.*
Telefonista	Un momento, por favor. No cuelgue . . . ¿Oiga?
Tú	*Yes, am I speaking to señorita Toñi?*
Telefonista	La extensión de la señorita Toñi está comunicando. ¿Quiere Vd. esperar?
Tú	*It's all right. Say you will wait.*
Telefonista	¿Oiga? Le pongo con la señorita Toñi.
Srta. Toñi	¿Sí, dígame?
Tú	*Say good morning, give your name and say you have seen the advertisement in the newspaper and that you would like to have more information about the job.*
Srta. Toñi	Bueno, se trata de una editorial y necesitamos vendedores a domicilio para ofrecer nuestra nueva enciclopedia. ¿Tiene Vd. experiencia en este tipo de trabajo?
Tú	*Yes, you worked as a salesman/woman for a time although you have never sold books. But you are willing to learn. You are living in Spain now and you need to earn some money and this is the sort of job you are looking for. You are very interested in it.*
Srta. Toñi	Bueno, nosotros daremos formación al personal que seleccionemos. Si Vd. quiere le puedo dar nuestra página web donde encontrará más detalles sobre la empresa, nuestros productos y las condiciones de trabajo. Además, tendrá acceso al formulario de solicitud en línea, y si le interesa el puesto, luego nos puede enviar una solicitud formal con una fotografía reciente. ¿Tiene con qué apuntar?
Tú	*Yes, what is your website?*

5 Roberto Urrutia from Chile needed a letter from his boss to get a loan. This is part of the letter written by Roberto's boss to the company that requested the references.

> **García y Cía.**
> **Calle Miraflores 546, Santiago, Chile**
>
> Santiago, 20 de octubre de 2014
>
> Señora Carmen Aldunate
> Gerente PROCASA S.A.
> Avenida El Bosque 321, Las Condes, Santiago
>
> Estimada señora:
>
> En respuesta a su carta del 15 del corriente, me es muy grato confirmar que el señor Roberto Urrutia trabaja como jefe de ventas en nuestra empresa desde hace cinco años. El señor Urrutia gana actualmente un sueldo bruto de ochocientos mil pesos mensuales.

GOING FURTHER – FORMS OF ADDRESS IN LETTER WRITING

All set to write a formal letter?

a One of the two forms of address Estimado señor: and Muy señores míos: leaves no doubt that the writer knows nothing about the recipient. Which one is it?

b Which phrase are you more likely to see in a job offer letter: Nos es muy grato . . . or Me alegro de decirle que . . . ?

Formal

Muy señor mío:	*Dear Sir,*
Muy señora mía:	*Dear Madam,*
Muy señores míos:	*Dear Sirs,*
Estimado señor:	*Dear Sir,*
Estimada señora:	*Dear Madam,*

Less formal

Estimado señor Díaz/Juan:	*Dear Mr Díaz/Juan,*
Estimada señorita Pérez/Ana:	*Dear Miss Pérez/Ana,*

Informal (for close relationships)

Querido Carlos:	*Dear Carlos,*
Querida María:	*Dear Maria,*

Introductory phrases

En respuesta a . . .	*In reply to . . .*
Me es muy grato . . .	*I am pleased to . . .*

Acuso recibo de su carta de fecha . . .	*I acknowledge receipt of your letter of . . .*
En contestación a su carta de fecha 12 de marzo . . .	*In answer to your letter of 12th March . . .*
El objeto de la presente es . . .	*This is to . . .*

Formal close
Atentamente or Le(s) saluda (muy) atentamente	*Yours truly or Yours sincerely*

Less formal
Un cordial/afectuoso saludo (de) . . .	*Best wishes (from) . . .*

Informal close
Un (fuerte) abrazo (de) . . .	*Love (from) . . .*

> **LANGUAGE TIP**
>
> Spanish uses a colon instead of a comma after phrases such as **Muy señor mío** *Dear Sir*. The words **señor**, **señora** and **señorita** are usually found in their abbreviated form, each followed by a full stop: **Sr., Sra., Srta.**
>
> The word **Estimado/a** is preferred when the name of the person is known. You can use this with the surname or even with the first name when the relationship is more informal. With friends, however, use **Querido/a** or simply **Hola (Diego/Teresa)**.

 Imagine your boss is giving similar information about you. Write the letter you are likely to get. Give your own or an imaginary occupation and salary.

¡A escuchar!

A journalist from a Spanish magazine conducted a series of interviews with people at work. Here are two of those interviews.

  6 03.04 **First, look at the vocabulary for any unknown words. Then listen to the first interview.**

publicarse	*to be published*
artículo (m)	*article*
agradar	*to like*
terreno (m)	*field*
lector/a	*reader*
satisfacer	*to satisfy*
exigir	*to demand*
estar dispuesto/a a	*to be ready or willing to*

Complete the questionnaire with the information given by María del Carmen Salas. You can also check the transcript in the ¡A escuchar! section.

MARÍA DEL CARMEN SALAS

Edad: ....

Profesión: ....

Deberes: ....

Aspectos que considera positivos en su profesión: ....

....

....

Aspectos que considera difíciles en su profesión:....................................

....

....

....

7 Now give the Spanish for the following phrases used by María del Carmen and the interviewer.

   a Could you tell me what you do for a living?

   b I am in charge of . . .

   c What do you like most about your profession?

   d field work

   e That is what I like most.

   f Is there anything you don't like about your work?

   g They are very demanding.

   h You have to renew yourself constantly.

8 03.05 **In the second interview, Javier Molina talks about his job at the tourist information office in Alicante. Listen and then answer the questions in Spanish.**

funcionario (m)	*official*
tener suerte	*to be lucky*
propiedad (f)	*property*
seguro/a	*safe* (adjective)

   a ¿Cuánto tiempo hace que trabaja Javier en la Oficina de Turismo de Alicante?

   b ¿Dónde trabajaba antes?

   c ¿Por qué decidió cambiarse?

   d ¿Cómo describe su nuevo puesto?

   e ¿En qué consiste su trabajo?

   f ¿Qué tipo de información piden los turistas?

9 Rephrase the sentences using an alternative word order, making any changes that are necessary. Give two alternatives for each.

Remember that changes in word order affect the emphasis you give to different elements within the sentence.

Ejemplo: Fue María la que me lo dijo. *La que me lo dijo fue María / María fue la que me lo dijo.*

   a Llegó a Madrid el viernes por la tarde.
   b Su madre le llamó por teléfono a las cinco de la mañana.
   c El teléfono móvil lo dejé en el restaurante donde comimos.
   d La noticia la supimos por Pepe, que nos llamó.
   e Antonia recibió el email de César el sábado.

10 The following article looks at youth unemployment in Spain through the story of María Soledad, one of thousands of young people who are looking for their first job. Read the text and answer the questions.

licenciatura (f)	*degree*
ingresos (m pl)	*income*
escasos/as	*low, poor, scarce*
paro (m)	*unemployment*
el anuncio (m)	*advertisement*

La búsqueda del primer empleo

María Soledad P. tiene 23 años y una licenciatura en traducción e interpretación de una universidad madrileña, que completó hace dos años con excelentes resultados. Domina perfectamente el inglés y el francés, pero María Soledad, como muchos otros jóvenes españoles, no ha podido encontrar trabajo en su especialidad. Actualmente trabaja vendiendo libros a domicilio y sus ingresos, escasos y fluctuantes, no le permiten alquilar un piso y vivir independientemente, lo que la obliga a seguir viviendo en casa de sus padres, donde comparte habitación con dos de sus hermanos.

El caso de María Soledad no es único, puesto que son miles los jóvenes españoles que se encuentran en similar situación. El paro, que en el último tiempo ha alcanzado niveles nunca antes vistos, afecta mayormente a los jóvenes y a las mujeres. El haber hecho estudios universitarios no es garantía de que se pueda conseguir un empleo estable y bien remunerado.

Las posibilidades de que esta situación cambie son escasas por ahora, y María Soledad quizá deba seguir esperando un tiempo largo antes de que consiga un trabajo que tenga relación con lo que estudió. Mientras tanto, y día a día, sigue mirando los anuncios de trabajo del periódico y enviando su currículum con la esperanza de que la llamen, al menos para una entrevista. El día que ello suceda, María Soledad sabe que deberá enfrentarse a una dura competencia con tantos otros que, como ella, buscan cambiar su situación.

a What did María Soledad study?

b What does she do at present?

c Who is she living with and why?

d What does she do day by day?

11 How are the following ideas expressed in the text?

    a She's completely fluent in English and French.

    b She works selling books door-to-door.

    c Having done university studies . . .

    d . . . in the hope that she may at least be called for an interview.

Now can you find in the text expressions with a similar meaning as:

    e una universidad de Madrid

    f ya que

    g obtener un trabajo

    h con un buen sueldo/salario

    i cuando esto ocurra.

 Test yourself

1 How would each of the following people say what their occupation is and what it is they do? Look up the occupations in your dictionary if necessary, and fill in the blank spaces with an appropriate verb: **fabricar**, **cuidar**, **enseñar**, **conducir**, **construir**, **dirigir**, **apagar**, **repartir**.

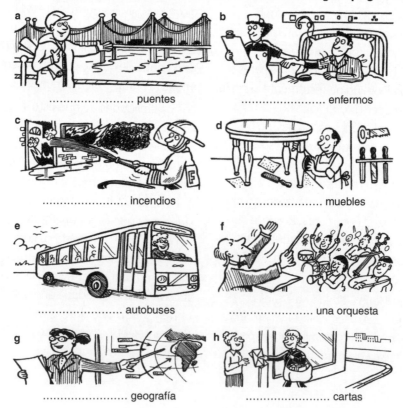

a .... puentes

b .... enfermos

c .... incendios

d .... muebles

e .... autobuses

f .... una orquesta

g .... geografía

h .... cartas

2 How would you express the following in Spanish?

 a They have been living on the Costa del Sol for five years. (use **llevar**)

 b How long have you been working for this company? (informal, use **hace**)

 c Victoria is going to New York on business but I'm going on holiday. I'm also going shopping.

 d What she likes most about teaching is the contact with people. She's been teaching Spanish for a long time. (use **llevar**)

 e It's normally my boss who does the buying but today it's my turn. (more than one possibility)

 f What I don't much like about my job is the salary, although I do like travelling. (more than one possibility)

Test 1 checks language related to professions and occupations that you are probably already familiar with. If not, this is a good chance to increase your vocabulary. Test 2 focuses on a number of language points covered in this unit. The uses of llevar and hace in time phrases are particularly important here. If you are satisfied with your performance, go on to the next unit; if not, go through the New expressions and Language discovery once again.

SELF CHECK

	I CAN . . .
○	. . . describe my job.
○	. . . discuss working conditions.
○	. . . say what I like or dislike about my job.
○	. . . refer to events which began in the past and which are still in progress.

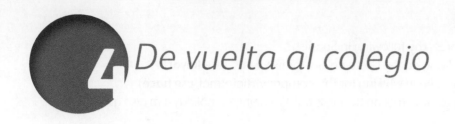

4 De vuelta al colegio

In this unit you will learn how to:
▶ *talk about your studies and the languages you speak.*
▶ *refer to past events and how long ago something happened.*
▶ *make detailed enquiries.*

CEFR: *Can synthesize information from a variety of sources (B2); can write clear connected text following established conventions, e.g. a business letter (B2); can understand correspondence given the occasional use of a dictionary (C1).*

Conversations

1 USTED HABLA MUY BIEN ESPAÑOL *YOU SPEAK SPANISH VERY WELL*

En una reunión social en un país de habla española, hablan dos desconocidas, Francisca Bravo y Sarah Parker.

1 04.01 **First, look at the vocabulary and practise the key language on the audio. Then listen to the conversation. Whose husband comes from a bicultural family, Francisca's or Sarah's?**

ha sido enviado/a	*he has been sent*
un par (m)	*a couple*
todavía me falta mucho por aprender	*I (still) have a lot to learn*
me da vergüenza (f)	*I feel ashamed*
lo domina perfectamente	*he is perfectly fluent*

Francisca	Vd. es inglesa, ¿verdad?
Sarah	Sí, soy inglesa, de Bath. ¿Conoce Vd. Inglaterra?
Francisca	Sí, estuve en Londres con mi marido hace un par de años. Nos gustó mucho. Es una ciudad muy bonita. Me gustaría mucho volver. ¿Y Vd. está aquí de vacaciones?
Sarah	No, mi marido ha sido enviado aquí por su empresa y nos quedaremos tres años.
Francisca	¡Estupendo! Vd. habla muy bien español.
Sarah	Gracias. Estudié español en la escuela y antes de venirme, hice un curso intensivo de tres meses. Pero todavía me falta mucho por aprender. Espero tomar algún curso en una escuela de idiomas. ¿Y Vd. habla inglés?
Francisca	¡Uy! Lo hablo, pero muy mal. Me da vergüenza decirlo. Mi marido sí, él habla inglés bastante bien. Lo aprendió en Estados Unidos. Vivió allí antes de que nos casáramos. También habla algo de alemán, y el francés lo domina perfectamente. Su madre es francesa.
Sarah	¡Qué bien! A mí me encantan los idiomas.

> **LANGUAGE TIP**
>
> Note the following two constructions: **antes de** + infinitive (**antes de venirme** *before coming away*), and **antes de que** + subjunctive (**antes de que nos casáramos** *before we got married*). The use of a preposition, **de** in this case, requires the use of the infinitive, while **que** calls for the use of the subjunctive. The verb form **casáramos** is the imperfect subjunctive (more on this in Unit 9).

2 ¿Verdadero o falso?

  a Francisca está en Londres con su marido desde hace un par de años.

  b Londres les agradó mucho.

  c El marido de Sarah es empresario.

  d Los primeros estudios de español de Sarah los hizo en la escuela.

  e Francisca vivió en Estados Unidos antes de que se casara.

  f Su marido domina el inglés, el alemán y el francés.

2 PIDIENDO INFORMACIÓN *ASKING FOR INFORMATION*

Sarah Parker pide información sobre cursos de español en una escuela de idiomas.

1 04.02 **Listen for the following information: What is Sarah's level of Spanish, intermediate or advanced?**

al final del pasillo (m)	*at the end of the corridor*
curso abreviado (m)	*short course*
no dispongo de …	*I haven't got …*
nivel superior (m)	*advanced level*
matrícula (f)	*registration*
folleto informativo (m)	*information brochure*
alojamiento (m)	*accommodation*

Secretaria	Buenos días. ¿Qué desea?
Sarah	Buenos días. ¿Podría darme información sobre los cursos de español para extranjeros?
Secretaria	¿Quiere usted pasar a la oficina número veinte, por favor? Allí le darán toda la información que necesite. Está al final del pasillo.
Sarah	Gracias.
	(En la oficina N°. 20)
Encargado	Buenos días, ¿dígame?
Sarah	Buenos días. He venido a pedir información sobre los cursos de español para extranjeros.
Encargado	¿Vd. es profesora de español? Se lo pregunto porque para profesores extranjeros de español tenemos cursos especiales.
Sarah	No, no, estoy interesada en un curso general.
Encargado	Bueno, en ese caso le puedo recomendar el curso general que empieza el 31 de julio y termina el 26 de agosto.
Sarah	¿Del 31 de julio al 26 de agosto me ha dicho?

Encargado	Exactamente. Son cuatro semanas en total. También tenemos un curso intensivo que va del 3 al 29 de julio y un curso abreviado del 28 de agosto al 16 de septiembre.
Sarah	Prefiero el curso general. No dispongo de mucho tiempo como para hacer el curso intensivo y el curso abreviado no es suficiente. ¿Cuál es el horario de clases?
Encargado	Bueno, en el caso del nivel superior, que es el que le correspondería a Vd. por su nivel de español, las clases de lengua son de 9.00 a 1.00. Y por la tarde, de 5.00 a 7.00, hay un ciclo de conferencias sobre cultura y civilización hispánicas.
Sarah	Perdone, no he entendido lo último que me ha dicho.
Encargado	He dicho que entre las 5.00 y las 7.00 de la tarde hay una serie de conferencias sobre cultura y civilización.
Sarah	¿Y . . . puede decirme cuánto cuesta la matrícula?
Encargado	Un momento, por favor, le daré un folleto informativo que incluye los precios y el boletín de inscripción. También tiene aquí información sobre alojamiento en caso de que lo necesite.
Sarah	Muchas gracias.

2 Answer the following questions in Spanish.
   a ¿Por qué le pregunta el encargado a Sarah si ella es profesora de español?
   b ¿Qué duración tiene el curso general? ¿Y el curso abreviado?
   c ¿Por qué no desea hacer el curso intensivo Sarah?
   d ¿Qué le da el encargado a Sarah?

3 Find the expressions in the dialogue which mean:
   a Could you give me . . . ?
   b There they'll give you . . .
   c in case you need it
   d I'm asking you (about it) . . .

04.03 **Now practise the key language from the conversation, trying to imitate the pronunciation and intonation of the speaker.**

NEW EXPRESSIONS

Look at the Spanish then complete the missing translations. Then hide either column and test your memory.

Saying what you have studied and what languages you speak

Estudié español en la escuela.	*I studied Spanish _____*
Hice un curso avanzado.	*I took an _____ course.*
Lo hablo (el inglés), pero muy mal.	*I speak it, but very badly.*
Lo hablo (el inglés), pero no lo domino.	*I speak it, but not fluently.*
Él habla inglés bastante bien.	*He speaks English very well.*

Referring to past events

Estudié español.	*I studied Spanish.*
Lo aprendió en EE. UU.	*He learnt it in the United States.*
Vivió allí antes de que nos casáramos.	*He lived there before we got married.*

Saying how long ago something happened

Estuve en Londres con mi marido hace un par de años.	*I was in London with my husband _____*
El año pasado estuvimos en Edimburgo.	*Last year we were in Edinburgh.*
Hace varios años hice un viaje a EE.UU.	*A few years ago I took a trip _____*

Making enquiries

¿Podría darme información sobre los cursos de español?	*Could you give me information about the Spanish courses?*
¿Puede decirme cuánto cuesta la matrícula?	*Can you tell me what the registration fees are?*

Language discovery

 You have seen this language in action. Now can you work out the rules?

1 **How would you say that you did these things at some point in the past?**
   a jugar al baloncesto (*play basketball*)
   b asistir a un congreso (*attend a conference*)
   c hacer un curso de baile (*take a dance class*)

2 **How do you say in Spanish?**
   a a few days ago   b a month ago   c two years ago

3 **What direct or indirect pronouns can you substitute for the underlined words in each sentence?**
   a ¿Ya conoces <u>a Joaquín</u>?
   b No recordaron <u>tu cumpleaños</u>.
   c Me da vergüenza contarte <u>la verdad</u>.
   d Sandra me explicó <u>cómo llegar a su casa</u>.
   e Sí, puedo dar <u>la noticia a tus padres</u>.

1 THE PRETERITE TENSE

Usage

To refer to events which are past and complete and to events which lasted a definite period of time and ended in the past, you use the preterite tense or simple past tense. For example:

Lo *aprendió* en Estados Unidos.	*He learnt it in the United States.*
***Estudié* español durante dos años.**	*I studied Spanish for two years.*

Formation

The preterite tense has two sets of endings, one for **-ar** verbs and another one for **-er** and **-ir** verbs. Here are two fully conjugated verbs: **estudiar** *to study* and **aprender** *to learn*.

estudié	*I studied*	**estudiamos**	*we studied*
estudiaste	*you studied* (familiar)	**estudiasteis**	*you studied* (familiar)
estudió	*he/she/you studied*	**estudiaron**	*they/you studied*

aprendí	*I learnt*	**aprendimos**	*we learnt*
aprendiste	*you learnt*	**aprendisteis**	*you learnt* (familiar)
aprendió	*he/she/you learnt*	**aprendieron**	*they/you learnt*

For irregular verbs in the preterite, such as **hacer** *to do, make*: **hice**, **hiciste**, **hizo** …, **estar** *to be*: **estuve**, **estuviste**, **estuvo** …, see the Irregular verbs section.

2 HACE *AGO*

With a verb in the preterite tense, **hace** translates into English as *ago*.

***Estuve* en Londres con mi marido *hace* un par de años.**	*I was in London with my husband two years ago.*

Compare this construction with the one you learnt in Unit 3, such as:

***Hace* un año que vivo en Madrid.**	*I have been living in Madrid for a year.*

3 DIRECT OBJECT PRONOUNS

The word **lo** in **lo hablo** *I speak it*, **lo aprendió** *he learnt it*, is a direct object pronoun. You use a direct object pronoun to avoid the repetition of a noun, in this case the word **el inglés**, *English*.

¿Y usted habla inglés?	*And do you speak English?*
Lo hablo, pero muy mal.	*I speak it, but very badly.*

Here is the complete set of direct object pronouns:

Singular		Plural	
me	*me*	**nos**	*us*
te	*you* (familiar)	**os**	*you* (familiar)
lo/le	*you, him, it* (m)	**los/les**	*you, them* (m)
la	*you, her, it* (f)	**las**	*you, them* (f)

Here are some further examples:

***La* vi ayer.**	*I saw her/it yesterday.*
***Nos* llamó.**	*He/She called us.*

In many parts of Spain you will now hear **le**, **les**, instead of **lo**, **los**, for human males – singular and plural respectively – all of which are considered correct. It may be easier for you to memorize the following simple rule when using the masculine form of direct object pronouns: use **lo** and **los** for things and **le** and **les** for people.

¿Conoces a Juan?	*Do you know Juan?*
Sí, *le* (or *lo*) conozco.	*Yes, I know him.*

4 INDIRECT OBJECT PRONOUNS

To say *to/for me*, *to/for you*, *to/for him*, *her*, etc., you use the following set of words which are called indirect object pronouns.

Singular		Plural	
me	*me, to me, for me*	**nos**	*us, to us, for us*
te	*you, to you, for you* (familiar)	**os**	*you, to you, for you* (familiar)
le	*you, him/her, to you, him/her, for you, him/her*	**les**	*you, them, to you, them, for you, them*

Examples:

¿Podría dar*me* información . . . ?	*Could you give me information . . . ?*
Allí *le* darán toda la información.	*There they will give you all the information.*

In some areas, notably in Madrid, you may hear **la** for **le** for feminine:

¿La dijiste?	*Did you tell her?*
La di todo.	*I gave her everything.*

This usage is rare in Latin America.

If you have two object pronouns, one direct and one indirect, the indirect one comes first.

Él *me* lo explicó.	*He explained it to me.*

When the indirect object **le** (or **les**) precedes **lo**, **la**, **los** or **las**, the indirect object becomes **se**. For example:

Le pregunto.	*I ask you.*
Lo pregunto.	*I ask about it.*
Se lo pregunto.	*I ask you (about it).*

Notice that object pronouns normally precede the verb, but in phrases where a verb precedes an infinitive, the object pronouns may either precede the main verb or be attached to the infinitive. For example: **¿Podría darme información . . .?** or **¿Me podría dar información?**

Practice

1 **Complete the sentences with the correct object pronouns: me, te, lo, le, etc.**

   a '¿_____ puedes explicar lo que significa esta frase? No entiendo muy bien el español.' 'Por supuesto, yo _____ _____ explicaré.'

   b '¿Habla Vd. español?' '_____ hablo, pero no muy bien.'

   c 'Carlos habla demasiado rápido. No _____ entiendo casi nada.'

   d 'Por favor, cuando llegue María diga _____ que _____ llame. Necesito preguntar _____ algo.' 'Muy bien, _____ _____ diré.'

   e 'Por favor, ¿podría dar _____ información sobre los cursos de español?' 'Un momento, por favor, _____ _____ daré en seguida, y _____ daré también un folleto informativo'.

2 Read a portion of an email written by Alfonso to his penfriend in England and complete the text with a verb from the box. (Use the preterite tense.)

estudiar	aprender	asistir	abrir	alegrarse	merecer
conseguir	ir	tener que	tener	hacer	

Querida Bárbara:

(a) _____ mucho de recibir carta tuya nuevamente y de saber que te **(b)** _____ bien en tus exámenes. Por lo que me cuentas, el curso que **(c)** _____ era bastante difícil.

Me preguntas si he estudiado inglés. Bueno, la verdad es que lo **(d)** _____ durante varios años, pero nunca **(e)** _____ hablarlo correctamente. Creo que no **(f)** _____ un buen profesor y además éramos muchos en la clase y no teníamos oportunidad de practicarlo. Pero hace unos seis meses **(g)** _____ a un curso intensivo en una escuela de idiomas que se **(h)** _____ aquí en Segovia y **(i)** _____ bastante. **(j)** _____ estudiar mucho, pues teníamos seis horas diarias de clases, pero creo que **(k)** _____ la pena, ya que ahora, al menos puedo comunicarme y entiendo casi todo. Espero que cuando te visite en Inglaterra me puedas ayudar . . .

---

3 At a conference in a Spanish-speaking country you engage in informal conversation with one of the participants.

Señor   Vd. habla muy bien español.

Tú   **(a)** *Thank him. Say that is very kind of him.*

Señor   ¿Dónde lo aprendió?

Tú   **(b)** *Say you learnt it at school, but you also spent six months in Spain. Ask him if he speaks English.*

Señor   Lo hablo, pero bastante mal. Lo encuentro muy difícil. Pero el francés sí lo hablo muy bien.

Tú   **(c)** *Ask him where he studied French.*

Señor   Bueno, mis padres vivieron en París cuando yo era pequeño. Lo aprendí allí. ¿Y Vd. habla francés?

Tú   **(d)** *Yes, you did several years of French at school and you had an excellent teacher. And you also go to France every summer. Last year you were in Cannes. You liked it very much.*

Señor   Sí, a mí me encanta Cannes también. Mi mujer y yo estuvimos allí hace unos cinco años. Lo pasamos estupendamente.

4 You are going to make enquiries about Spanish courses at a language school in Spain. Write the necessary questions to get the information you need.

  a Ask if they do summer courses in Spanish.

  b Ask when they start.

  c Ask what levels they offer.

  d Ask how much they cost.

  e Ask about the timetable.

  f Ask if they can help you find accommodation.

5 Pamela Johnson wrote to a school in Malaga asking for information about Spanish courses.

First, read the letter and then answer the questions.

El objeto de la presente es ...	*This is to ...*
En espera de sus gratas noticias	*I look forward to hearing from you*

---

26 Devonshire Street
Londres W3 7HF
Inglaterra

26 de mayo de 2014

Señor Director de Estudios
Cursos para extranjeros
Universidad de Málaga
San Agustín, 6
29080 – Málaga
España

Muy Señor mío:

El objeto de la presente es solicitar a Vd. que me envíe información sobre los cursos de español para extranjeros, que ofrecerá la Universidad de Málaga este verano.

Le ruego que me dé información detallada sobre las fechas en que estos se realizarán, los niveles que se ofrecen, el horario de clases y el importe de la inscripción.

Le agradeceré además, que me informe sobre la posibilidad de conseguir alojamiento a través de ustedes con una familia española.

En espera de sus gratas noticias, le saluda atentamente,

Pamela Johnson

---

a What information did Pamela ask for in the letter?

b Does she know in which level she wants to enrol?

c What sort of hosting arrangement is she interested in?

 Now have a go at translating the letter into your own language.

> **LANGUAGE TIP**
>
> Note the use of the present subjunctive in: **. . . solicitar a Vd. que me envíe información . . .** literally, *to request that you send me information . . .*, **Le ruego que me dé . . .** *Please give me . . .* (literally, *I beg you that you give me . . .*), **Le agradeceré que me informe . . .** *I shall be grateful if you would inform me . . .* (literally, *I shall be grateful that you inform me . . .*).

6 Here is part of the information Pamela Johnson received from the school of languages in Malaga. Read it through and make a note in English of the following points:

a How can you register?

b What certificates or diploma can you obtain?

c What sort of accommodation can they help you find?

d How are the students grouped?

e How many hours a week do you have to attend?

f What activities can students take part in during the course?

CURSOS DE ESPAÑOL PARA EXTRANJEROS
CURSO DE VERANO

El Curso se dirige a extranjeros que deseen iniciar o ampliar sus conocimientos en lengua y cultura españolas.

Duración
Se desarrolla en tres ciclos, pudiéndose inscribir en uno, dos o los tres.

Ciclo I	03.07 – 30.07
Ciclo II	01.08 – 30.08
Ciclo III	02.09 – 27.09

Inscripción y matrícula
El Curso de verano es un curso abierto: no es necesario ningún título académico para inscribirse, solo se precisa tener 16 años.

Enviar a la Secretaría la ficha de inscripción, dos fotografías y fotocopia del documento de pago.

Exámenes y certificados
Los exámenes son obligatorios solo para los alumnos que deseen obtener uno de estos títulos:
▶ Certificado de Lengua Española;
   Permanencia mínima: un mes.

> ▶ Diploma de Estudios Hispánicos;
> Permanencia mínima: dos meses.

Alojamiento
La Secretaría del Curso facilitará direcciones de familias o apartamentos a los alumnos inscritos que lo soliciten.

Horario de clases y niveles
Los alumnos se dividen en niveles según sus conocimientos de la lengua: básico, intermedio y superior. Se imparten cuatro clases diarias de lunes a viernes, desde las 9.00 hasta las 13.15.

Otras actividades
Durante el curso se organizan conciertos, espectáculos y sesiones de cine. Asimismo, hay visitas a los principales monumentos de la ciudad y excursiones a ciudades de interés (Granada, Córdoba, Sevilla y Ronda).

También se organiza un viaje a Marruecos. Durante el mes de agosto son las fiestas de la ciudad con actos folclóricos y culturales de gran interés.

7 In a Spanish magazine, you see the following courses advertised and you decide to write an email to enquire about one of them.

anuncio (m)	*advertisement*
ofrecer	*to offer*
información referente a . . .	*relevant information about* . . .
realizarse	*to be held*
inscribirse	*to register*
lo antes possible	*as soon as possible*
estar interesado/a	*to be interested*

GRADUADO ESCOLAR	GUITARRA
Preparación para la obtención del Titulo del Estado.	Método seguro. Por solfeo o por cifra. Incluye tutoría en internet gratis.
CULTURA GENERAL	**ORDENADORES Y BASIC**
Los conocimientos que toda persona debe poseer hoy.	Lograrás un conocimiento completo de lo que da de sí un Ordenador Personal y su programación.
DECORACIÓN	**CONTABILIDAD**
Podrás decorar desde una habitación de niños a una tienda.	Muy sencillo y práctico. Diploma de Contable.

Follow these guidelines to structure your email:

a Say you have seen the advertisement for courses offered by the Centro de Estudios Eva and state which course you are interested in.

b Ask them to send you all the relevant information about the course, including the date when it is held, registration fees, timetable and how you can register.

c Ask them to send you the information as soon as possible.

¡A escuchar!

In an interview on the subject of education, Gloria Díaz from Spain talked about the school she went to.

8 04.04 **Study the key words, then listen to the conversation.**

recuerdos (m pl)	*memories*
olvidado/a	*forgotten*
disfruté	*I enjoyed it*
nos llevábamos mal	*we didn't get on*
simpatiquísimo/a	*very nice*
asignatura (f)	*(school) subject*
suspendí	*I failed*
guardar	*to keep*

How well have you understood the conversation: ¿Verdadero o falso?

a Hace casi dos años que Gloria está en el colegio.

b Gloria estudió en un colegio religioso para chicas.

c Ella fue allí porque prefería estar solo con chicas.

d La profesora que más le gustaba era la de matemáticas.

e Con la profesora de historia se llevaba muy bien.

f Sus asignaturas favoritas eran Matemáticas y Ciencias.

9 04.05 **Role play – This conversation brings together the language you've already learnt. Listen to it first, then follow the prompts and play the part of the person being interviewed.**

> **LEARNING TIP**
> Occasionally, there is no text to follow as you listen; this is to help you develop real-world listening and speaking skills.

10 **Five writers talk about some of their childhood experiences. Look at the vocabulary first, then read the texts and answer the questions which follow.**

tirar	*to throw away*
mono/a	*pretty*
engañar	*to deceive*
aguantar el llanto	*to hold back one's tears*
enfermizo/a	*unhealthy, morbid*
autoestima (f)	*self-esteem*
amenazado/a	*threatened*
reponerse	*to recover*
quiebra (f)	*bankruptcy*
redundar en	*to have as a consequence*
huellas profundísimas (f pl)	*deep marks*
Edad Dorada (f)	*Golden Age*

a Rosa Montero, España

De pequeña, cuando tenía cinco años, me enfermé de tuberculosis. Estuve en casa sin ir al colegio durante muchos años. Entonces, mi distracción era leer y escribir muchísimo. La escritura era un juego: empezaba una novela del Oeste o de asesinatos y al día siguiente la tiraba y escribía otra. A los nueve o diez años, cuando volví al colegio, mi sorpresa fue descubrir que las demás niñas no jugaban a eso.

b Ana María Matute, España

Me sentía fea. . . ¡Y no lo era! Era muy mona. Digo, las fotografías no engañan, ¿no? Pero mis hermanas eran unas bellezas. . . Así, yo vivía en mi soledad, tranquila, tímida, aguantándome siempre el llanto.

c Isabel Allende, Chile

Yo tuve una infancia bien infeliz. Llena de terrores, de preguntas sin respuestas. Con una sensibilidad enfermiza y un orgullo ilimitado, que provenía de una muy baja autoestima y de sentirme muy amenazada, muy vulnerable.

d Mario Benedetti, Uruguay

A mi padre le fue mal con una farmacia que había comprado en Tacuarembó y durante años no pudimos reponernos de esa quiebra. Eso redundó en una infancia sin juguetes, y eso nunca fue un buen recuerdo.

e Mario Vargas Llosa, Perú

La peor marca quedó a partir de los diez años, cuando conocí a mi padre, en una relación espantosa que me dejó huellas profundísimas. Pero, tal vez, también me marcaron esos primeros diez años vividos con la familia de mi madre, que son algo así como la Edad Dorada.

> **CULTURE TIP**
>
> **Rosa Montero** (Madrid, 1951), a journalist and writer, is the author of a number of successful books, including several novels. **Ana María Matute** (Barcelona, 1925), a well-known Spanish novelist, was only ten years old at the outbreak of the Spanish Civil War (1936–9). The war and life in post-war Spain had a profound influence on her writing. **Isabel Allende** (Perú, 1942), a Chilean and best-selling novelist, has done most of her writing in the United States. **Mario Benedetti** (Uruguay, 1920–2009), a journalist, novelist and poet, was one of the most outstanding writers in the Hispanic world. **Mario Vargas Llosa** (Perú, 1936), a novelist, essayist and playwright, won the 2010 Nobel Prize for Literature.

Now answer these questions:

a What did Rosa Montero do during her illness, and what did she discover when she returned to school?

b How does Ana María Matute describe herself in her childhood?

c What does Isabel Allende say about her childhood?

d What event marked Mario Benedetti's life?

e How does Mario Vargas Llosa describe the relationship with his father? And with his mother's family?

❓ Test yourself

1 Complete each sentence with the preterite tense of the verb in brackets.
   a Cristóbal _____ sus estudios en Madrid. Alberto y Mercedes los _____ en Barcelona. Yo también los _____ allí. (hacer)
   b Esteban _____ cinco días en París y Luis y yo _____ en Londres una semana. (estar)
   c (Yo) le _____ a Gloria que viniera, pero (ella) me _____ que no podía. (decir)
   d ' ¿Dónde (tú) _____ mi libro? ' (Yo) lo _____ en tu biblioteca. (poner)
   e Jorge _____ un buen estudiante. Marta y Paca también lo _____, pero nosotros _____ los mejores. (ser)
   f José _____ en el coche. Sara y Ramón _____ en el autobús y yo _____ en la bici. (venir)

2 How would you express the following in Spanish?
   a Could you give me information about the Spanish summer courses, please?
   b Will you send us information about accommodation too? We'll give you our emails.
   c I feel ashamed to say it, but my Spanish is not as good as my French, although I studied it for a year.
   d My son is completely fluent in French and Spanish. He learnt them at school and also spent some time in France and Spain.

3 The following phrases are typical of formal letter writing. What do they mean?
   a El objeto de la presente es pedir un folleto informativo . . .
   b Le ruego que me indique cuál es el importe de la inscripción . . .
   c Les agradeceré que me consignan alojamiento con una familia española . . .
   d En espera de sus gratas noticias . . .

Did you manage to get all the verb forms right in Test 1? If you did, congratulations! These verbs are very common. If you are still uncertain about them, check the Irregular verbs section. Don't be discouraged if you made a few mistakes in Tests 2 and 3. Communication is the first step, accuracy will follow.

SELF CHECK

	I CAN . . .
⚪	. . . talk about my studies and the languages I speak.
⚪	. . . refer to past events and how long ago something happened.
⚪	. . . make detailed enquiries.

5 De vacaciones

In this unit you will learn how to:
▸ *describe places and people you knew in the past.*
▸ *express hope, intention and regret.*
▸ *talk about future events and plans.*
▸ *report and discuss the weather.*

CEFR: *Can understand specialized articles and technical instructions, e.g. weather bulletins (C1); can present clear detailed descriptions on a range of subjects, e.g. talk about an organized tour (B2).*

Conversations

1 UN VIAJE A CUBA *A JOURNEY TO CUBA*

Pablo Dávila y Ana Ramírez hablan de sus últimas vacaciones.

1 05.01 **As you listen to the conversation, try answering this question: Did Ana and her friends plan their holiday themselves or did they go with a tour group?**

agencia de viajes (f)	*travel agency*
majo/a	*nice (Spain)*
por mi cuenta	*by myself, independently*
nos habría resultado caro/a	*it would have been expensive (for us)*

Pablo	¿El año pasado también viniste aquí de vacaciones?
Ana	No, el año pasado fui a Cuba con unas amigas. Estuvimos en La Habana y en Varadero.
Pablo	¿Y qué tal?
Ana	Nos gustó muchísimo. Estuvimos tres días en La Habana y una semana en Varadero. Varadero es un lugar muy bonito y tiene unas playas estupendas. Y el hotel donde nos quedamos era excelente. Estaba a cinco minutos de la playa. Tenía piscina, discoteca . . .
Pablo	¿Fuisteis a través de alguna agencia de viajes?
Ana	Sí, porque de otra manera nos habría resultado demasiado caro. Mereció la pena, y la gente del grupo era muy maja, la mayoría era gente joven.
Pablo	La verdad es que a mí los viajes organizados no me gustan nada. Prefiero viajar por mi cuenta.

2 **Find the phrases in the conversations which mean:**

   a Last year I went to Cuba.

   b The hotel where we stayed was excellent.

   c Through a travel agency

   d otherwise

   e It was worth it.

3 **Answer the following questions in Spanish.**

   a ¿Dónde pasó sus vacaciones Ana el año pasado?

   b ¿Cuánto tiempo estuvo allí?

   c ¿Qué dice Ana del hotel?

   d ¿Fue por su cuenta? ¿Por qué sí/no?

   e ¿Cómo describe Ana a la gente con que viajó?

   f ¿Qué dice Pablo de los viajes organizados?

4 05.02 **Role play – Imagine that you are visiting Chile and someone asks you about last year's holiday. Follow the prompts and answer his questions.**

2 ESPERO IR A MÉXICO *I HOPE TO GO TO MEXICO*

Pablo y Ana hablan de sus planes para las próximas vacaciones.

1 05.03 **Listen and answer: How much holiday is Pablo planning on taking next summer?**

espero ir	*I hope to go*
pienso irme	*I'm thinking of going*
hacia finales de	*towards the end of*
así podré conocer . . .	*that way I'll be able to see . . .* (lit. *to know*)
me contó maravillas de . . .	*she spoke wonderfully about . . .*
. . . que me entusiasman	*. . . which I am very tempted by*
ya veremos	*we'll see*

Ana	¿El año que viene vendrás aquí otra vez?
Pablo	No, el próximo verano espero ir a México. Un amigo mexicano que conocí en Salamanca, me ha invitado a su casa. Pienso irme hacia finales de julio y me quedaré allí todo el mes de agosto. Él tomará sus vacaciones en la misma fecha y viajaremos juntos. Así podré conocer un poco del país.
Ana	¡Estupendo! Te gustará mucho. Mi hermana estuvo en México hace un par de años y me contó maravillas de los sitios que visitó y de la gente.
Pablo	Bueno, ¿y tú que harás? ¿Volverás aquí otra vez?
Ana	No lo creo. Espero ir a algún lugar diferente. Hay unos viajes al oriente que me entusiasman mucho y que no son nada caros. Ya veremos. Aún falta mucho tiempo . . .

2 If *aún falta mucho tiempo* means *There is still a long time to go*, how would you translate: *Falta mucho para mi cumpleaños* and *Faltan dos meses para la Navidad*?

3 Complete these phrases with information from the conversation.

    a El próximo verano Pablo irá de vacaciones a _____.

    b Él ha sido invitado por _____.

    c Piensa viajar en (mes) _____.

    d Estará allí todo el mes de _____.

    e Viajará con _____.

    f A Ana le gustaría ir a (lugar) _____.

4 05.04 **Role play – Your Chilean friend wants to know if you will visit Chile again next year. Speak in the pauses and listen to confirm your answers.**

3 HABLANDO DEL TIEMPO *TALKING ABOUT THE WEATHER*

En la recepción del Hotel El Conquistador, dos turistas sudamericanos hablan del tiempo.

1 05.05 **Practise the key sentences on the audio before listening to the conversation. What plan does the man say has been derailed by the weather?**

Señor	¿Sigue lloviendo?
Señorita	Lamentablemente sí, no ha parado de llover en toda la noche. Está lloviendo a cántaros en este momento.
Señor	¡Qué lástima! Y yo que pensaba salir de paseo. Tendré que quedarme en el hotel.
Señorita	¡Es una pena! Pero probablemente mañana hará buen tiempo.
Señor	¡Ojalá!

y yo que pensaba . . .	*and I was thinking of . . .*
hará buen tiempo	*the weather will be good*
lamentablemente	*unfortunately*

2 **What phrases are used in the conversation to say the following?**

    a It hasn't stopped raining.

    b It's pouring with rain.

    c What a pity!

    d It's a pity.

    e I hope so.

> **LANGUAGE TIP**
>
> After **seguir** and **continuar**, the verb must be in the gerund: **¿Sigue lloviendo?** *Is it still raining?* **Continúa nevando.** *It is still snowing.* **¿Sigues trabajando?** *Are you still working?*

NEW EXPRESSIONS

Look at the new expressions, and then check your understanding:

1 **How would you say:** *Today it's sunny, but tomorrow the weather will be bad?*

2 **What two ways do you know of saying:** *It's still snowing?*

3 **What is the correct verb form (present tense) to use in: La mayoría de la gente _____ (viajar) acompañada?**

56

Describing places and people you knew in the past

El hotel era excelente.	*The hotel was excellent.*
Tenía piscina.	*It had a swimming pool.*
La gente era muy maja.	*The people were very nice.*
La mayoría era gente joven.	*The majority were young people.*

Expressing hope

Espero ir a México.	*I hope to go to Mexico.*
¡Ojalá!	*I hope so.*

Expressing intentions

Pienso irme hacia finales de julio.	*I intend to go towards the end of July.*
Yo pensaba salir de paseo.	*I was thinking of going out.*

Talking about the future

Me quedaré allí todo el mes de agosto.	*I will stay there for all of August.*
Él tomará sus vacaciones en la misma fecha.	*He will take his holidays on the same date.*
Voy a viajar a España.	*I am going to travel to Spain.*
Vamos a quedarnos aquí.	*We are going to stay here.*
Mañana salgo para Londres.	*I am leaving for London tomorrow.*

Talking about the weather

Hace frío/calor.	*It is cold/warm.*
Hace buen/mal tiempo.	*The weather is good/bad.*
Está despejado.	*It is clear/cloudless.*
Llueve/Está lloviendo.	*It rains./ It is raining.*
Está lloviendo a cántaros.	*It's pouring with rain.*
Hace viento/sol.	*It is windy/sunny.*
Hace bueno.	*The weather is good.*
Mañana hará buen tiempo.	*The weather will be good tomorrow.*
Está nublado.	*It is cloudy/overcast.*
Está nevando.	*It is snowing.*
Nieva.	*It snows./ It is snowing.*

Expressing regret

Lamentablemente, sí.	*Unfortunately/Regrettably yes!*
Desafortunadamente/Desgraciadamente . . .	*Unfortunately . . .*
¡Qué lástima!	*What a pity!/ What a shame!*
¡Es una pena!	*It is a pity!/ It is a shame!*
¡Qué desgracia!	*What a shame!*

> **LANGUAGE TIP**
> Exclamations which use *how* in English translate in Spanish with **qué**:
> **¡Qué terrible!** *How terrible!* **¡Qué increíble!** *How incredible!*

Language discovery

You have seen this language in action. Now can you work out the rules?

1 **Three out of these four phrases refer to the future. Which ones?**
   a saldremos para Ibiza
   b cuando saldríamos para Ibiza
   c vamos a salir para Ibiza
   d salimos para Ibiza mañana

2 **Which form of pasar (*to spend time*) does not take a written accent in the future tense: tú, nosotros or vosotros?**

3 **Using the preterite, how would you say the following?**
   a Her parents were very nice.
   b They were ready to go out.

4 **What difference in perspective do you notice in these two sentences?**
   a Espero pasarlo bien.
   b Espero que lo pases bien.

1 LOOKING AHEAD

To refer to the future you can use:

a the future tense:

Me quedaré allí todo el mes.	*I'll stay there the whole month.*
¿Vendrás aquí otra vez?	*Will you come here again?*

b the construction ir with a + the infinitive:

Va a llover.	*It's going to rain.*
¿Qué vas a hacer?	*What are you going to do?*

c the present tense, particularly with verbs which indicate movement:

Él llega mañana.	*He's arriving tomorrow.*
Esta tarde voy a Madrid.	*I'm going to Madrid this afternoon.*

2 THE FUTURE TENSE

Formation

The future tense is formed with the whole infinitive, to which the endings are added. The same endings are used for the three conjugations: **-ar**, **-er** and **-ir** verbs. Here is an example:

tomar	to take
tomaré	*I will take*
tomarás	*you will take* (familiar)
tomará	*he, she, it, you will take*
tomaremos	*we will take*
tomaréis	*you will take* (familiar)
tomarán	*they, you will take*

A few verbs, such as **venir** *to come*, are irregular in the future tense: **vendré**, **vendrás**, **vendrá**, **vendremos**, **vendréis**, **vendrán**. For other irregular verbs in the future, see the Irregular verbs section.

3 THE IMPERFECT TENSE FOR PAST DESCRIPTION

To describe places or people you knew in the past, you normally use the imperfect tense, for example:

El hotel era excelente.	*The hotel was excellent.*
Estaba a cinco minutos de la playa.	*It was five minutes away from the beach.*
La gente era muy maja.	*The people were very nice.*

Formation

There are two sets of endings for the imperfect tense, one for **-ar** verbs and another one for **-er** and **-ir** verbs. Here are two examples:

estar	to be
estaba	*I was*
estabas	*you were* (familiar)
estaba	*he, she, it was, you were*
estábamos	*we were*
estabais	*you were* (familiar)
estaban	*they, you were*

tener	to have
tenía	*I had*
tenías	*you had* (familiar)
tenía	*he, she, it, you had*
teníamos	*we had*
teníais	*you had* (familiar)
tenían	*they, you had*

Ser *to be* is irregular in the imperfect tense: **era**, **eras**, **era**, **éramos**, **erais**, **eran**. For other irregular verbs in the imperfect tense, see the Irregular verbs section.

4 EXPRESSING HOPE

Notice the use of the infinitive after **esperar** *to hope* when expressing hope not involving others or something outside ourselves.

Espero ir a México.	*I hope to go to Mexico.*
Esperamos volver pronto.	*We hope to come back soon.*

For hope involving others, or something outside ourselves, use **esperar** + **que** + subjunctive:

Espero que vayas conmigo.	*I hope you come with me.*
Espero que no llueva.	*I hope it doesn't rain.*

 Practice

1 **Give the correct form in the future tense of the verbs in brackets.**

Querida Paloma:

Te mando este mail para contarte que el lunes que viene, John
y yo _____ (viajar) a España. _____ (salir) de aquí a las
2.00 de la tarde y _____ (llegar) a Madrid a las 5.00. Aún no
sabemos cuánto tiempo _____ (quedarse), pero esperamos
estar allí por lo menos dos semanas. ¿ _____ (poder) venir
a vernos al hotel el lunes por la noche? _____ (estar) en el
Hotel Gran Vía. Tengo un regalo para ti de Paul y te lo _____
(dar) cuando nos veamos . . . A propósito, ¿qué _____
(hacer) tú en tus próximas vacaciones? Nos gustaría mucho
que vinieras a Inglaterra . . .

2 **Complete the sentences with the correct form of the verbs in brackets, using
either the preterite or the imperfect.**

a El año pasado Isabel y Javier _____ (ir) al Perú. _____ (estar) allí diez días en total.

b _____ (ser) la primera vez que (ellos) _____ (ir) allí y ambos _____ (estar)
fascinados con la idea de conocer Cusco y el Machu Picchu.

c El vuelo desde Madrid les _____ (resultar) bastante largo, pero el avión _____
(llegar) a la hora. En el aeropuerto les _____ (esperar) Antonio, un amigo de Javier
que _____ (vivir) desde hacía dos años en Lima.

d Los primeros dos días los _____ (pasar) en Lima. Antonio, que _____ (conocer)
bien la ciudad les _____ (llevar) a conocer los principales sitios de interés.

e Al tercer día, Isabel y Javier _____ (tomar) un vuelo a Cusco. La llegada a la ciudad
les _____ (parecer) espectacular. _____ (ser) mediodía cuando el avión aterrizó.

f La estancia en la ciudad y la posterior visita al Machu Picchu _____ (ser) los
momentos culminantes de un viaje que ambos _____ (soñar) con realizar desde
hacía mucho tiempo.

 3 **A Spanish friend asks you about your last holiday. Answer his questions.**

Amigo	¿Dónde pasaste tus últimas vacaciones?
Tú	*Say you spent them in San Sebastián, in northern Spain.*
Amigo	¿Y qué tal? ¿Te gustó?
Tú	*Say you liked San Sebastián very much. It is a very nice town, and the hotel where you stayed was excellent. It was opposite the beach, it had a swimming pool and an excellent restaurant. And you were very lucky with the weather. It wasn't too hot.*
Amigo	¿Con quién fuiste?

Tú	*Say you went with some friends. You got on very well together, they were very nice people.*
Amigo	¿Y cuánto tiempo estuvisteis allí?
Tú	*Say you didn't stay long. Unfortunately, you all had to come back to work.*
Amigo	Supongo que volverás allí otra vez el próximo verano.
Tú	*Say you would love to go back, but next year you hope to visit South America. You are thinking of travelling to Argentina and Chile. If you have money, you'll stay a couple of months there. You are thinking of taking on another job to pay for your holiday. Ask your friend if he went anywhere on holiday.*
Amigo	No, desgraciadamente no, no tenía dinero.
Tú	*What a shame!*

4 You are going on holiday to Mexico. The holiday, which starts in Madrid, will take you to Cancún and Mexico City (México D. F.). Read the programme from the travel agency's website.

mostrador (m)	*counter, flight desk*
escala (f)	*stopover*
estancia (f)	*stay*
facultativo/a	*optional*
recogida (f)	*pick-up*

www.viajes-yucatan.com

CANCÚN/MÉXICO D.F.

DÍA 1.°: MADRID/CANCÚN

Presentación en salidas internacionales del aeropuerto de Barajas en el mostrador de Club Vacaciones, dos horas antes de la salida del vuelo. Viajarás en un Boeing 767 de la compañía Spanair en vuelo sin escala a Cancún. A la llegada te espera personal de nuestra organización que te trasladará en autobús privado al hotel. Alojamiento.

DÍAS 2.° AL 6.°: CANCÚN

Estancia en los hoteles en el régimen de pensión elegido, atendidos por nuestro personal que te informará además de las excursiones facultativas, que puedes hacer durante tu estancia.

DÍA 7.°: CANCÚN/MÉXICO D.F.

Recogida en el hotel y traslado al aeropuerto para salir en avión hacia México D.F. Llegada y traslado en autobús privado al hotel. Alojamiento.

DÍAS 8.° AL 13.°: MÉXICO D.F.

Estancia en los hoteles en régimen de alojamiento. Posibilidad de excursiones facultativas.

DÍA 14.°: MÉXICO D.F./CANCÚN

Recogida en el hotel y traslado al aeropuerto para salir hacia Cancún. Traslado al hotel y alojamiento.

DÍA 15.°: CANCÚN/MADRID

Recogida en el hotel y traslado al aeropuerto a la hora que te indique nuestro personal, para embarcarte en un Boeing 767 de la compañía Spanair hacia Madrid donde finaliza nuestro servicio.

Your travelling companion wants to know the following:

   a Which airline are we flying with?

   b Is there a stopover on the way to Cancún?

   c How are we getting from Cancún airport to the hotel?

   d How are we travelling from Cancún to Mexico City?

   e How long are we staying in Mexico City?

   f Are we flying back to Madrid from Mexico City?

 5 **You are talking about your next holiday in Mexico with a Spanish-speaking friend. Answer your friend's questions.**

   a ¿A qué parte de México irás?

   b ¿Qué lugar visitarás primero?

   c ¿Cuántos días te quedarás en total?

   d ¿Te quedarás en casa de amigos?

> **CULTURE TIP**
>
> With just over 100 million people, Mexico is the largest Spanish-speaking country in the world. Mexico City, which Mexicans call **el D. F.** (**Distrito Federal** *Federal District*), is one of the largest cities in the world. Mexico is a top-ten destination worldwide with over 20 million visitors annually.

 6 **During a flight to Madrid you are given a Spanish newspaper which has a weather chart for the whole of Spain and the forecast for the following day. What will the weather be like in Madrid? Study the following information and then answer the questions.**

calima (f)	*haze*
neblina (f)	*mist*
nuboso/a	*cloudy*
nube (f)	*cloud*
ventolina (f)	*light and variable wind*
se pondrá . . .	*it will set . . .*
luna (f)	*moon*

EL TIEMPO EN MADRID

MAÑANA

Área urbana: (Máxima: 33 / Mínima: 18). Cielo despejado. Calimas. Neblinas a primeras horas y calimas posteriormente. Sin cambios térmicos.

Área de la Sierra: Despejado por la mañana con nieblas a primeras horas. Algo nuboso por la tarde con nubes altas. Ventolinas del suroeste.

CONTAMINACIÓN

Los índices de contaminación se mantienen relativamente bajos. La contaminación, por tanto, estacionaria.

El sol saldrá hoy domingo a las 7 horas y 48 minutos y se pondrá a las 20 horas y 36 minutos.

La luna saldrá a las 20 horas y 46 minutos y se pondrá a las 7 horas y 20 minutos.

Fase de la luna: Estamos en luna nueva.

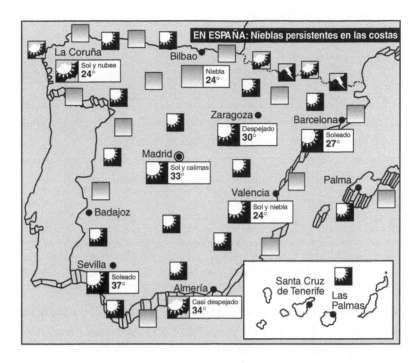

a Will it be overcast in Madrid tomorrow?

b What will the weather be like early in the morning? And later on in the day?

c If you wanted to drive up to the Sierra, what will the weather be like there early in the morning? And in the afternoon?

d With all the traffic that there is in Madrid, the air becomes very polluted at times. What will the situation be like tomorrow?

e If you spend the day at the Sierra tomorrow, you want to return to the city before sunset, as you don't like driving at night. What time will the sun set?

LANGUAGE TIP

Note the ending **-oso** in **nuboso** *cloudy*. A number of Spanish adjectives can be formed in the same way: **caluroso** *warm* (from **calor**), **ruidoso** *noisy* (from **ruido**), **amoroso** *loving, affectionate* (from **amor**). Like all adjectives, such words will agree in gender and number with the noun that they go with: **una noche calurosa** *a warm night*, **unos vecinos ruidosos** *noisy neighbours*.

¡A escuchar! El pronóstico del tiempo

Now that you are familiar with some of the terminology used in Spanish weather forecasts, you should be able to follow a broadcast about the weather in Santiago de Chile.

7 05.06 **First, familiarize yourself with some words and phrases which did not appear in the previous exercise. Then, as you listen, focus on the information which will help you answer the questions in Spanish.**

llovizna (f)	*drizzle*
grado (m)	*degree*
nubosidad (f)	*cloudiness*
humedad (f)	*humidity*

a ¿Cómo estará el tiempo hoy en Santiago, según la Dirección Meteorológica de Chile?
b ¿Cuál será la temperatura mínima probable? ¿Y la máxima?
c ¿Cuáles fueron las temperaturas mínima y máxima ayer en la capital? ¿A qué hora fueron?
d ¿Cuáles son las perspectivas para el viernes 21 de febrero?
e ¿Cuál es la temperatura del momento?

> **LANGUAGE TIP**
> Referring to degrees of temperature with a decimal: **trece grados, una décima** is only one of the variants you will hear in the Spanish-speaking world. Others are: **trece grados y una décima**, or **trece grados con una décima**. When writing figures, the decimal separator usually is a comma, but it is not mentioned in the spoken language.

8 **What sort of holidays do most people in your country prefer, organized tours or independent travel? And what do they like to do when they go on holiday? Read the following passage and compare their preferences with those of Spaniards.**

guía (m/f)	*guide* (person)
viaje organizado (m)	*package tour*
responsabilizarse	*to take responsibility*
paquete turístico (m)	*package tour*
ofertado/a	*offered*
inquietud (f)	*interest*

No nos gusta ir todo el día detrás de un guía

A los españoles nos encanta el viaje organizado, pero mucho menos que al resto de los europeos. Buscamos la seguridad de que alguien se responsabilice de nosotros, aunque los paquetes turísticos ofertados a los españoles son bastante abiertos: dejan tiempos libres y dan opciones diferentes dentro de un mismo viaje, porque se sabe que nuestra idiosincrasia hace que no nos guste ir a todas horas detrás de un guía. Por otra parte, a los españoles nos interesa visitar monumentos, museos, parques naturales . . . Hay una inquietud cultural manifiesta.

How well have you understood? Answer these questions:
a ¿Qué prefieren los españoles, el viaje organizado o el viaje independiente?
b ¿Qué prefieren hacer en sus vacaciones?

Test yourself

1 Change the verbs in brackets into the appropriate forms of the future tense.

a Andrés _____ sus vacaciones en Italia. Sofía y Julio las _____ en Egipto, y yo _____ todo el verano en casa. (pasar)

b El pronóstico del tiempo dice que hoy _____ mucho calor. Adela y yo _____ una excursión a la sierra para escapar de la ciudad. (hacer)

c Debido a la enfermedad de su madre Sandra _____ que cancelar el viaje y lamentablemente (yo) _____ que viajar solo. (tener)

d – ¿Dónde _____ (vosotros) el regalo que os hizo Elena?

– Creo que (nosotros) lo _____ en el salón. (poner)

e – ¿(Tú) le _____ a Paco lo que ocurrió?

– Yo no se lo _____, pero seguramente Victoria se lo _____. (decir)

f David y Lucía _____ a pasar sus vacaciones con nosotros, pero su hijo Pablo no _____. ¿(Tú) _____ conmigo al aeropuerto a recogerlos? (venir)

2 How would you express the following in Spanish?

a The hotel where they stayed was excellent. It wasn't far from the beach and it also had a swimming pool, but unfortunately it poured with rain most of the time.

b But it was worth going. The town was interesting, although it was a bit noisy.

c We're thinking of travelling to Brazil next year. Patricia was there two years ago and she told me wonderful things about Rio.

d No, we're not taking an organized tour. We prefer to travel independently, otherwise it will be too expensive. We'll book our tickets through a travel agency.

e Well, I hope to go on holiday at the end of August. There are some holidays in the Caribbean which are not at all expensive. We'll see. It's still a long way off.

f – Is it still raining?

– Unfortunately, yes. It hasn't stopped raining since we got up.

– What a pity! I was thinking of playing tennis.

The main focus in these tests is verbs, the future tense in Test 1 and the imperfect, preterite and future tenses in Test 2. Note that all but one of the verbs in Test 1 are irregular. For their full forms, see the Irregular verbs section. Test 2 also assesses your knowledge of the vocabulary and expressions from Conversations 1–3. Go back to the conversations and New expressions if necessary, or continue on to Unit 6.

SELF CHECK

	I CAN . . .
○	. . . describe places and people I knew in the past.
○	. . . express my hopes, intentions and regrets.
○	. . . talk about future events and plans.
○	. . . report and discuss the weather.

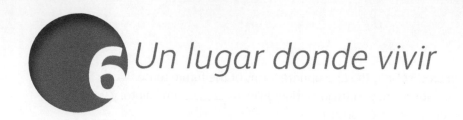

6 Un lugar donde vivir

In this unit you will learn how to:
▶ *enquire about accommodation and book into a hotel.*
▶ *state your personal requirements.*
▶ *describe a place.*
▶ *ask and say how much something costs.*

CEFR: *Can understand and pass on detailed information reliably, e.g. give and take messages about reservations; can scan quickly through a variety of texts to locate information, e.g. infographics (B2).*

Conversations

1 RESERVANDO UNA HABITACIÓN *BOOKING A ROOM*

Martin Baron y su familia están de vacaciones en España. Desde Madrid, Martin llama por teléfono al Hotel San Marcos de Marbella para reservar una habitación.

 1 06.01 **Look at the vocabulary and read the hotel advertisement before you listen. How many people are there in Martin's family and how many rooms will they require?**

disponible	*available*
tengo entendido que …	*I understand that …*
descuento (m)	*discount*
a partir de …	*starting on …*

———— HOTEL SAN MARCOS ————

COMODIDAD, ELEGANCIA Y DISTINCIÓN EN PLENO CENTRO DE MARBELLA Y A SOLO CINCUENTA METROS DE LA PLAYA

▶ Habitaciones individuales y dobles (Descuentos especiales para niños)
▶ Media pensión o pensión completa
▶ Aire acondicionado
▶ TV color vía satélite
▶ Tres grandes piscinas
▶ Discoteca
▶ Tiendas para uso exclusivo de nuestros clientes

PARA INFORMACIÓN Y RESERVAS LLAME AL TELÉFONO 95 83 41 02
DE MARBELLA O CONSULTE A SU AGENCIA DE VIAJES

Recepcionista	Hotel San Marcos, ¿dígame?
Martin	Buenos días. ¿Podría decirme si tiene habitaciones disponibles para la última semana de agosto?
Recepcionista	Sí señor, sí tenemos. ¿Qué tipo de habitación desea Vd.? ¿Individual o doble?
Martin	Perdone, pero no se oye bien. ¿Podría repetir?
Recepcionista	Le pregunto si quiere una habitación individual o doble.
Martin	Bueno, somos dos adultos y dos niños pequeños. Necesitamos una habitación con una cama de matrimonio y dos camas individuales para los chicos.
Recepcionista	Perfectamente.
Martin	Tengo entendido que hay un descuento especial para los niños. ¿No es así?
Recepcionista	Sí, efectivamente, hacemos un descuento del 25 por ciento por cada niño. En total, incluido el descuento, la habitación le saldría a 80 euros.
Martin	¿El desayuno está incluido en el precio de la habitación?
Recepcionista	No, señor, el desayuno se paga aparte. El desayuno continental vale seis euros. Y también tenemos un servicio de restaurante en caso de que Vd. prefiera tomar media pensión o pensión completa.
Martin	No, solo tomaremos la habitación con desayuno.
Recepcionista	Muy bien, ¿y para qué fecha la quiere Vd.?
Martin	A partir del 24 de agosto.
Recepcionista	¿Y para cuántas noches?
Martin	Siete noches en total. Hasta el 30 de agosto inclusive.
Recepcionista	Del 24 . . . al . . . 30 de agosto . . . ¿Me dice su nombre, por favor?
Martin	Martin Baron.
Recepcionista	Perdone, ¿cómo ha dicho?
Martin	Martin Baron.
Recepcionista	¿Cómo se escribe, por favor?
Martin	B-a-r-o-n, Baron.
Recepcionista	Muy bien, señor Baron.
Martin	Ah, ¿oiga?
Recepcionista	Sí, ¿dígame?
Martin	¿Tienen Vds. aparcamiento en el hotel? Vamos a viajar en coche.
Recepcionista	Sí señor, tenemos un aparcamiento para uso exclusivo de los clientes.
Martin	¡Estupendo! Adiós, muchas gracias.
Recepcionista	De nada, adiós.

LANGUAGE TIP

Notice this special use of the verb **salir** here meaning *to come to, to cost.*

Le saldría a ochenta euros.	*It would cost you 80 euros.*
Me salió muy caro.	*It cost me a lot of money.*
¿Cuánto sale?	*How much does it come to?*
La cena salió a 35 euros.	*Dinner came to 35 euros.*

2 **Answer the following questions in Spanish.**
   a ¿Qué tipo de habitación necesita Martin Baron?
   b ¿Para cuándo quiere la habitación y para cuánto tiempo?
   c ¿Cuánto cuesta la habitación?
   d ¿Está incluido el descuento para los niños?
   e ¿Hay aparcamiento en el hotel?

3 **Find the phrases in the conversation which have the same meaning as:**
   a No oigo bien.
   b Entiendo que . . .
   c No está incluido.
   d Si usted prefiere . . .
   e Desde el 24 de agosto.
   f Solo para los clientes.

4 06.02 **Role play – You've been sent by your company to Madrid, and you decide to stay at the Hotel Los Ingleses.**

Listen to the model conversation first, then follow the prompts to make your own booking.

2 BUSCANDO UN APARTAMENTO *LOOKING FOR AN APARTMENT*

Elizabeth Reed trabaja para una empresa multinacional en Barcelona. Elizabeth necesita alquilar un apartamento y llama por teléfono a una inmobiliaria.

alquilar	*to rent*
inmobiliaria (f)	*accommodation agency, estate agent*
encargado/a	*person in charge*
tal como pone el anuncio (m)	*just as the advertisement says*
aseo (m)	*small bathroom*
cocina americana (f)	*open-plan kitchen*
amueblado/a	*furnished*
estado (m)	*condition*
pasar por	*to come round*

1 06.03 **Now listen to the conversation. What sort of flat is Elizabeth looking for, large or small? Furnished or unfurnished?**

Empleada	Sí, ¿dígame?
Elizabeth	Buenas tardes. He visto en La Vanguardia un anuncio de un apartamento que se alquila en la calle Pelayo. ¿Podría decirme si está disponible todavía?
Empleada	Sí, ¿quiere esperar un momento, por favor? Ahora le pongo con la persona encargada.
Empleado	Sí, ¿diga?
Elizabeth	Buenas tardes, llamo por el anuncio del apartamento que se alquila en la calle Pelayo. ¿Estará disponible todavía?

Empleado	Sí, un momento, por favor . . . pues, tal como pone el anuncio, es un apartamento muy pequeño, de veinticinco metros cuadrados, tiene un aseo con ducha y cocina americana. Y está amueblado. Está muy bien de precio, cuatrocientos cuarenta euros solamente.
Elizabeth	Es justamente lo que busco. Necesito algo que no sea demasiado caro y que esté cerca de mi oficina. Yo trabajo en el centro. ¿En qué piso está?
Empleado	Está en el cuarto piso, pero tiene ascensor. Es un apartamento muy bonito, es exterior y está en perfecto estado. Lo acaban de pintar. Tiene agua caliente, teléfono . . .
Elizabeth	¿Sería posible verlo esta misma tarde?
Empleado	Sí, no creo que haya problema. ¿Por qué no pasa Vd. por aquí entre las tres y las cuatro y le acompañaré yo mismo? ¿Tiene Vd. nuestra dirección?
Elizabeth	Sí, sí, la tengo, gracias.

> **LANGUAGE TIP**
>
> Note the uses of the present subjunctive in **Necesito algo que no sea demasiado caro y que esté cerca . . .** *I need something which is not too expensive and which is near* (need) and **No creo que haya problema** *I don't think there'll be any problem* (uncertainty).

2 ¿Verdadero o falso?

   a El apartamento de la calle Pelayo está alquilado.

   b El apartamento tiene un gran baño.

   c Tiene una cocina con muebles americanos.

   d El apartamento da a la calle.

   e Está en el centro de Barcelona.

3 What phrases are used in the conversation to say the following?

   a I'm calling/phoning about the advertisement.

   b Is it available? (two phrases)

   c I'll put you through to . . . right now.

   d It's a very good price.

   e It's just what I'm looking for.

   f They have just painted it.

NEW EXPRESSIONS

Asking for information about accommodation

¿Podría decirme si tiene habitaciones disponibles . . .?	*Could you tell me if you have rooms available?*
¿Podría decirme si está disponible todavía?	*Could you tell me if it is still available?*
¿Estará disponible todavía?	*Is it still available?*

Booking into a hotel

Tomaremos la habitación con desayuno.	We'll take the room with breakfast.
¿Para qué fecha?	For what date?
a partir del 24 de agosto	starting on 24th August
una habitación doble/individual	a double/single room
con cama de matrimonio/cama doble / con camas individuales	with a double bed / with single beds
una habitación exterior	a room with a view
con vistas al mar / con terraza	with a sea view / with balcony

Stating requirements

Necesitamos una habitación con una cama de matrimonio.	We need a room with a double bed.

Describing a place

Está en el cuarto piso.	It is on the fourth floor.
Es un apartamento muy pequeño.	It is a very small apartment.
Tenemos un aparcamiento.	We have a car park.

Asking and saying how much something costs

Vale seis euros.	It costs six euros.
Le saldría a ochenta euros.	It would come to/cost 80 euros.
¿Cuánto cuesta/vale?	How much does it cost?
¿Qué precio tiene? / ¿Cuál es el precio?	What is the price?
Cuesta/vale 100 libras.	It costs £100.
¿Cuánto sale?	How much does it come to?

 Using what you know and some intuition, how would you say the following in Spanish?

    a Could you tell me if it is a two-bedroom flat? Is it on the top floor?

    b I'm looking for a flat in a building that has parking.

Language discovery

 You have seen this language in action. Now can you work out the rules?

1 ¿Ser o estar? Which one do you use to ...

    a tell the time?

    b ask where something is?

    c describe people, places and things?

    d give personal information, such as your nationality?

    e describe a temporary state or condition?

2 What is the Spanish equivalent of: *English is spoken here*?

3 ¿Por o para?

    a Necesito una habitación _____ cinco noches.

    b Hay un descuento del 10 _____ ciento _____ cada niño.

    c Pase usted _____ nuestra oficina hoy _____ la tarde.

    d Tenemos aparcamiento _____ los clientes.

1 SER AND ESTAR

Observe the use of **ser** in these sentences from the conversations:

To denote characteristics:

Es un apartamento pequeño.   *It is a small apartment.*

With impersonal expressions such as **es posible**, **es mejor**, **es difícil**:

¿Sería posible verlo?   *Would it be possible to see it?*

With figures:

Somos dos adultos.   *We are two adults.*

Consider now the use of **estar** in these sentences:

To indicate position:

Está en el cuarto piso.   *It is on the fourth floor.*

To denote a temporary state or condition:

Está en perfecto estado.   *It is in perfect condition.*

Before a past participle to denote a condition resulting from an action:

Está amueblado.   *It is furnished.*

2 USE OF SE

Notice how **se** has been used in the dialogues.

In a passive sentence:

El desayuno *se* paga aparte.   *Breakfast is paid for separately.*

In passive sentences with **se**, the verb agrees in number (singular or plural) with the subject. Compare the previous sentence with this one:

Las bebidas *se pagan* aparte.   *The drinks are paid for separately.*

In an impersonal sentence:

No *se* oye bien.   *One can't hear well.*

3 PARA AND POR

Observe the use of **para** in these phrases from the dialogues.

To denote length of time:

¿*Para* cuántas noches?   *For how many nights?*

With time phrases:

¿*Para* qué fecha?   *For what date?*

To indicate destination:

Dos camas *para* los chicos.   *Two beds for the children.*

Notice how **por** has been used in these phrases:

With the meaning of *per*:

Un descuento del 25% *por* cada niño.   *A 25% discount per child.*

With the meaning of *about*:

Llamo *por* el anuncio.   *I am calling about the advertisement.*

To indicate movement:

¿*Por* qué no pasa Vd. por aquí?   *Why don't you come round?*

Practice

1 ¿Ser o estar? Complete the hotel description with the correct verb forms.

El Hotel Doña Bárbara **(a)** _____ situado en pleno centro de Caracas y **(b)** _____ uno de los mejores de la ciudad. El Hotel Doña Bárbara **(c)** _____ dotado de todo lo necesario para el turista exigente. El servicio de restaurante y de bar **(d)** _____ de excelente calidad y a pesar de su elegancia, sus precios **(e)** _____ relativamente módicos para el turista europeo. En el Hotel Doña Bárbara le **(f)** _____ posible disfrutar de un verdadero descanso y si Vd. **(g)** _____ acompañado de sus hijos, la dirección del hotel le ofrecerá generosos descuentos para ellos.

2 ¿Por o para? Choose the correct word to complete the conversation.

A   Buenos días. Llamo (por/para) reservar una habitación (por/para) este fin de semana.
B   ¿Es (por/para) una persona solamente?
A   No, quiero una habitación doble.
B   ¿(Por/para) cuántas noches la quiere?
A   (Por/para) tres noches solamente, de viernes a domingo. Llegaremos allí el viernes (por/para) la tarde. ¿Tienen Vds. aparcamiento (por/para) los clientes?
B   No, nosotros no tenemos. Pero enfrente del hotel hay un aparcamiento. Me parece que vale siete euros (por/para) día ...
A   ¿Y cuánto cobran Vds. (por/para) la habitación doble con media pensión?
B   Ciento veinte euros (por/para) persona ...

3 Carol Wilson sent an email to the Hotel Don Quijote in Gandía to book a room. Read her email and then use it as a model to make your own hotel booking.

Les ruego que me confirmen ...   *Please confirm* (lit. *I beg you that you confirm ...*)
a la brevedad posible
lo más pronto posible   *as soon as possible*
cuanto antes

Estimados señores:

El objeto de la presente es solicitar a Vds. la reserva de una habitación doble, con dos camas y con baño, a partir del sábado 28 de agosto próximo y hasta el 13 de septiembre inclusive.

Les ruego que me confirmen la reserva a la mayor brevedad posible.

Les saluda muy atentamente.

Carol Wilson

4 06.04 **Role play – You are going to a Spanish-speaking country for an extended stay and you want to rent an apartment. You decide to call una agencia inmobiliaria (*an estate agent*) to get more information about a listing in the local newspaper.**

Agente	Sí, ¿dígame?
Tú	**(a)** *Say good morning. Tell him you are phoning about the advertisement.*
Agente	Sí, sí. Por el anuncio del periódico, ¿no?
Tú	**(b)** *Yes, the apartment which is for rent on Avenida La Marina.*
Agente	Sí, sí. Todavía está disponible. ¿Quiere verlo?
Tú	**(c)** *Ask how many rooms it has.*
Agente	Tiene dos habitaciones solamente.
Tú	**(d)** *Say it's just what you are looking for. You need something which is not too big.*
Agente	Y está muy bien de precio. ¿Cuándo desea verlo?
Tú	**(e)** *Ask if it will be possible to see it this afternoon?*
Agente	Sí, por supuesto. Le daré la dirección.

5 Tony, a student from London, received the following letter from his Spanish correspondent in Barcelona. Read the letter and then answer the questions.

en pleno centro (m)	*right in the centre*
siglo pasado (m)	*last century*
bien conservado/a	*well-preserved*
grandes almacenes (m pl)	*department store*
tiene mucha marcha (f)	*there's a lot going on there*
por cierto	*of course, naturally*
puesto que	*as*

Querido Tony:

En mi carta anterior te escribí sobre mi familia. Hoy te contaré algo sobre el lugar donde vivimos, que es muy especial.

Como te decía, vivo con mis padres y mis dos hermanos menores. Tenemos un piso muy grande y muy antiguo en el Paseo de Gracia, una de las calles principales de Barcelona, en pleno centro de la ciudad. Aquí vivió mi padre cuando era niño y aquí he vivido siempre.

El piso está en un edificio muy bonito, de principios del siglo pasado, que está muy bien conservado. Tiene un gran salón, un comedor también muy grande, y cinco habitaciones más. Una de ellas la utiliza mi padre como despacho. Mis dos hermanos comparten uno de los dormitorios, yo tengo mi propia habitación y cuando tú vengas a Barcelona, tenemos una habitación para las visitas también.

El salón da a la calle, una calle muy ruidosa, pero con una arquitectura muy interesante. Mi habitación, afortunadamente, es interior, de manera que no me despierta el ruido del tráfico por la mañana. Los fines de semana suelo dormir hasta muy tarde.

En el barrio tenemos todo lo que necesitamos: supermercados, tiendas de ropa, grandes almacenes –el Corte Inglés está muy cerca de aquí-, buenos restaurantes, cafés, etc. En la esquina hay una estación de metro, la de Paseo de Gracia, donde cojo el metro para ir al instituto. Allí también cogemos el tren para ir a Sitges el fin de semana. Te llevaré allí cuando vengas a verme. Estoy seguro de que te gustará. ¡Tiene mucha marcha!

Me preguntas si seguiré viviendo con mi familia cuando vaya a la universidad. Por supuesto que me gustaría mucho vivir independientemente, pero no creo que pueda hacerlo ya que aquí alquilar un piso cuesta una fortuna. No es como en Inglaterra. Aquí no tenemos más alternativa que seguir viviendo con la familia. Cuando trabaje, quizá sí. Entonces tendré dinero suficiente para alquilar mi propio piso o compartirlo con algún amigo, pero de momento no. Tampoco me puedo quejar puesto que en casa estoy muy bien.

¿Y tú, qué tal? Me dices que el próximo año te irás a vivir fuera de Londres y que tendrás que encontrar un lugar donde vivir. Espero que tengas suerte. Algún día iré a visitarte. Mientras tanto, escríbeme y cuéntame de ti.

Un abrazo
Paco

LANGUAGE TIP

In **Cuando tú vengas a Barcelona** *When you come to Barcelona*, **Cuando vengas a verme** *When you come and see me*, **Cuando vaya a la universidad** *When I go to university*, **Cuando trabaje . . .** *When I work . . .*, the subjunctive is used because **cuando** refers to an action which is not yet a reality. The subjunctive is also needed in **No creo que pueda hacerlo** *I don't think I'll be able to do it* (uncertainty) and **Espero que tengas suerte** *I hope you are lucky* (hope).

Answer the following questions in Spanish.

   a ¿Con quién vive Paco?

   b ¿Cómo es el piso donde vive?

   c ¿Cómo es el edificio?

   d ¿Cuántas habitaciones tiene?

   e ¿Comparte habitación Paco?

   f ¿Cómo es la calle donde vive?

   g ¿Dónde está la estación de metro más cercana?

   h ¿Por qué seguirá viviendo con su familia Paco cuando vaya a la universidad?

¡A escuchar!

Un nuevo piso: Pablo is going to share a flat with some friends. In a conversation with Soledad he described the place where he is going to live. Later that day Soledad emails a mutual friend a rather inaccurate description of Pablo's flat.

6 06.05 **Listen first, then read. Can you correct the factual errors?**

| búsqueda (f) | search |
| mudado | moved (house) |

Pablo se ha mudado a un piso estupendo a solo veinticinco minutos de la Plaza Mayor. Es un piso de dos habitaciones, pero no tiene vistas. Va a compartirlo con un amigo y van a pagar doscientos sesenta euros mensuales.

7 06.06 *Hotel O'Higgins – The Hotel O'Higgins in Viña del Mar, Chile, is announcing a special offer.*

Listen to this radio advertisement and then answer the true/false questions.

| impuesto (m) | tax |
| merecido/a | deserved |

¿Verdadero o falso?

   a La oferta especial es válida para niños menores de doce años.

   b Los niños se pueden quedar con dos adultos por la mitad del precio.

   c La oferta es válida solo por tres noches.

   d El desayuno y el impuesto están incluidos en el precio.

8 **A group of young Europeans were asked why many of them continued living with their parents after leaving school.**

  Can you think of some reasons why young people might stay at home? Try listing them in Spanish in order of importance and then compare your answers with those in the following chart.

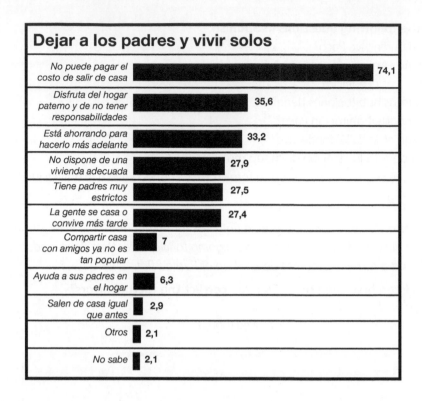

Dejar a los padres y vivir solos

No puede pagar el costo de salir de casa	74,1
Disfruta del hogar paterno y de no tener responsabilidades	35,6
Está ahorrando para hacerlo más adelante	33,2
No dispone de una vivienda adecuada	27,9
Tiene padres muy estrictos	27,5
La gente se casa o convive más tarde	27,4
Compartir casa con amigos ya no es tan popular	7
Ayuda a sus padres en el hogar	6,3
Salen de casa igual que antes	2,9
Otros	2,1
No sabe	2,1

9 The following article looks at this issue from the point of view of young Spanish people. Why do you think many of them continue living with their parents well into their twenties? Read and find out.

insólito/a	*unusual*
si acaso	*if*
en el peor de los casos (m pl)	*at worst*
truncarse	*to cut short*
ahorrar	*to save*
carga (f)	*burden*
doloroso/a	*painful*
asombro (m)	*surprise*
progenitores (m pl)	*parents*
romperse	*to break*

> **WORD FORMATION**
>
> The suffix **-miento** serves to form nouns from verbs: **casar(se)** *to marry* – **casamiento** *marriage*; **aparcar**, **estacionar** *to park* – **aparcamiento**, **estacionamiento** *car park*; **almacenar** *to store* – **almacenamiento** *storage*, etc.
>
> The suffix **-ario/a** added to a noun indicating a place designates an occupation: **universidad** *university* – **universitario/a** *university student*; **biblioteca** *library* – **bibliotecario/a** *librarian*; **parlamento** *parliament* – **parlamentario/a** *member of parliament*, etc.

VIVIR CON MAMÁ A LOS 30, UNA MODA IMPUESTA POR LAS CIRCUNSTANCIAS

En España, es muy normal que los jóvenes de 25 a 30 años e incluso de más edad vivan aún con los padres, hecho insólito para otras culturas como la europea o americana. Allí, los jóvenes no suelen quedarse con sus padres más allá de los 20 años.

En Estados Unidos, cuando el chico cumple los 18 años e inicia sus estudios universitarios, se marcha de casa. Normalmente, suele matricularse en una universidad que queda lejos de su ciudad e incluso fuera de su Estado. Las chicas y muchachos americanos se van de sus casas a una edad temprana, en la mayoría de los casos para siempre, pues si acaso regresan a su ciudad para trabajar, vivirán solos en un apartamento, o en el peor de los casos compartiéndolo con algún amigo.

En España esa mentalidad independentista se inició años atrás, pero se ha truncado. Alfonso de Hohenlohe, 30 años, aristócrata y conspicuo representante de la jet española, piensa que vivir con los padres resulta más cómodo. Él aún comparte techo con su madre y afirma, 'mi relación con ella es perfecta, tiene una mentalidad jovencísima y es fácil convivir con ella, si no, no dudaría en vivir solo. Desde luego es más cómodo vivir en familia porque no te tienes que ocupar de nada, ahorras y tienes independencia, como es mi caso. La casa además es amplia y confortable'.

Para el español Alfonso Ibáñez, administrativo, 33 años viviendo con sus padres, esa es otra historia. Él sigue todavía viviendo en la casa que le vio nacer y eso le supone una carga difícil de llevar. 'La situación – dice – es a menudo exasperante, notas una asfixia que impide desarrollar tu personalidad. No se trata, por supuesto, de que a mis 33 años me limiten la libertad, sino que uno necesita más que un cuarto de tres por dos en donde tener su propia intimidad.'

Y es que en España, las cosas son diferentes. Para asombro de extraños, es muy normal encontrar en este país hombres y mujeres que, superada ampliamente ya la etapa de juventud, aún comparten vivienda con sus progenitores. 'Ahora (señala el sociólogo Amando de Miguel) se ha invertido la tendencia que se daba en los años sesenta y principios de los setenta cuando los jóvenes buscaban su independencia y marchaban a vivir solos o en grupos de amigos en viviendas de alquiler. La vocación emancipadora se ha roto y se ha reinstaurado la costumbre de no salir de la casa paterna hasta el casamiento.'

La cuestión económica es la principal responsable de esta situación. Los jóvenes son los principales afectados por el paro y sin un salario mensual y estable es imposible vivir independientemente.

a Read the text again and see how the following phrases have been used. For each of them write an alternative phrase expressing the same idea. In the Key to the exercises you will find some examples.

    1 Comparte techo con su madre.

    2 Se van de sus casas a una edad temprana.

    3 Mi relación con ella es perfecta.

    4 No te tienes que ocupar de nada.

    5 La casa que le vio nacer.

    6 Aún comparten vivienda con sus progenitores.

    7 La vocación emancipadora se ha roto.

b How are the following expressed in the text?

    1 They don't normally stay.

    2 beyond the age of 20

    3 He usually registers at a university.

    4 forever

    5 if they return to their (home) town

    6 Of course, it's not a question of . . . but . . .

Test yourself

1 Complete the sentences with **por** or **para**, as appropriate.

    a Llamo _____ el anuncio de su página web. Queremos una habitación _____ tres personas, _____ cinco días, _____ el 10 de julio.

    b Una habitación individual _____ nuestro hijo y una doble _____ nosotros.

    c ¿Cuánto es _____ día?

    d ¿El precio que se paga es _____ persona o _____ la habitación?

    e Y _____ llegar allí, ¿qué carretera tenemos que tomar?
       Pueden venir _____ la A45.

    f Podemos confirmar su reserva _____ correo electrónico o _____ fax, o _____ teléfono, si prefiere.

2 Choose between **ser** and **estar** and give the Spanish for the words in brackets.

    a El apartamento (*which is for rent*) en la calle Pelayo, ¿es/está (*still available*)?

    b Es/Está un apartamento (*furnished*).

    c Es/Está (*in very good condition*) y es/está muy bonito. (*They have just painted it.*)

    d Es/Está (*facing on to the street*).

    e Es/Está (*just what I'm looking for*).

    f ¿(*On which floor*) es/está?
       No soy/estoy seguro, pero (*I'll put you through to the person in charge now*).

3 You and some friends would like to spend a month in Fuengirola. In a local newspaper you see this advertisement and you decide to phone to ask for more information.

> FUENGIROLA Alquilo, por meses o larga temporada, o vendo apartamento Paseo Marítimo (Torreblanca), 2 dormitorios, baño, gran salón-comedor. Teléfono (952) 473078

Señora	¿Dígame?
Tú	**(a)** *Say you are ringing about the ad in the newspaper.*
Señora	Ah, por el apartamento.
Tú	**(b)** *That's it. Say you are looking for something to rent. Ask her to give you more information about the apartment.*
Señora	Pues, es un apartamento nuevo, con vistas al mar y muy tranquilo. Tiene dos habitaciones, además del salón-comedor, la cocina y el baño.
Tú	**(c)** *Say you need something which is available immediately.*
Señora	El apartamento está disponible ahora mismo.
Tú	**(d)** *Well, you are also looking for something which is not too expensive. Ask how much the monthly rent is.*
Señora	Bueno, es un precio muy razonable. Mil ciento cincuenta euros por mes.
Tú	**(e)** *Thank her and say that is too much for you.*

Por, para, ser, estar and booking accommodation are the focus of these tests. Even if you did well, make sure you understand why you used one form instead of another before you go on to the next unit. Most grammar books will have references to such words.

SELF CHECK

	I CAN ...
○	. . . enquire about accommodation and book into a hotel.
○	. . . state my personal requirements.
○	. . . describe a place.
○	. . . ask and say how much something costs.

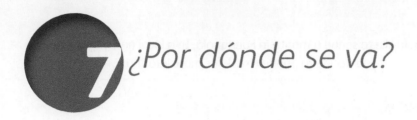

7 ¿Por dónde se va?

In this unit you will learn how to:
▶ *ask how to get to a place.*
▶ *give directions.*
▶ *ask and give information about transport.*

CEFR: *Can explain the advantages or disadvantages of various options, e.g. coach vs. train travel; can deliver announcements clearly and spontaneously, e.g. communicate that travel plans have changed (B2).*

Conversations

1 ¿QUÉ LÍNEA TENGO QUE TOMAR? *WHAT LINE DO I HAVE TO TAKE?*

Mark Johnson, un turista de visita en Madrid, pregunta cómo ir a la estación de Chamartín. Mark está en la estación de metro Sol.

 1 07.01 Listen to and practise the conversation. How many changes will Mark have to make?

línea (f)	*line*
coger	*to take*

Mark	Perdone, ¿qué línea tengo que tomar para ir a la estación de Chamartín?
Empleado	Coja la línea 1 hasta Plaza de Castilla y allí, cambie a la línea 8 en dirección a Fuencarral.
Mark	Gracias.
Empleado	De nada.

> **LANGUAGE TIP**
> **Coger** and **tomar** are interchangeable in this context. **Coger** seems to be more frequent in Spain. In some Latin American countries, it is a taboo word and it is better to avoid it. **Tomar** will be understood everywhere.

2 ¿Verdadero o falso?
   a Mark desea ir a la estación de Chamartín.
   b La línea 1 va directo a Chamartín.
   c Mark tiene que cambiar a la línea 8 en Fuencarral.

3 What expressions are used in the dialogue to say the following?

　　a Take line 1.

　　b as far as . . .

　　c Change on to line . . .

2 ¿A QUÉ HORA LLEGA EL EXPRESO? *WHAT TIME DOES THE EXPRESS TRAIN ARRIVE?*

Mark ha ido a la estación de Chamartín a buscar a un amigo que viene de Zaragoza. En información, Mark pregunta por la llegada del tren.

1 07.02 **As you listen to the conversation, try answering this question: What two pieces of information does Mark want to know?**

llegada (f)	*arrival*
retraso (m)	*delay*
andén (m)	*platform*
tablero (m)	*board*

Mark	Por favor, ¿a qué hora llega el expreso que viene de Zaragoza?
Empleada	La hora de llegada es a las catorce treinta, pero hoy viene con veinte minutos de retraso. Llegará a las catorce cincuenta.
Mark	¿A qué andén llega?
Empleada	No lo sé, tiene que mirar el tablero de llegadas.
Mark	Gracias.
Empleada	De nada.

> **CULTURE TIP**
>
> The **AVE** (**Alta Velocidad Española**, literally *Spanish High Speed*) is a fast train which links Madrid with Spain's other major cities at a top speed of 300 km per hour. Travelling to Seville on the **AVE** takes about two and a half hours and to Barcelona about three hours. The **AVE** is operated by **RENFE** (**Red Nacional de los Ferrocarriles Españoles**), the state-owned railway company.

2 Answer the following questions in Spanish, using the 12-hour clock.

　　a ¿A qué hora llega normalmente a Madrid el expreso de Zaragoza?

　　b ¿Con cuántos minutos de retraso llegará hoy?

　　c ¿A qué hora llega?

3 What phrases are used in the conversation to say the following?

　　a the arrival time

　　b Which platform does it arrive at?

　　c the arrivals board

4 07.03 **Role play – You are in Madrid and have gone to the railway station to meet a friend coming from Barcelona. He's coming in on the Talgo, a train which is much faster and more comfortable than the Expreso.**

Speak in the pauses and listen to confirm your answers.

3 SIGAN TODO RECTO *GO STRAIGHT AHEAD*

Mark y su amigo Robert están en un hotel en la calle de la Magdalena. En su segundo día en Madrid deciden visitar el Museo del Prado. En la recepción del hotel preguntan cómo llegar hasta allí.

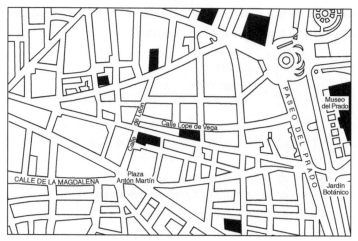

¿por dónde se va a . . .?	*which is the way to . . .?*
sigan todo recto	*go straight on*
tuerzan (torcer)	*turn (to turn)*
hasta llegar a. . .	*until you get to*

 1 07.04 **Listen to the conversation and practise asking and giving directions.**

Robert	Buenos días.
Recepcionista	Buenos días, señor. Dígame.
Robert	Por favor, ¿nos puede decir por dónde se va al Museo del Prado?
Recepcionista	Sí, miren, al salir del hotel tuerzan ustedes a la derecha y vayan hasta la Plaza Antón Martín que está a cien metros de aquí. Allí, cojan la calle de León que está a la izquierda y sigan hasta la calle Lope de Vega. Sigan todo recto por Lope de Vega hasta llegar al Paseo del Prado. Al otro lado del Paseo está el Museo.
Robert	Muchas gracias.

After leaving the hotel, Robert repeated the directions given by the receptionist to Mark in English. Complete Robert's version of the directions: *First we have to turn . . .*

 2 What expressions from the conversation mean the same as:
   a ¿Qué desea?/¿En qué puedo ayudarle?
   b ¿Puede decirnos . . .?

c Cuando salgan . . .

d Giren a la derecha.

e Sigan de frente.

f . . . hasta que lleguen . . .

3 07.05 **Role play – Practise giving some simple directions. In a Spanish town you know well, a Spanish tourist asks you the way to the station. Follow the prompts and take part in the conversation. Then listen to confirm your answers.**

4 SE PUEDE IR EN TREN O EN AUTOCAR *YOU CAN GO BY TRAIN OR COACH*

Mark y Robert quieren viajar a Toledo, ciudad que está a 70 km de Madrid. En una agencia de viajes piden información.

autocar (m)	*coach*
folleto informativo (m)	*information brochure*
quedar	*to be left*
quizá puedan conseguir uno	*perhaps you can get one*
no hay de qué	*you're welcome*

1 07.06 **As you listen to the conversation, try answering this question: Do trains and coaches leave from the same station in Madrid?**

Empleada	Buenos días, ¿qué desean?
Mark	Por favor, ¿podría decirnos cómo podemos viajar a Toledo?
Empleada	A Toledo se puede ir en tren o en autocar. Los trenes salen de la estación de Atocha y los autocares de la estación Sur, en la calle Canarias.
Mark	¿Sabe usted cuál es el horario de los trenes?
Empleada	Hay trenes cada hora, a la hora en punto, a partir de las siete de la mañana y hasta las veintitrés horas.
Mark	¿Dónde está la estación de Atocha?
Empleada	Pues, tienen que coger la línea 1 del metro. Pueden cogerla aquí, en Sol. Les llevará directo.
Mark	¿Tiene usted un folleto informativo sobre Toledo?
Empleada	No, de Toledo no nos queda ninguno, pero en la estación quizá puedan conseguir uno.
Mark	Muchas gracias. Adiós.
Empleada	No hay de qué.

2 Complete these sentences with information from the conversation:

a A Toledo se puede ir en (means of transport) . . .

b Los trenes salen de (name of station) . . .

c Los autocares salen de (name of coach station) . . .

d Hay trenes (frequency) . . .

e El primer tren sale a las (time) . . .

f El último tren sale a las (time) . . .

> **LANGUAGE TIP**
> Note the impersonal construction **Se puede ir en tren . . .**, literally *One can go by train . . .* Compare this with **Pueden ir en tren.** *You can go by train.*

3 What phrases are used in the dialogue to say the following?
   a Could you tell us . . .?
   b the train timetable
   c every hour on the hour
   d from 7 o'clock in the morning
   e We don't have any left.

4 07.07 **A traveller stops by the tourist office to ask how to get from Barcelona to Sitges. Listen and answer.**
   a From which station do the trains for Sitges leave?
   b How frequently do they run?
   c How does one get to the station from the tourist office?

 NEW EXPRESSIONS

 Work out the missing words in the English translations. Then hide either column and test your memory.

Asking the way

¿Dónde está . . .?	*Where is it?*
¿Nos puede decir por dónde se va a . . .?	*_____ how we can get to . . .?*
¿La ruta/carretera/autopista para . . . por favor?	*The road/highway/motorway for . . . please?*
¿En qué dirección está . . .?	*In which direction is . . .?*

Giving directions

Tuerza a la derecha.	*Turn right.*
Doble a la izquierda.	*Turn left.*
Vaya hasta . . .	*Go as far as . . .*
Siga hasta la calle . . .	*Continue as far as . . . street.*
Siga todo recto.	*Go straight on/ahead.*
Tome/coja . . .	*Take . . .*
Suba/baje por esta calle.	*Go up/down _____*
Está al lado de/junto a . . .	*It is next to . . .*
Está en la esquina de . . . con . . .	*It is on the corner of . . . with . . .*
Cruce la avenida.	*Cross the avenue.*
Está al lado de . . .	*It is next door to . . .*
Está enfrente de . . .	*It is opposite . . .*
Está entre . . . y . . .	*It is between . . . and . . .*

Asking and giving information about transport

¿Qué línea tengo que tomar/ coger?	*_____*
Tome/coja la línea 1.	*Take line 1.*
Cambie/transborde a . . . en . . .	*Change on to . . . at . . .*
¿Podría decirme/nos cómo puedo/ podemos viajar a . . .?	*Can you tell me/us how I can/we can travel to . . .?*

¿A qué hora llega el expreso?	What time does _____ arrive?
La hora de llegada es a las . . .	The _____ is . . .
Llega/llegará a las . . .	It arrives/it will arrive at . . .
Sale(n) de . . .	It leaves/they leave from . . .
Hay (trenes) cada hora.	There are trains every hour.

Language discovery

You have seen this language in action. Now can you work out the rules?

1 Which of these two commands addresses more than one person?
   a Dobla a la izquierda.   **b** Doblad al a derecha.

2 If *no dobléis* is a negative command (*don't turn*), how would you give the opposite command to *hablad entre vosotros*?

3 What vowel change is required to give the subjunctive of these verb forms?
   a comes (*you eat*, fam.)   **b** leemos (*we read*)   **c** vengo (*I come*)

1 THE IMPERATIVE – GIVING DIRECTIONS

Directions are normally given with the imperative, e.g. **cruce la calle** *cross the street*, **suba por esta avenida** *go up along this avenue*. The imperative is the same as the third person singular of the present subjunctive (see Unit 1). As with the subjunctive, you use the stem of the first person singular of the present tense plus the appropriate ending. In Spanish, you use different imperative forms depending on who you are talking to (polite or familiar) and whether you are speaking to one, or more than one, person (singular or plural).

a Polite imperatives

Here are the polite imperatives of three regular verbs: **doblar** *to turn*, **retroceder** *to go back*, **subir** *to go up*:

Present tense (1st person)	Imperative	
doblo	**doble**	*turn* (sing)
	doblen	*turn* (pl)
retrocedo	**retroceda**	*go back* (sing)
	retrocedan	*go back* (pl)
subo	**suba**	*go up* (sing)
	suban	*go up* (pl)

The negative imperative is formed by placing **no** before the verb, e.g. **no doble aquí** *don't turn here*. As the imperative is formed with the stem of the first person singular of the present tense, verbs which are irregular or stem-changing in the present are also irregular or stem-changing in the imperative, e.g. **vengo** *I come*, **venga** *come*, **vuelvo** *I come back*, **vuelva** *come back*.

b Positive familiar imperatives

Familiar imperatives have different positive and negative forms:

Present tense (yo)	Imperative (tú/vosotros)	
doblo	dobla/d	*turn*
retrocedo	retrocede/d	*go back*
subo	sube/id	*go up*

Irregular forms: **di** (**decir**), **haz** (**hacer**), **ve** (**ir**), **oye** (**oír**), **pon** (**poner**), **sal** (**salir**), **ten** (**tener**), **ven** (**venir**), **sé** (**ser**).

c Negative familiar imperatives

Present tense (yo)	Imperative (tú/vosotros)	
doblo	no dobles	*don't turn*
	no dobléis	*don't turn*
retrocedo	no retrocedas	*don't go back*
	no retrocedáis	*don't go back*
subo	no subas	*don't go up*
	no subáis	*don't go up*

Latin Americans do not use the **vosotros** forms of the imperative: **hablad – no habléis**; **subid – no subáis**, etc. The **ustedes** form of the imperative is used in formal and informal address: **hablen – no hablen, suban – no suban**, etc. In the River Plate area (Argentina, Uruguay and Paraguay), where **vos** replaces **tú**, positive informal imperative forms are: **doblá, retrocedé, subí**. Negative informal forms are: **no doblés, no retrocedás, no subás**. Plural forms are as above.

d Pronouns with imperatives

If the imperative includes a pronoun, this must go at the end of the positive form but before the negative one. Positive imperatives which carry a pronoun may need to add an accent, e.g. **bajarse** *to get off*: **bájese** *get off*, **no se baje** *don't get off*.

When the pronoun **os** is added to the **vosotros** form of the imperative, the final **-d** of the imperative is dropped: **cuidarse** *to take care*, **cuidaos** *take care of yourselves*; **callarse** *to be quiet*, **callaos** *be quiet*. In colloquial speech, however, imperative forms such as these are often replaced by the infinitive: **cuidaros, callaros**.

2 USING THE PRESENT TENSE TO GIVE DIRECTIONS

Directions can also be given with the present tense, using the **usted** or the **tú** form of the verb, as appropriate.

Sigue todo recto por la calle Mayor y luego toma la segunda a la izquierda. (formal)

You go straight on along the high street and then you take the second turning on the left.

Sigues todo recto hasta el parque, cruzas el parque y luego tomas la primera calle a la derecha. (informal)

You go straight on as far as the park, you go across the park and then you take the first street on the right.

The present tense seems to be just as frequent as the imperative in giving directions and it is a useful alternative to know if you have difficulty using the different imperative forms. You must, however, make an effort to understand directions or instructions given to you in forms other than the present tense.

 Practice

1 Change the imperatives in bold type into the familiar (tú) form.

Para llegar a mi oficina, **coja** _____ el autobús número 4 y **bájese** _____ en la plaza Isabel La Católica. **Cruce** _____ la plaza en dirección a la Catedral y **suba** _____ por la calle de la Catedral hasta el primer semáforo. La empresa donde trabajo está justo en la esquina. **Suba** _____ en el ascensor hasta la quinta planta. Al salir del ascensor hay un pasillo. **Siga** _____ por el pasillo hasta el fondo. Mi oficina es la 510 y está a la mano izquierda.

2 *You have been in Madrid for a few days and you are now familiar with **el metro** (the underground system). Someone you have met at your hotel near the opera metro needs assistance with directions.*

 Role play – Look at the map of the Madrid underground and answer his questions.

Conocido	Buenos días, ¿cómo está Vd.?
Tú	**(a)** *Reply to his greeting.*
Conocido	Muy bien, gracias. Hoy tengo que ir a visitar a unos amigos que viven cerca de la estación de Goya. ¿Sabe Vd. qué línea tengo que tomar?
Tú	**(b)** *Study the map of the underground and tell him how to get there.*
Conocido	¿Va directo?
Tú	**(c)** *Tell him whether it does or not.*
Conocido	Gracias. Y después tengo que ir a una tienda que está cerca de la estación de Colombia. ¿Podría decirme qué línea tengo que tomar para ir allí desde la estación de Goya?
Tú	**(d)** *Study the map and tell him how to get there.*
Conocido	Muchas gracias. Aún no entiendo el metro de Madrid. ¿Y Vd. qué planes tiene para hoy?
Tú	**(e)** *Say you are going to the Prado Museum and then you'll have lunch with a Spanish friend.*
Conocido	Bueno, espero que nos veamos esta noche. Podríamos salir a tomar una copa, ¿qué le parece?
Vd.	**(f)** *Why not! You'll be back at the hotel about 7.00.*

Note: There is more than one way to give the directions above. The Key to the exercises provides a model.

3 **With the help of the street map, try building up simple dialogues showing different ways of asking and giving directions. Use some of the words and phrases from the conversations.**

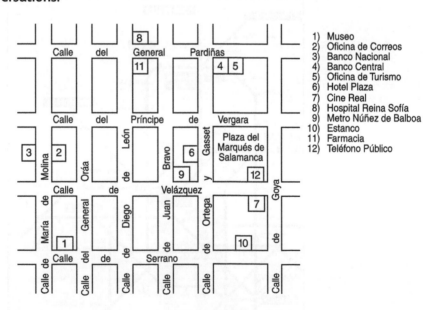

1) Museo
2) Oficina de Correos
3) Banco Nacional
4) Banco Central
5) Oficina de Turismo
6) Hotel Plaza
7) Cine Real
8) Hospital Reina Sofía
9) Metro Núñez de Balboa
10) Estanco
11) Farmacia
12) Teléfono Público

a You get out of the metro station at Nuñez de Balboa (No. 9 on the map) and someone stops you to ask the way to the Banco Central (No. 4 on the map).

b You have been to a museum (No. 1) and, as you go out, someone stops you to ask the way to the Hotel Plaza (No. 6).

4 **Someone who is visiting a South American country received a letter with directions. Complete it with the most appropriate word. Notice it is a formal letter.**

Estimada señora Peña:

El objeto de la presente es explicarle brevemente cómo llegar hasta nuestras oficinas desde su hotel.

Al _____ del hotel _____ a la derecha y _____ hasta la estación de metro _____ próxima, que es la estación de Moneda. Allí _____ la línea 1 que va en _____ a Las Condes y _____ en la estación de Pedro de Valdivia que _____ en la Avenida Providencia. A dos _____ de allí, en _____ oriente, está la calle Concepción. Allí _____ a la izquierda y _____ por esa misma calle _____ el final. Nuestra oficina se encuentra justo en la _____ a la mano derecha.

Atentamente,

Julián García

5 **Christine lives in London and today her friend Antonio is coming to visit her. This is the email Christine sent to Antonio with directions to get to her place.**

First, make sure you understand the directions:

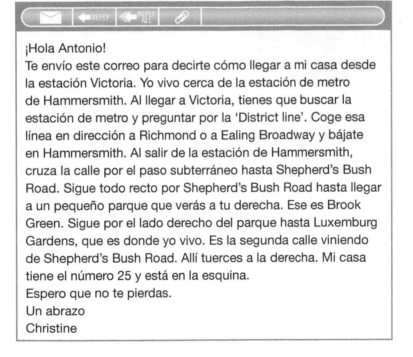

¡Hola Antonio!

Te envío este correo para decirte cómo llegar a mi casa desde la estación Victoria. Yo vivo cerca de la estación de metro de Hammersmith. Al llegar a Victoria, tienes que buscar la estación de metro y preguntar por la 'District line'. Coge esa línea en dirección a Richmond o a Ealing Broadway y bájate en Hammersmith. Al salir de la estación de Hammersmith, cruza la calle por el paso subterráneo hasta Shepherd's Bush Road. Sigue todo recto por Shepherd's Bush Road hasta llegar a un pequeño parque que verás a tu derecha. Ese es Brook Green. Sigue por el lado derecho del parque hasta Luxemburg Gardens, que es donde yo vivo. Es la segunda calle viniendo de Shepherd's Bush Road. Allí tuerces a la derecha. Mi casa tiene el número 25 y está en la esquina.

Espero que no te pierdas.

Un abrazo
Christine

Imagine the directions are for somebody much older than Christine whom she doesn't know well. She would need to use the polite form. Rewrite the note using the polite imperative, making other necessary changes.

6 A tourist phones a travel information centre in Madrid to ask about train travel to Paris. The following are the answers given to him/her. What were his/her questions?

EC (m)   *Eurocity*
RENFE (Red Nacional de los Ferrocarriles Españoles)   *Spanish railways*

HORARIO DE TRENES

MADRID -PARIS- LISBOA
2 DE JUNIO AL 28 DE SEPTIEMBRE **26**

RENFE

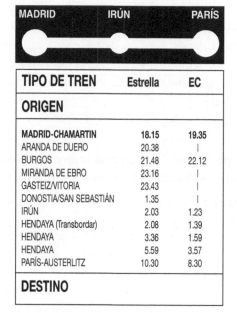

MADRID   IRÚN   PARÍS

TIPO DE TREN	Estrella	EC
ORIGEN		
MADRID-CHAMARTIN	18.15	19.35
ARANDA DE DUERO	20.38	I
BURGOS	21.48	22.12
MIRANDA DE EBRO	23.16	I
GASTEIZ/VITORIA	23.43	I
DONOSTIA/SAN SEBASTIÁN	1.35	I
IRÚN	2.03	1.23
HENDAYA (Transbordar)	2.08	1.39
HENDAYA	3.36	1.59
HENDAYA	5.59	3.57
PARÍS-AUSTERLITZ	10.30	8.30
DESTINO		

a El Eurocity a París sale de la estación de Chamartín.
b Sale de Madrid a las 19.35.
c Hace cinco paradas.
d Tarda trece horas en total.
e Llega a París a las 8.30 de la mañana del día siguiente.
f Llega a la estación de Austerlitz.
g Sí, sí, se puede reservar por teléfono con su número de tarjeta.

¡A escuchar!

En viaje al aeropuerto – A driver stops a policeman to ask the way to the airport.

7 07.08 **First, make notes in English of the directions you hear. Then read the ones the confused driver thought he heard. Can you rewrite them correctly?**

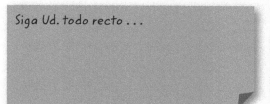

Siga Ud. todo recto . . .

Siga Ud. todo recto hasta el primer semáforo y allí doble a la derecha y continúe por esta calle hasta el segundo semáforo. Para ir al aeropuerto tiene que torcer a la izquierda.

¿Sabe Vd. cómo llegar a . . .? A tourist asks a passer-by the way to the tourist office.

 8 07.09 **Listen to the directions once and try answering the tourist's questions.**

9 **Your Spanish-speaking friend wants to take a holiday abroad. What advice would you give him/her to travel cheaply? Read the article and see if you can find more suggestions than occured to you.**

a precio de oro	*a fortune*
con antelación	*in advance*
por libre	*independently*

TRUCOS PARA HACER TURISMO SIN ARRUINARTE

- Viaja fuera de las fechas que se consideran temporada alta. Un par de días de diferencia pueden significar precios más baratos.

- Elige agencias especializadas en el destino escogido. Además de conocer todas las tarifas, y acceder a precios más baratos, te ayudarán a planear mejor el viaje. Las oficinas de turismo de cada país tienen listados de estas agencias.

- Pide los precios por separado si prefieres contratar un paquete turístico (viaje, traslados con guía y alojamiento): a veces, la tarifa global oculta que te cobran a precio de oro los transportes del aeropuerto al hotel, y viceversa. En estos casos, ir en taxi te puede salir mucho más económico.

- La fórmula más barata suele ser 'avión + alojamiento'. Si eres un viajero experimentado y sabes moverte con soltura en otros países, no dudes en contratarla.

- Haz tu reserva con antelación y, para mayor tranquilidad, contrata en la propia agencia un seguro de cancelación del viaje.

- Aprovecha las ofertas de última hora, si tienes la suerte de no tener que ajustar tus vacaciones a unas fechas determinadas. Pero ten en cuenta que, contratando una semana antes de salir, difícilmente podrás elegir el destino que más te guste.

- Si quieres hacer un 'tour' por varios países, siempre te saldrá más económico contratar un viaje organizado que ir por libre.

Read the article again, and:

    a Find all the imperative forms used in the passage and list them with their corresponding infinitive.

    b Find equivalent expressions for the following words and phrases:

tener acceso	planificar	lista
separadamente	el precio total	con facilidad/sin dificultad

    c Find the Spanish for:

high season	a package tour	It can be much more economical for you.
Don't hesitate to . . .	cancellation insurance	Take advantage of last-minute offers.
But bear in mind that . . .		

Test yourself

1 Complete the statements with a verb from the box using the polite imperative form **usted** (**Vd.**).

girar	seguir	coger	cruzar	mirar	bajarse

    a _____ la línea 2.

    b _____ el tablero de llegadas.

    c _____ a la izquierda.

    d _____ todo recto.

    e _____ en la estación de metro Sol.

    f _____ al otro lado de la calle.

2 Make the following sentences negative.

    a Dáselos.

    b Díselo.

    c Ponedla aquí.

    d Por favor, hazlo.

    e Envíasela por email.

    f Bájate aquí.

Don't be discouraged if you made a few mistakes. The different forms of the imperative in Spanish require a lot of practice. The most important thing is that you are able to understand people when they give you directions or instructions. But when it comes to being the active participant and you need to tell others what to do, the present tense is just as appropriate and common as the imperative in this context.

SELF CHECK

	I CAN . . .
○	. . . ask how to get to a place.
○	. . . give directions.
○	. . . ask and give information about transport.

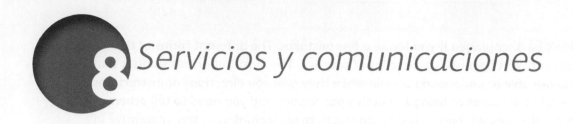

8 Servicios y comunicaciones

In this unit you will learn how to:
▶ *talk about events that happened recently.*
▶ *use reported speech.*
▶ *make complaints and respond to complaints.*
▶ *offer advice and recommendations.*
▶ *give instructions.*
▶ *express certainty and uncertainty.*

CEFR: *Can convey degrees of emotion and highlight the personal significance of events, e.g. a botched reservation (B2); can explain a problem which has arisen and make it clear that the service provider must make a concession (B2); can appreciate registers of language, e.g. a formal letter (C1).*

Conversations

1 UNA RECLAMACIÓN *A COMPLAINT*

Pamela Miles ha pedido una transferencia de dinero desde su banco en Inglaterra, pero la transferencia aún no ha llegado.

1 08.01 **Listen to the key language and the conversation. Does the bank clerk offer a solution to Pamela's problem?**

| reclamación (f) | *complaint* |
| estar seguro/a | *to be sure* |

Pamela	Buenos días.
Empleado	Buenos días. ¿Dígame?
Pamela	He pedido una transferencia de dinero a mi banco en Inglaterra y quisiera saber si ha llegado.
Empleado	¿Su nombre, por favor?
Pamela	Pamela Miles. M-i-l-e-s. Miles.
Empleado	Un momento, por favor. Veré si ha llegado.

(El empleado revisa la documentación y se dirige a la clienta.)

	Aún no ha llegado. ¿Cuándo la pidió usted?
Pamela	La pedí hace una semana. Me dijeron que la enviarían inmediatamente y que tardaría solo dos días. ¿Está seguro de que no hay nada?
Empleado	Estoy completamente seguro. He revisado todas las transferencias que han llegado en los últimos días y la suya no está.

Pamela	¡No es posible! ¿Qué puedo hacer? Necesito ese dinero urgentemente.
Empleado	Pues, lo siento mucho, pero lamentablemente yo no puedo hacer nada. ¿Por qué no vuelve Vd. mañana sobre el mediodía para ver si la hemos recibido? Y si no ha llegado, es mejor que llame Vd. por teléfono o escriba a su banco en Inglaterra para saber qué ha ocurrido.
Pamela	Bien, volveré mañana. Adiós.
Empleado	Adiós. Buenos días.

> **LANGUAGE TIP**
>
> Note the use of the conditional in indirect speech: **Me dijeron que la enviarían . . . y que tardaría solo dos días.** *They told me they'd send it . . . and that it would only take two days.*

2 How are the following expressed in the conversation?

- **a** I've asked for a transfer.
- **b** I'd like to know if it has arrived.
- **c** It hasn't arrived yet.
- **d** I've checked all transfers.
- **e** tomorrow about midday
- **f** You'd better phone or write to your bank.

3 08.02 **Role play – You are spending some time in a Spanish-speaking country and you have ordered a money transfer from your bank back home.**

Follow the prompts and take part in the conversation.

2 UNA LLAMADA INTERNACIONAL *AN INTERNATIONAL TELEPHONE CALL*

Pamela Miles quiere llamar a Londres para informar a sus padres de que ha llegado a casa de sus anfitriones en Suramérica. Pregunta a la operadora cómo marcar un número internacional.

marcar	*to dial*
prefijo (m)	*code*
abonado/a	*subscriber*

1 08.03 **How many digits does Pamela need to dial before the regular number?**

Pamela	Por favor, ¿podría decirme qué prefijo tengo que marcar para llamar a Londres?
Operadora	Primero tiene que marcar el cero cero que es internacional. Después marque el cuarenta y cuatro que corresponde a Inglaterra. Luego marque el número del abonado.
Pamela	Vale, gracias.

2 What words and phrases are used in the dialogue to say the following?

a What code do I have to dial . . . ?

b Then dial . . .

c the subscriber's number

3 EN CORREOS *AT THE POST OFFICE*

Robert Davies, un hombre de negocios, desea enviar unas muestras desde Bilbao a Madrid. En Correos pide información sobre el servicio de paquetería (parcel service) más adecuado.

hombre de negocios (m)	*businessman*
muestra (f)	*sample*
envío (m)	*package, parcel*
domicilio (m)	*home, address*
entrega (f)	*delivery*

1 08.04 **Are the samples going to a business or a home address?**

Sr. Davies	Buenos días. Quisiera enviar unas muestras a Madrid. ¿Qué servicio me recomienda? Las necesitan con urgencia.
Empleada	Pues, en ese caso, le recomiendo que utilice el servicio postal express. Es un servicio de urgencia y además tiene la ventaja de que el envío es certificado. Es el servicio más seguro y rápido que tenemos.
Sr. Davies	¿Y lo llevan a domicilio?
Empleada	Sí, la entrega se hace a domicilio. Es un poco más caro que los otros servicios, pero en este caso creo que es lo que más le conviene.
Sr. Davies	Gracias. Este es el paquete que quiero enviar.

2 Study the conversation once more, then complete this passage with the most suitable words and phrases. (Try not to refer back to the conversation.)

El señor Davies va a _____ porque quiere enviar unas _____ a Madrid. La empleada le _____ que utilice el servicio _____ express, porque este es un servicio de _____ y además tiene la _____ de que el envío es _____. Por otra parte, la _____ se hace a domicilio. Este servicio es más _____ que los otros, pero, en este caso, cree la empleada, es lo que más le _____ al señor Davies.

4 UNA QUEJA *A COMPLAINT*

John y Helen Brown, dos turistas de vacaciones en España, han alquilado un coche a través de una agencia en Inglaterra. Al llegar al aeropuerto en Palma de Mallorca, John y su mujer se dirigen al mostrador de la agencia de alquiler.

recoger	*to pick up, collect*
yo mismo/a	*I . . . myself*
no me cabe duda . . .	*I have no doubt . . .*
es el colmo (de) . . .	*it's the height of, it's the limit . . .*
exigir	*to demand, insist*
aconsejar	*to advise*

1 08.05 **What went wrong with the reservation? Was it an error in the customers' name or a mix-up in the dates?**

Sr. Brown	Buenas tardes.
Empleada	Buenas tardes.
Sr. Brown	Me llamo John Brown. Hemos alquilado un coche a través de su agencia en Manchester. ¿Dónde podemos recogerlo?
Empleada	¿Cómo me ha dicho que se llama?
Sr. Brown	John Brown. B-r-o-w-n. Brown.
Empleada	Un momento, por favor . . . Sí, aquí tenemos una reserva a su nombre, pero es para el día quince y hoy estamos a catorce.
Sr. Brown	¿Cómo? ¿Para el día quince ha dicho Vd.? Mire Vd., yo mismo hice la reserva y no me cabe duda que era para el catorce. ¡Esto es el colmo de la incompetencia! Exijo que me entreguen el coche que pedí, inmediatamente.
Empleada	Lo siento, pero en este momento no tenemos ningún coche disponible.
Sra. Brown	¡Es increíble! Es la primera vez que nos sucede algo así.
Empleada	Pues, les aconsejo que hablen con el encargado. A lo mejor él les puede solucionar el problema. Yo no puedo hacer nada. ¿Quieren esperar un momento, por favor? Iré a buscarle.

2 Which expressions from the conversation have the following meanings?
   a I demand that you hand me the car.
   b I suggest you speak to the manager.

3 Answer the following questions in Spanish.
   a ¿Dónde alquilaron el coche los Brown?
   b ¿Quién hizo la reserva?
   c ¿Por qué no puede darle otro coche la empleada?
   d ¿Qué les aconseja la empleada?

NEW EXPRESSIONS

Talking about events that happened recently

He pedido una transferencia.	*I've asked for a transfer.*
Aún no ha llegado.	*It hasn't arrived yet.*

Using reported speech

Me dijeron que la enviarían inmediatamente.	*They told me they would send it immediately.*
Me dijeron que tardaría solo dos días.	*They told me it would take only two days.*

Making complaints

¡No es posible!	*That's impossible!*
¡Es increíble!	*It's incredible!*
¡Esto es el colmo de la incompetencia!	*This is the height of inefficiency!*
Quiero hacer una reclamación.	*I want to make a complaint.*
Tengo una queja.	*I have a complaint.*
Quisiera quejarme de . . .	*I'd like to complain about . . .*

Offering advice and recommendations

Es mejor que llame Vd. por teléfono a su banco.	*You'd better telephone your bank.*
Le recomiendo que utilice el servicio postal express.	*I recommend you use the postal express service.*

The verbs most frequently used to give advice and recommendations are **aconsejar** *to advise*, **recomendar** *to recommend*, **sugerir** *to suggest*.

Giving instructions

Primero tiene que marcar el 00.	*First you have to dial 00.*
Siga las instrucciones de la pantalla.	*Follow the on-screen instructions.*

In writing, instructions and procedures are often expressed with the infinitive, e.g. **introducir su tarjeta** *insert your card*, **tomar su recibo** *take your receipt*.

Expressing certainty and uncertainty

¿Está seguro/a de que no hay nada?	*Are you sure there is nothing?*
Estoy (completamente) seguro/a.	*I'm (absolutely) sure.*
Me parece que . . .	*It seems to me (that) . . .*
Creo que . . .	*I think (that) . . .*
No creo que . . . (+ subjunctive)	*I don't think (that) . . .*

 Can you match the complaints with the corresponding recommendations?

a Quiero quejarme del olor en el coche. Apesta a cigarrillo.

b Esto es el colmo, ¡el ascensor está fuera de servicio otra vez!

c Nos dijeron que el servicio de habitaciones tardaría solo quince minutos y aún no ha llegado el desayuno.

1 Les recomiendo que bajen al restaurante.

2 Le aconsejo que encienda el aire acondicionado.

3 Le sugiero que suba por la escalera.

Language discovery

You have seen this language in action. Now can you work out the rules?

1 **How would you say in Spanish that the following things have occurred?**
  a We have already had dinner.
  b I've asked for the bill.
  c But you've told me this already!

2 **Which is the correct verb form to use in these sentences?**
  a Me han llamado y me dijeron que (llegaran / llegarían / habrían llegado) tarde.
  b Me prometió que nos (llamará / llamaría / llamó) a las ocho en punto.

3 **Give the correct verb form of the verb: indicative or subjunctive?**

¿Estás segura de que _____ (tú/tener) la llave del coche? No creo que la _____ (tener/tú)

1 THE PERFECT TENSE

This is used to refer to the recent past and to events which have happened in a period of time which includes the present.

Sentences such as:

He pedido una transferencia.	*I have asked for a transfer.*
Hemos alquilado un coche.	*We have hired a car.*

refer to the recent past and are normally expressed in Spanish in the perfect tense.

Events which have happened in a period of time which includes the present, e.g. **hoy** *today*, **esta mañana** *this morning*, **esta semana** *this week*, **todavía, aún** *still, yet*, **ya** *already*, etc., are also normally expressed in the perfect tense, as in:

Hoy he hablado con él.	*Today I've spoken to him.*
Aún no ha llegado.	*It hasn't arrived yet.*

a In Latin America and in the North-Western regions of Spain, notably Galicia and Asturias, the preterite tense, e.g. **Hoy hablé con él** *Today I spoke to him*, is much more common than the perfect tense.

b The Spanish perfect tense often translates into English as simple past, e.g. **Lo he llamado hace un rato.** *I phoned him a while ago.*

Formation

To form the perfect tense you use the present tense of **haber** *to have* followed by a past participle which does not change. The past participle of **-ar** verbs ends in **-ado** while **-er** and **-ir** verbs form the past participle by adding **-ido** to the stem. Here are two verbs, **llegar** *to arrive* and **pedir** *to ask for*, in the perfect tense.

he llegado	*I have arrived*
has llegado	*you have arrived* (familiar)
ha llegado	*he/she/it has arrived, you have arrived*
hemos llegado	*we have arrived*
habéis llegado	*you have arrived* (familiar)
han llegado	*they/you have arrived*

he pedido	*I have asked (for)*
has pedido	*you have asked (for)* (familiar)
ha pedido	*he/she/it has asked (for), you have asked (for)*
hemos pedido	*we have asked (for)*
habéis pedido	*you have asked (for)* (familiar)
han pedido	*they/you have asked (for)*

2 THE CONDITIONAL TENSE IN REPORTED SPEECH

Compare these sentences:

La enviaremos inmediatamente.	*We'll send it immediately.*
Me han dicho/Dicen que la enviarán inmediatamente.	*They've told me/They say they will send it immediately.*
Me dijeron que la enviarían inmediatamente.	*They told me (that) they would send it immediately.*

The first sentence is a direct statement while the other two are reported speech. Verbs such as **decir** *to say*, **prometer** *to promise* and **asegurar** *to assure* are often used in reported speech. As in English, there is no fixed way in which to do this, but normally, if the direct statement is in the future tense, the reported one can start with a verb in the present, the perfect or the preterite tense. With the first two, the verb in the second clause will normally not change tense, but if the reported statement is introduced by the preterite, the second verb will be in the conditional tense.

Tardará solo dos días.	*It will only take two days.*
Me dijeron que tardaría solo dos días.	*They told me it would only take two days.*
Os devolveré el dinero la semana que viene.	*I'll return the money to you next week.*
Nos prometió que nos devolvería el dinero la semana que viene.	*He/she promised to return the money to us next week.*

Note the similarity between Spanish and English when reporting a direct statement that refers to the past:

La enviamos ayer.	*We sent it yesterday.*
Dicen que la enviaron ayer.	*They say they sent it yesterday.*
Me dijeron que la habían enviado ayer.	*They told me they had sent it yesterday.*

Formation of the conditional tense

Like the future tense, the conditional is formed with the infinitive, to which the endings are added. The endings of the three conjugations are the same as those of the imperfect tense of **-er** and **-ir** verbs (see Unit 5). Here is the conditional tense of a regular verb, **enviar** *to send*.

enviaría	*I would send*
enviarías	*you would send* (familiar)
enviaría	*he/she/you would send*
enviaríamos	*we would send*
enviaríais	*you would send* (familiar)
enviarían	*they/you would send*

Note that **-er** and **-ir** verbs have the same endings as **-ar** verbs.

 # Practice

1 Complete this note with the correct form of the perfect tense of the verb shown.

> Antonio:
> Esta mañana te _____ (llamar) Ricardo.
> Dice que él y su mujer _____ (llegar)
> hoy a Madrid y que _____ (reservar)
> una habitación en el Hotel El Escorial.
> Volverá a llamar esta tarde. Yo _____ (ir)
> a Correos a revisar mi apdo, pero espero
> volver antes de las 2.00. Te _____ (dejar)
> la comida en la nevera.
> No te olvides de que mi madre nos _____
> (invitar) a cenar esta noche.
> Mari Carmen

CULTURE TIP

Among the services offered by Correos de España, **el apartado postal** (*P. O. Box*) is used by many individuals who run a business from home. In writing, you are more likely to see the abbreviation **apdo**: **Voy a revisar mi apdo** *I'm going to check my P. O. Box*. Other services include **el servicio de paquetería** (*parcel service*) and **el buzón de vacaciones** (*post held during your holidays*). To drop a letter in the box, you'd say **echar una carta**.

---

2 Make indirect statements using the introductory phrases given.

    a El envío llegará mañana. El empleado me dijo que . . .

    b Tardará dos días en llegar. Ella me aseguró que . . .

    c El paquete estará allí el lunes. En Correos me dijeron que . . .

    d Les entregaremos el coche esta tarde. En la agencia nos prometieron que . . .

e Le repararemos el coche ahora mismo. El mecánico me prometió que . . .

f Te llamaré por teléfono esta noche. Alfonso me dijo que . . .

 3 **You arrive in a hotel in a Spanish-speaking country and you are told that there is no record of your booking and that there are no rooms available. How would you say the following in Spanish?**

a I made the reservation myself. (Use the perfect tense.)

b I have no doubt it was for today.

c Are you sure there isn't any reservation in my name?

d This is the height of inefficiency!

e This is incredible!

f I demand that you give us a room immediately.

g Well, I'd like to make a complaint.

h It's the first time something like this has happened to us. (Use the present tense for the second verb.)

4 **Rosa had many reasons to complain about the flat she rented. Can you match the complaints with the drawings?**

a ¡No puede ser! Uno de los cristales está roto.

b ¡Esto es el colmo! La nevera no funciona.

c ¡No me lo puedo creer! Hay una gotera en el techo.

d Me tengo que quejar del vecino. Hace mucho ruido.

e Tengo una reclamación: La bañera está atascada. Por favor, envíe un fontanero en seguida.

f ¡No es posible! Uno de los grifos está estropeado. Necesito que lo reparen ahora mismo.

5 **Diana, a Spanish-speaking friend who is visiting you at home, needs to withdraw some cash. She has never used a cash machine in your country before. Give her some instructions based on the user's notice. Use the correct verb forms and the phrases in the box.**

cajero automático (m)	*cash machine*
ranura (f)	*slot*
ingresar su PIN	*insert your PIN*
clave (secreta) (f)	*(secret) user password or code*
en pantalla (f)	*on screen*
un monto	*an amount*
libra (f)	*pound sterling*
recibo (m)	*a receipt*
transacción (f)	*a bank transaction*
cuenta corriente (f)	*a current account*

> **Para hacer un retiro**
> 1 introducir su tarjeta
> 2 seleccionar un idioma
> 3 ingresar su PIN
> 4 seguir las instrucciones en pantalla
> 5 retirar su dinero
> 6 tomar su recibo

Diana   Dime, ¿Cómo hago para retirar dinero de un cajero automático?

Tú   Primero, introduce tu tarjeta en la ranura y _____

08.06 **There is more than one way to give these instructions. Listen for a model answer.**

¡A escuchar!

¡Dígalo por la PR! This is the title of a public announcement from Radio la Romántica, XHPR, in Veracruz, Mexico.

6 08.07 **Listen to the announcement or, alternatively, read the transcript of the text, and then explain:**
   a What kind of service does Radio la Romántica offer its listeners?
   b How does this service operate?

¡Quejas y más quejas! Some people like to complain!

7 08.08 **Listen to three different complaints then, for each one, say where it takes place and what it is about.**
   a _____
   b _____
   c _____

8 Have you ever written a complaint to a newspaper or magazine? Here are two emails sent by people in Chile and Spain. What are they complaining about? Read the emails to find out and then write a brief summary of their content in Spanish.

sobreventa (f)	*overbooking*
mesón (m)	*counter*
enterarse	*to find out*
ley (f)	*law*

Sobreventa en línea aérea

Hace unos días mi mujer y yo íbamos a viajar a Londres vía Nueva York, pero al presentarnos en el mostrador de Aerosur, nos informaron de que no podríamos viajar, ya que el vuelo estaba completo, hecho insólito, ya que habíamos hecho y pagado nuestras reservas hacía un mes.

Nos quejamos al encargado de la línea aérea en el aeropuerto, pero sin éxito. Después de esperar más de dos horas, este prometió enviarnos en un vuelo que salía al día siguiente.

Regresamos a nuestra casa, y al otro día, antes de iniciar nuestro viaje al aeropuerto, llamamos por teléfono a la línea aérea para reconfirmar nuestras reservas. Grande fue nuestra sorpresa e indignación al enterarnos de que solo estaba confirmado el vuelo hasta Nueva York, y que en el vuelo de conexión de Nueva York a Londres estábamos en lista de espera. ¡No podíamos creerlo! Nunca nos había sucedido una cosa así, por lo que decidimos anular nuestras reservas y viajar en otra empresa.

La sobreventa, según nos hemos enterado, es una práctica habitual en Aerosur. Ello nos causó grandes molestias y pérdida de tiempo y dinero. Aparte de eso, el trato que recibimos por parte del personal de la línea aérea fue descortés y su actuación incompetente. No volveremos a utilizar sus servicios.

Juan Carlos Reyes, Santiago de Chile

LANGUAGE TIP

Look at the word order in: **Grande fue nuestra sorpresa, Nunca nos había sucedido.** By placing **grande** and **nunca** in initial position the writer highlights their meanings. More usually, you would say **Nuestra sorpresa fue grande** and **No nos había sucedido nunca**.

El inglés en Ibiza

Es el colmo que en España no nos permitan leer en nuestro propio idioma.

Este verano pasé mis vacaciones en un hotel en Ibiza, y todas la indicaciones estaban en inglés. Me pareció increíble. Me dio la impresión de que estaba en Inglaterra o en Estados Unidos en lugar de España. Estoy segura de que esto no sucede en otros países. Al menos en mis viajes nunca lo había experimentado. Sentí que era una suerte de discriminación ejercida contra los españoles en su propio país. ¿Dónde están las autoridades que no hacen nada al respecto? Debería haber una ley que prohibiera situaciones como esta. Defendamos nuestra lengua.

María de la Luz García, Madrid

 9 Read the letters again and find the expressions which mean the following:
   a puesto que
   b raro, extraño
   c presentamos una queja
   d empezar, comenzar
   e rabia, ira
   f poco cortés, poco amable
   g nunca me había pasado
   h una especie de

 Test yourself

1 Change the verbs in brackets into an appropriate form. For some of the sentences there is more than one possibility.
   a Marta aún no (volver). Dijo que (venir) sobre las seis.
   b Le he (escribir) un email a Pablo y le he (aconsejar) que lo (hacer) lo antes posible.
   c Me han (recomendar) que (contratar) un seguro de viaje, y así lo he (hacer).
   d – Es mejor que Vd. mismo se lo (decir).
      – Se lo he (decir) hace un momento.
   e Exijo que Vds. me (entregar) el dinero ahora mismo. Vds. me dijeron que lo (hacer).
   f Para llamar a Inglaterra (marcar) Vd. el 00 44. ¿Me ha (entender)?

2 Complete the sentences with a suitable word from the box.

| seguro encargado cajero automático anular colmo |
| código entrega reclamación ventaja |

a ¿Cuál es el _____ internacional para llamar a Estados Unidos?

b Hay un banco Santander en la esquina. Allí encontrará Vd un _____.

c El servicio postal express es un servicio _____ y la _____ se hace a domicilio. Esa es una gran _____.

d El servico fue tan malo que decidimos _____ nuestra reserva..

e Estoy muy descontento con la atención y quiero hacer una _____. ¿Me puede poner con el _____, por favor?

f ¡Esto es el _____ de la ironía!

Test 1 focuses on the use of the perfect tense, the conditional in indirect speech and the subjunctive after certain verbs. In Test 2 the main focus is on vocabulary. Check your answers in the key to Test yourself and go on to the next unit if most of your answers were correct. Don't be discouraged if you made a few mistakes, as the important thing is that you are able to communicate.

SELF CHECK

I CAN . . .
. . . talk about events that happened recently.
. . . use reported speech.
. . . make complaints and respond to complaints.
. . . offer advice and recommendations.
. . . give instructions.
. . . express certainty and uncertainty.

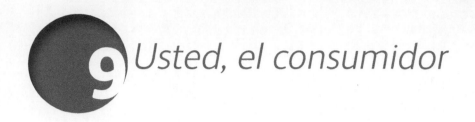

Usted, el consumidor

In this unit you will learn how to:

▶ *enquire about forms of payment.*
▶ *describe things.*
▶ *express open and remote conditions.*
▶ *express obligation and needs.*
▶ *express surprise.*

CEFR: *Can understand clear and detailed descriptions on a range of subjects, e.g. saving tips for shopping (B2); can extract specific information from broadcasts, e.g. long answers to a marketing survey (C1).*

Conversations

1 EN UNA TIENDA DE ARTÍCULOS DE PIEL *IN A LEATHER SHOP*

Una señora entra en una tienda de artículos de piel para comprar un regalo para su hija.

 1 09.01 **As you listen to the conversation, try answering these questions:**

    a Why does the lady turn down the first article that she is shown?
    b Is her gift selection within or beyond her self-imposed budget in the end?

bolso (m)	*handbag*
gastar	*to spend*
artículos de piel	*leather goods*
factura (f)	*the till receipt*

Clienta	Buenas tardes. Quisiera comprar un bolso. Es para regalo.
Dependienta	¿Es para una persona joven?
Clienta	Sí, es para mi hija que está de cumpleaños.
Dependienta	¿Cuánto desea gastar aproximadamente?
Clienta	Unos cien euros.
Dependienta	Pues, tenemos estos que están de oferta y están muy bien de precio. Los tenemos a ochenta y cinco euros. Este marrón, por ejemplo, es muy bonito y es de muy buena calidad. Mire Vd.
Clienta	Sí, es precioso. Pero no creo que a mi hija le guste ese color. Prefiero llevar uno blanco. Aquel, por ejemplo, ¿vale lo mismo?
Dependienta	Sí, tiene el mismo precio. Y si no le gusta puede cambiarlo, pero deberá traer la factura.
Clienta	De acuerdo. Me lo quedo.

Dependienta	¿Va a pagar en efectivo?
Clienta	No, ¿puedo pagar con tarjeta de crédito?
Dependienta	Sí, sí, claro.
Clienta	¿Me lo puede envolver para regalo, por favor?
Dependienta	Sí, por supuesto.

> **LANGUAGE TIP**
>
> Note the conditional sentence: **Si no le gusta, puede cambiarlo** *If you don't like it, you can change it.*
> More on this in the Language discovery section.

 2 **There are a number of words and phrases related to shopping in this conversation. Can you find the Spanish for the following?**

a It's for a present.
b She's having a birthday.
c They are on offer.
d You can change it.
e I'll take it.
f To pay cash
g To pay with a credit card
h Can you wrap it up for me?

 3 09.02 **Role play – You want to buy una cartera *a wallet* for your father. Follow the prompts and take part in a conversation with the shopkeeper. Then listen to check your answers.**

2 DESCRIBIENDO UN COCHE *DESCRIBING A CAR*

Javier y su amiga Trini hablan de coches.

 1 09.03 **Look at the key words and phrases, then read the conversation and do Exercise 2 before listening.**

¿de veras?	*really?*
beca (f)	*scholarship*
¡no me digas!	*you don't say!*
¿cuánto pide por él?	*how much is he asking for it?*
tener ganas (f pl)	*to want, be longing to*

Javier	¿Sabes que Cristóbal va a vender su coche?
Trini	¿De veras? Es un coche estupendo y está casi nuevo. ¿Por qué lo piensa vender?
Javier	Se ha ganado una beca para Estados Unidos y necesita el dinero.
Trini	¡No me digas! ¿Y sabes tú cuánto pide por él?
Javier	Tres mil euros.
Trini	¡Hombre! ¡Y con las ganas que tengo yo de tener un coche! Si tuviera dinero, se lo compraría.

2 Check your understanding: ¿Verdadero o falso?

    a Cristóbal ha vendido su coche.

    b Critóbal necesita el dinero para obtener una beca.

    c El coche está bien de precio.

    d Trini piensa comprar el coche de Javier.

> **LANGUAGE TIP**
> Note another sort of conditional sentence:
> **Si tuviera dinero, se lo compraría** *If I had money I'd buy it.*

3 EN UN TALLER DE REPARACIONES *IN A REPAIR SHOP*

Un cliente lleva su televisor a un taller de reparaciones.

1 09.04 **Go over the vocabulary then listen to the conversation.**

imagen (f)	*picture (TV)*
presupuesto (m)	*estimate*
estar conforme	*to be in agreement*

Cliente	Buenas tardes. ¿Podría repararme este televisor?
Empleado	¿Qué le pasa?
Cliente	La imagen no se ve muy bien.
Empleado	Bien, pero habrá que revisarlo primero y después le daré un presupuesto por la reparación. Y si Vd. está conforme, haremos el trabajo.
Cliente	De acuerdo. ¿A qué hora puedo volver?
Empleado	Vuelva Vd. esta tarde después de las seis.

> **LANGUAGE TIP**
> **Habrá que revisarlo** *We'll have to check it* is an impersonal sentence expressing need, and using the verb **haber** *to have* in the future tense. You may be familiar with the present tense form **hay que: Hay que repararlo** *We need to repair it.*

2 Answer the following questions in Spanish.

    a ¿Cuál es el problema con el televisor?

    b ¿Qué tendrá que hacer el empleado antes de repararlo?

    c ¿Con qué tiene que estar conforme el cliente para que empiece el trabajo?

 NEW EXPRESSIONS

Asking for something in a shop and enquiring about forms of payment

Quisiera comprar un bolso.	*I'd like to buy a handbag.*
¿Va a pagar en efectivo?	*Are you going to pay cash?*
¿Puedo pagar con tarjeta de crédito?	*May I pay with a credit card?*
No llevo dinero./No tengo efectivo.	*I don't have cash on me.*
No llevo (dinero) suelto.	*I don't have the exact change.*

Describing things

Es muy bonito y es de muy buena calidad.	*It is very nice and the quality is very good.*
Es un coche estupendo y está casi nuevo.	*It is an excellent car and it is almost new.*

Expressing open and remote conditions

Si no le gusta, puede cambiarlo (open condition).   *If you don't like it, you can change it.*
Si tuviera dinero, se lo compraría (remote condition).   *If I had money, I would buy it from him.*

Expressing obligation and needs

Deberá traer la factura.   *You'll have to bring the receipt.*
Habrá que revisarlo.   *It will be necessary to check it.*
No hace falta que te invite formalmente.   *It's not necessary that I invite you. /*
   You don't need to wait for me to invite you.

Expressing surprise

¿De veras?	*Really?*
¡No me digas!	*You don't say!*
¡Hombre!	*Good heavens!, I never!*
¡Qué sorpresa!	*What a surprise!*
Es sorprendente.	*It is surprising/amazing.*
¡Me parece imposible que . . . !	*I can hardly believe . . . !*
Me sorprende.	*It surprises me.*
¡Quién lo hubiera creído!	*Who would have thought it!*
¡No (me) lo puedo creer!	*I can't believe it!*

> **LANGUAGE TIP**
>
> The word **¡Hombre!** used as an exclamation is extremely common in Peninsular Spanish and it has a number of meanings depending on the context: *Good heavens!, I never!, Of course!, You bet!, (Oh) come on!, Oh please!, Hey!, Dear oh dear!,* etc.

What two Spanish words can have the meaning of *cash*?

Using what you know and some intuition, how would you say:

– *Who would have thought this restaurant doesn't take credit cards!*

– *You don't say! Fortunately I've got enough cash. Don't worry.*

Language discovery

1 CONDITIONAL SENTENCES

You have seen this language before. Now can you work out the rules?

1 **Which of these verb forms carry an imperfect subjunctive ending?**

perdieran	tuviera	tuvimos
querremos	perdieron	quisieras

2 **Can you supply the verb in the main part of the sentences?**
   a Si está conforme, _____ empezar ahora mismo.
   b Si estuviera/estuviese conforme, _____ empezar ahora mismo.

3 How about in the que (*that*) part of these sentences?

   a Me gustaría que (tú) _____ (pasar) por mí.

   b Te pido que lo _____ (hacer), por favor.

4 Do these sentences have a similar or different meaning?

   a Deberemos traer la factura.

   b Tendremos que traerla.

   c Habrá que traerla.

Open conditions

These are sentences in which the condition may or may not be fulfilled, as in:

Si Vd. está conforme, haremos el trabajo.   *If you are in agreement, we shall do the job.*

The combination of tenses used in these sentences is the same as it is in English, e.g. present tense plus future tense, as in the previous sentence, present tense plus present tense, as in:

Si llueve, es mejor no ir.   *If it rains, it is better not to go.*

Notice that **si** is followed by a verb in the indicative, not the subjunctive.

Remote conditions

Most sentences of this type express a condition which is contrary to fact, i.e. which may not be fulfilled, as in:

Si tuviera dinero, se lo compraría.   *If I had money, I would buy it from him.*

The verb which follows **si** must be in the imperfect subjunctive while the verb in the second clause is normally in the conditional (for the conditional tense, see Unit 8).

This same construction is sometimes used to express conditions which may be fulfilled (as in open conditions). Consider, for example:

Si fueras ahora, la verías.   *If you went now, you would see her.*

which is practically equivalent to:

Si vas ahora, la verás.   *If you go now, you will see her.*

2 IMPERFECT SUBJUNCTIVE TENSE

Formation

The imperfect subjunctive, used in remote conditions, can be formed in two ways. The first is directly derived from the third person plural of the preterite (see Unit 4), for example:

Infinitive	Preterite	Imperfect subjunctive (1st and 3rd person sing)
comprar *to buy*	**compraron**	**comprara**
vender *to sell*	**vendieron**	**vendiera**
escribir *to write*	**escribieron**	**escribiera**

The same derivation occurs with irregular and stem-changing verbs:

tener *to have*	**tuvieron**	**tuviera**
ser/ir *to be/go*	**fueron**	**fuera**
querer *to want*	**quisieron**	**quisiera**

Verbs of the second and third conjugation (**-er** and **-ir**) form the imperfect subjunctive in the same way. First conjugation verbs (**-ar**) have a different set of endings. Here are two examples:

comprar:	(sing)	**comprara**	**compraras**	**comprara**
	(pl)	**compráramos**	**comprarais**	**compraran**
vender:	(sing)	**vendiera**	**vendieras**	**vendiera**
	(pl)	**vendiéramos**	**vendierais**	**vendieran**

The imperfect subjunctive has a second set of endings which appear to be less frequent than the first. The two forms are generally interchangeable. Again, **-er** and **-ir** verbs share the same endings.

comprar:	(sing)	**comprase**	**comprases**	**comprase**
	(pl)	**comprásemos**	**compraseis**	**comprasen**
vender:	(sing)	**vendiese**	**vendieses**	**vendiese**
	(pl)	**vendiésemos**	**vendieseis**	**vendiesen**

Sequence of tenses with the imperfect subjunctive

Other than in remote conditions such as the above, the imperfect subjunctive normally occurs in sentences which carry a main clause in the:

a Imperfect:
Él *quería* que yo lo *comprara*.   *He wanted me to buy it.*

b Preterite:
Ella me *pidió* que lo *cambiara*.   *She asked me to change it.*

c Pluperfect:
Yo le *había pedido* que me *diera* un presupuesto.   *I had asked him to give me an estimate.*

d Conditional:
Me *gustaría* que lo *hicieras*.   *I'd like you to do it.*

e Perfect conditional:
Yo *habría preferido* que lo *hicieras*.   *I'd have preferred you to do it.*

3 VERBS WHICH EXPRESS OBLIGATION AND NEEDS

Tener que   *to have to*
Tendré que venderlo.   *I will have to sell it.*

Deber   *to have to, must*
Deberá traer la factura.   *You'll have to bring the receipt.*

Ser necesario *to be necessary*

¿Crees que es necesario?	*Do you think it is necessary?*
No es necesario esperar.	*We don't need to wait.*
No es necesario que esperes./No hace falta que esperes.	*You don't need to wait.*

> **LANGUAGE TIP**
>
> Notice how the translation of **no es necesario** and **no hace falta** is not word-for-word. These constructions with a subordinate clause introduced by **que** require the use of the subjunctive whenever the subjects of the main and the subordinate clauses are different: **no es necesario que (tú) esperes**; otherwise use the infinitive: **no es necesario esperar**, or **no hace falta esperar**.

Necesitar *to need*

Necesito un coche.	*I need a car.*
Necesito comprar un regalo.	*I need to buy a present.*
Necesito que me ayudes.	*I need you to help me.*

Hacer falta *to be necessary*

¿Hace falta tener visado?	*Does one need a visa?*
No hace falta que me lo digas.	*You don't need to tell me.*

Note again the use of the subjunctive in the subordinate clause in **No hace falta que (tú) me lo digas.**

Hay que *it is necessary – one has to, you/we have to*

Hay que hacerlo.	*One has to do it.*

Hay derives from **haber** (auxiliary verb *to have*), and it can be used in tenses other than the present.

Habrá que revisarlo.	*It will be necessary to check it.*
Hubo que repararlo.	*It was necessary to repair it.*
Habría que venderlo.	*It would be necessary to sell it.*

 ## Practice

1 Follow the example and express remote conditions.

Ejemplo: No iré porque no tengo dinero. *Si tuviera dinero, iría.*

  a No viajaré a España porque no tengo vacaciones.
  b No compraré el coche porque está en mal estado.
  c No lo haremos reparar porque no merece la pena.
  d No se quedarán porque tienen que volver al trabajo.
  e No los recibiré porque estoy ocupado.
  f Ella no le entiende porque él no habla bien español.

2 Say what you have or had to do:

Ejemplo: ¿Qué necesitas comprar? (un regalo) *Necesito comprar un regalo.*

    a ¿Qué tuviste que hacer? (vender el piso)

    b ¿Qué tenías que decirme? (algo importante)

    c ¿Qué hay que hacer? (nada)

    d ¿Qué debes llevar? (el pasaporte)

    e ¿Qué necesitabas comprar? (una maleta)

    f ¿Qué habrá que traer? (algo para beber)

3 Role play – You go into a shop to buy yourself a pair of trousers. Play the part of the customer in this conversation with the shop assistant.

pantalón/pantalones (m sing/pl)	*trousers*
tengo la talla 46	*I'm size 46*
probarse	*to try on*
quedar bien	*to fit*
no llevo dinero (m)	*I don't have cash on me*

Dependiente(a) ¿En qué puedo servirle?

Tú **(a)** *I'd like to buy some trousers. Have you got any on offer? I don't want to spend too much.*

Dependiente(a) Sí, tenemos dos o tres modelos de oferta. Son para usted, ¿verdad?

Tú **(b)** *Yes, they are for me. I'm looking for something of good quality.*

Dependiente(a) Tenemos estos de algodón, son de muy buena calidad y están de moda. ¿Qué le parecen?

Tú **(c)** *Yes, they are nice. I like them very much. Have you got them in black?*

Dependiente(a) Sí, y también en marrón y en gris. ¿Qué talla tiene Vd.?

Tú **(d)** *I'm size 46. Have you got any in that size?*

Dependiente(a) Sí, este es el último pantalón que nos queda en esa talla.

Tú **(e)** *I'd like to try them on. Where's the fitting room?*

Dependiente(a) Está al fondo a la derecha.

(Coming back to the sales person)

Tú **(f)** *They fit very well. How much are they?*

Dependiente(a) Cuestan cuarenta y ocho euros.

Tú **(g)** *They are a little expensive, but I like them. I'll take them. Do you accept credit cards? I haven't got any cash.*

Dependiente(a) Sí, por supuesto.

> **LANGUAGE TIP**
>
> **Quedar** has a number of meanings: **Me/Nos queda uno/quedan dos** *I/We have one/two left*; **Me queda grande** *It's too big for me*; **Estos zapatos me quedan bien** *These shoes fit (me) well*; **¿Dónde queda Andorra? Queda entre España y Francia** *Where's Andorra? It's between Spain and France*; **He quedado con Paco** *I've agreed to meet Paco.*

4 Pat, a friend of yours who has just started learning Spanish, has asked you to translate an email which she received from someone in Venezuela. Go for the overall meaning rather than a word-for-word translation.

quizás	maybe, perhaps
no hace falta que te invite	there's no need to wait for an invitation
ya que . . .	as, given that . . .

Querida Pat:

¡Qué agradable recibir un mail tuyo otra vez! Me alegro de que estés bien y espero que te vaya estupendamente en tus exámenes finales.

Te agradezco mucho tu invitación para este verano, pero desgraciadamente no tengo suficiente dinero para viajar. Si pudiera, naturalmente que iría a verte. ¡No sabes cómo me gustaría! El próximo año quizás, pero tendré que trabajar mucho para ahorrar dinero ya que el viaje es muy caro. Tú también tendrás que venir a Venezuela algún día. No hace falta que te invite formalmente. Te estaré esperando.

Un abrazo

Raúl

5 ¿Qué harías si ganaras la lotería?

Ana, Luis and Raquel each commented on what they would do or buy if they won a big prize in the lottery. Read their comments and match the names with the drawings.

V deuda (f)	debt	

deuda (f) — debt
tocar — to win
amueblar — to furnish
invertir — to invest
holgadamente — comfortably
instalar — to set up
bolsa (f) — stock exchange
soñar — to dream
donar — to give
malgastar — to squander

_____ **Ana, 18 años**

Si ganara la lotería, lo primero que haría sería pagar todas mis deudas y las de mis padres, con quienes vivo actualmente. También me compraría una gran casa en la playa y la amueblaría lujosamente y, además, compraría un yate, en el que mi novio y yo daríamos la vuelta al mundo. Al regresar nos casaríamos. Si todavía me quedara dinero, lo invertiría muy bien y viviríamos holgadamente. Pero no dejaría mi trabajo, ya que me gusta lo que hago . . .

_____ **Luis, 48 años**

Si a mí me tocara la lotería, mi vida cambiaría completamente. No sé si sería más feliz o no, pero sí sé que resolvería mis actuales problemas económicos. Para empezar, renunciaría a mi puesto de administrativo en la empresa donde trabajo e instalaría mi propia empresa, y la administraría personalmente. Ya no tendría un jefe, ni tendría que trabajar ocho horas diarias para ganar un sueldo miserable.

En lo personal, me mudaría con mi familia al mejor barrio de la ciudad. Mi mujer y yo tendríamos cada uno su propio coche, y enviaríamos a nuestro hijo al mejor de los colegios. En verano tomaríamos unas largas vacaciones en la playa y en invierno nos iríamos a esquiar a la montaña. Y todavía nos quedaría suficiente dinero para invertir en la bolsa y vivir bien el resto de nuestras vidas . . .

_____ **Raquel, 32 años**

Soy profesora y, si tuviera la suerte de ganar la lotería, haría una gran fiesta para celebrarlo. No dudaría en dejar mi actividad actual y dedicarme totalmente a escribir novelas, que es lo que siempre he soñado. Ayudaría también a mi familia y a la gente más necesitada de mi pueblo, especialmente a los niños y a los ancianos. Donaría una gran cantidad de dinero al colegio donde trabajo y donde yo misma hice mis estudios. No malgastaría el dinero, pero sí lo disfrutaría mucho . . .

6 Who said the following? Reread the comments and match these sentences with the appropriate person.

   a Dejaría mi trabajo.
   b No renunciaría a mi puesto.
   c Yo mismo estaría a cargo de ella.
   d Es lo que he querido hacer toda mi vida.
   e Antes que nada, pagaría todo lo que debo.

¡A escuchar!

¿Dónde compra Vd.? Where do people in your country normally buy their food: in traditional corner shops, or in small or large supermarkets? Compare their habits with those of Spanish people in the table.

TIENDAS DONDE LOS ESPAÑOLES SUELEN COMPRAR SUS ALIMENTOS (%)	
Hipermercados	37
Pequeños supermercados	32
Grandes supermercados	14
Tiendas tradicionales	9
Pequeños autoservicios	8

7 09.05 **Rosario Santos, a housewife, is asked about her shopping preferences. Look at the key words and, as you listen, focus on Questions a–c.**

grandes almacenes (m pl)	*department stores*
comestibles (m pl)	*foodstuff*
vecino/a	*neighbour*
cotillear	*to gossip*

  a ¿En qué ocasiones compra en la tienda de su barrio?

  b ¿Cuándo compra en grandes almacenes? ¿Por qué?

  c Y los comestibles, ¿dónde los suele comprar?

8 09.06 **Ana Belmar, a student, answers the survey. Listen to what she has to say, then decide if the following statements are verdaderos o falsos.**

rebajas (f pl)	*sale*
aprovechar	*to take advantage*
tratándose de . . .	*if it is to do with . . .*
a la moda	*fashionably*

  a Ana prefiere comprar en pequeñas tiendas porque es más barato.

  b Hoy ha comprado en unos grandes almacenes porque hay ofertas especiales.

  c Ana trabaja para comprar su ropa.

9 09.07 **Andrés Calle, an office clerk from Chile, is the third person to take the survey. Listen to the complete conversation a couple of times:**

lo cierto es . . .	*the truth is . . .*
encargarse de	*to be responsible for*
acompañar	*to accompany*

  a Complete the passage with the missing words. Try doing so as you listen without the help of the transcripts.

Pues, lo cierto es _____ prefiero ir a una _____ más pequeña donde el _____ sea más directo, más _____. Pero eso solo lo _____ hacer el fin de _____. Yo soy administrativo y _____ por la mañana y _____ la tarde y cuando _____ las tiendas ya están _____. Por eso vengo a _____ aquí, pues está abierto _____ mediodía. Aprovecho la _____ de la comida para _____ lo que necesito.

b Listen again to (or read) the answer given by Andrés Calle to the second question: **¿Y la compra de comestibles, la hace Vd. también?** Summarize his answer in English.

10 **A friend of yours who doesn't know any Spanish is thinking of renting a flat in Spain for the summer. Your friend has been sent the information on consumer protection and has asked you to translate it. Familiarize yourself with the new vocabulary before you do the translation in writing.**

combustible (m)	*fuel (gas)*
recogida de basuras (f)	*rubbish collection*
señal (f)	*deposit*
importe (m)	*cost, value*
antelación (f)	*time in advance*
aviso (m)	*notice*

ESTE VERANO
VIAJA
INFORMADO

✳ OMIC

APARTAMENTOS
TURÍSTICOS

En el precio del alojamiento van incluidos los siguientes servicios: agua, luz y combustible; recogida de basuras y servicios comunes.

En el momento de realizar la reserva se puede exigir, en concepto de paga y señal, una cantidad que va del 15 al 40% del importe total que corresponda al precio contratado.

Si el usuario decide anular la reserva tiene derecho a una devolución de la paga y señal con unas penalizaciones que van del 5 al 50%, según la antelación del aviso. Si la anulación se efectúa conmenos de 7 días de antelación no tendrá derecho a devolución alguna.

(Oficina Municipal de Información al Consumidor, Ayuntamiento de Toledo)

11 **Here is some advice given by a consumer magazine to its readers, in which some key words are missing.**

presupuesto (m)	*budget*
ceder	*to give in, yield*
cajero/a	*cashier*
estante (m)	*shelf*
romper	*to tear up, break*
pareja (f)	*partner*

Complete the text with an appropriate word from the box.

> precio   pena   bolsillo   lista   vergüenza   compra   tentación
> estantes   vacío   gastos

Cómo mantener el consumo bajo control

a Antes de salir a comprar, lo mejor es hacer una _____ de lo que necesitas y un presupuesto aproximado.

b No compres alimentos con el estómago _____. Caerías fácilmente en la tentación de adquirir más de lo necesario.

c Si en un gran almacén ves un artículo que no tenías previsto comprar y parece interesarte, trata de no ceder a la primera _____ y déjalo para la próxima vez. Solo así sabrás si merece la pena comprarlo.

d Muchas veces compramos cosas que no nos sirven para nada, solo porque están en oferta. Piensa que una oportunidad solo es real si se trata de un artículo que realmente necesitas y cuyo _____ es inferior al que suele tener habitualmente.

e Antes de pasar por el cajero de la tienda, compara el dinero que has gastado con el que habías previsto. Si excede, devuelve a los _____ los artículos menos necesarios.

f No sientas ningún tipo de _____ por salir de un establecimiento sin haber realizado compra alguna.

g Algunos expertos recomiendan, para luchar contra la adicción al crédito, romper la tarjeta o envolverla con el tícket de la última compra en la que se gastase mucho. Otro remedio es visualizar el dinero saliendo de tu _____ y llegando a las manos del dependiente cuando pagues con la tarjeta.

h Si tienes problema con el control de _____, divide con tu pareja el dinero disponible. De este modo evitarás llegar a un conflicto familiar.

---

12 **Which words and phrases from Cómo mantener el consumo bajo control can be defined as follows:**

a Cantidad de dinero calculado para hacer frente a ciertos gastos.

b Comidas o bebidas necesarias para subsistir.

c Establecimiento comercial dividido en departamentos.

d A precio rebajado.

e Persona que recibe el dinero en una tienda.

f Persona encargada de atender a los clientes en una tienda.

g Marido o mujer, o la persona con la que tienes una relación sentimental.

Test yourself

1 Complete the sentences on the left with an appropriate phrase on the right.

a Si me invitaran
b Si supiera dónde está
c Si mereciera la pena
d Si tuviera que elegir
e Si no le queda bien
f Si tuviese tiempo

1 escogería este
2 puede cambiarlo
3 te lo diría
4 te acompañaría
5 lo haría reparar
6 claro que aceptaría

2 Match each sentence on the left with a suitable phrase on the right.

a La chaqueta te ha quedado grande.
b El lector de DVD no funciona.
c A mi hija no le ha gustado el regalo.
d No tengo efectivo.
e ¡Qué sorpresa y qué alegría que hayáis venido!
f El alquiler es demasiado alto para nosotros.

1 Tengo que pagar con tarjeta (de crédito).
2 Esto hay que celebrarlo con unas copas.
3 Tendrás que cambiarla por otra talla.
4 Habrá que mudarse.
5 Tenemos que llevarlo al taller (de reparaciones).
6 Tendremos que comprarle otra cosa.

Test 1 focuses on conditional sentences, while Test 2 assesses vocabulary and some key expressions. Check your answers in the Key to the exercises before you go on to the next unit, or go back to the New expressions or the Language discovery if you feel you need to revise some of the new language. Having reached so far in the course is a sign of good progress, but it is a good idea to go back to those bits that give you more trouble.

SELF CHECK

	I CAN . . .
○	. . . enquire about forms of payment.
○	. . . describe things.
○	. . . express open and remote conditions.
○	. . . express obligation and needs.
○	. . . express surprise.

10 Estar en forma

In this unit you will learn how to:
▸ *describe minor ailments.*
▸ *refer to an action in progress.*
▸ *express indirect suggestions and commands.*

CEFR: *Can give clear and detailed descriptions on a range of subjects, e.g. telling a doctor about health issues; can follow the essentials of lectures or academic presentations, e.g. a talk on nutrition (B2).*

Conversations

1 EN EL CONSULTORIO *IN THE SURGERY*

A causa de un pequeño accidente, Carlos, un jugador de tenis, consulta a un médico.

caerse	*to fall*
tobillo (m)	*ankle*
torcerse	*to sprain*
doler, duele	*to hurt, it hurts*
hinchado/a	*swollen*
esguince (m)	*sprain, twist*
doloroso/a	*painful*
venda (f)	*bandage*
sanar	*to recover*
hinchazón (f)	*swelling*

1 10.01 **As you listen, try to answer this question: How long does the doctor think it will take for Carlos to get better?**

Paciente	Buenas tardes. Tengo hora con la doctora Martínez.
Recepcionista	¿Su nombre, por favor?
Paciente	Carlos González.
Recepcionista	Bien ..., tendrá que esperar un momento. La doctora está atendiendo a un paciente.
(Después de algunos minutos.)	
	Pase, por favor.
Paciente	Buenas tardes.
Doctora	Buenas tardes, señor. Siéntese, por favor. Dígame qué le pasa.
Paciente	Ayer, mientras estaba jugando al tenis me caí y me torcí un tobillo, el de la pierna derecha. Me duele mucho y lo tengo hinchado.

Doctora	A ver . . ., ¿le duele aquí?
Paciente	Ay, sí, me duele mucho.
Doctora	Bueno, por suerte no es más que un esguince, pero suelen ser bastante dolorosos y tardará unos días en sanar. Le pondré una venda para proteger el tobillo. Y trate de no mover mucho el pie. Si de aquí a quince días no se le ha pasado el dolor y la hinchazón, vuelva a verme, pero no creo que sea necesario.
Paciente	Gracias, doctora.

2 What phrases are used in the dialogue to say the following?

a I have an appointment.

b I fell and twisted my ankle.

c Does it hurt here?

d The right leg.

e It hurts very much.

f It's swollen.

g Come and see me again.

h I don't think it'll be necessary.

> **LANGUAGE TIP**
> The word **hora** is used for appointments with a fixed time such as those with doctors, dentists and hairdressers: **Quería pedir/Tengo hora con el doctor Santana** *I'd like to ask for/I have an appointment with Doctor Santana*. For other kind of appointments, use the word **cita**: **Tengo una cita con el/la gerente** *I have an appointment with the manager.*

2 ¿QUÉ TE DIJO EL DOCTOR? *WHAT DID THE DOCTOR SAY?*

María Luisa, una amiga de Carlos, le pregunta sobre la visita al doctor.

sentirse	to feel
aún no se me pasa el dolor (m)	the pain is still there
roto/a (from romper)	broken (to break)
puso (from poner)	she put, applied
juntos/as	together

1 10.02 **What won't the two friends be able to do now that Carlos is incapacitated?**

María Luisa	Hola, ¿cómo te has sentido?
Carlos	Pues, no muy bien, aún no se me pasa el dolor. Ayer por la tarde fui al médico.
María Luisa	Ay sí, ¿y qué te dijo?
Carlos	Bueno . . ., que no está roto el tobillo, es solo un esguince. Me puso una venda y me dijo que tratara de no mover mucho el pie, y que volviera si de aquí a unos días no estoy bien. Ya ves, no podremos jugar al tenis juntos.
María Luisa	¡Hombre! Lo siento.

2 Match the words from the conversation (a–g) with their equivalents.

a	sentirse	**1**	intentar
b	sentir	**2**	dentro de
c	pasarse	**3**	encontrarse
d	romper	**4**	lamentar
e	tratar	**5**	acabarse
f	volver	**6**	quebrar
g	He aquí a	**7**	regresar

NEW EXPRESSIONS

Describing minor ailments

Me torcí un tobillo.	*I twisted my ankle.*
Me duele mucho.	*It hurts very much.*
Lo tengo hinchado.	*It is swollen.*
Me duele la cabeza.	*I have a headache.*
Me duele el oído.	*I have an earache.*
Me duele la espalda.	*I have a backache.*
Me duele la garganta.	*I have a sore throat.*
Me duele una muela.	*I have a toothache.*
Tengo fiebre.	*I'm running a temperature.*
Tengo indigestión.	*I have indigestion.*
Tengo estreñimiento/diarrea.	*I have constipation/diarrhoea.*
Tengo dolor de estómago.	*I have a stomach ache.*
Tengo tos.	*I have a cough.*
Estoy enfermo/a.	*I'm ill.*
Estoy malo/a.	*I'm unwell.*
¿Cómo se/te encuentra(s)/ siente(s)?	*How are you feeling?* (formal/informal)
Me siento/encuentro mal. / No me siento/encuentro bien.	*I'm feeling unwell. I'm not feeling well.*
Estoy constipado/a.	*I have a cold.*
He cogido un catarro/la gripe.	*I've caught a cold/the flu.*
Me he roto la pierna.	*I've broken my leg/arm.*
Se quebró el brazo.	*He/She broke his/her arm.*

Referring to an action in progress

Está atendiendo a un paciente.	*She is looking after a patient.*
Estaba jugando al tenis.	*I was playing tennis.*

Expressing indirect suggestions or commands

Me dijo que tratara de no mover mucho el pie y que volviera ...	*She told me to try not to move my foot too much and to come back ...*

 How would you say in Spanish: *My back hurts and my arms hurt*? What two ways of saying *I have a stomach ache* do you know?

Beware of 'false friends'. You probably know that estar embarazada means *to be pregnant* (not *embarrassed*). Can you find another falso amigo: a health-related expression that reflects the state of your nose (not your digestive system)?

Language discovery

 You have seen this language in action. Now can you work out the rules?

1 **How do the different verb forms impact the meaning of these sentences? Explain what each one means.**
   a La doctora ayudaba a sus pacientes.
   b La doctora estaba ayudando a sus pacientes.
   c Trabajo como enfermero en un consultorio.
   d Estoy trabajando como enfermero en un dispensario.

2 **Does the choice of verb tense make any difference in these two sentences from a live conversation?**
   a Pero Miguel, ¿qué dices?
   b Pero Miguel, ¿qué estás diciendo?

3 **What is the gerund corresponding to each of these infinitives?**
   a traer   b ir   c venir   d poder

4 **Using Me pidió que ..., how would you report in Spanish what someone asked you?**
   a Ve a farmacia.
   b Cómprame unas pastillas para la tos.

1 ESTAR WITH THE GERUND: FOR ACTIONS IN PROGRESS

Estar with gerund, as in **Está atendiendo a un paciente**, refers to an action in progress at the time of speaking. To refer to an action which was in progress when something else happened, as in **Mientras estaba jugando al tenis me caí** *While I was playing tennis I fell*, you need to use the imperfect tense of **estar** (see Unit 5) followed by a gerund.

The gerund is formed by adding **-ando** to the stem of **-ar** verbs, e.g. **jugar** *to play*, **jugando** *playing*, and **-iendo** to the stem of **-er** and **-ir** verbs, e.g. **correr** *to run*, **corriendo** *running*, **subir** *to go up*, **subiendo** *going up*.

A few verbs undergo a change in their spelling when forming the gerund: **dormir** – **durmiendo, morir** – **muriendo, poder** – **pudiendo, pedir** – **pidiendo, decir** – **diciendo, venir** – **viniendo, ir** – **yendo, leer** – **leyendo**.

Note that the second action will normally be expressed in the preterite tense: **Cuando me caí** *When I fell*. Here are some further examples:

Estoy esperando al médico.	*I'm waiting for the doctor.*
Estábamos trabajando cuando sucedió.	*We were working when it happened.*

The continuous form (e.g. **estoy trabajando**), present or past, can often be replaced by a non-continuous verb form (e.g. **trabajo**) without altering its meaning, for example:

¿Qué estás haciendo?	*What are you doing?*
¿Qué haces?	*What are you doing?*
Estaba jugando al tenis.	*I was playing tennis.*
Jugaba al tenis.	*I was playing tennis.*

The continuous forms, however, are more specific, with the emphasis more on the action in progress than on the action alone.

2 EXPRESSING INDIRECT SUGGESTIONS AND COMMANDS

Look at the way this suggestion has been reported.

Vuelva si de aquí a unos días no está bien.	*Come back if within a few days you are not well.*
Me dijo que volviera si de aquí a unos días no estoy bien.	*She told me to come back if within a few days I'm not well.*

If the verb in the first clause is in the past (e.g. **me dijo** . . . *she told me* . . .), the verb form of the direct suggestion or command (e.g. **vuelva** . . . *come back* . . .) changes into the imperfect subjunctive tense (e.g. . . . **que volviera** . . . *to come back*) in the indirect sentence.

Now consider this example:

Vuelva dentro de dos semanas.	*Come back within two weeks.*
Quiere que vuelva dentro de dos semanas.	*She wants me to come back within two weeks.*

If the verb in the main clause is in the present tense (e.g. **quiere** . . ., *he/she wants* . . .), the verb form in the second clause will be in the present subjunctive tense, which is the same as that for the polite imperative, therefore there is no change. Notice, however, that the verb changes if the direct command is a familiar imperative, e.g. **Vuelve dentro de dos semanas; Quiere que vuelva dentro de dos semanas.**

(For the forms of the present subjunctive, see Unit 1, and for the imperfect subjunctive, see Unit 9.)

 Practice

1 Use the verbs in brackets to say what you or others were doing.

Ejemplo: Pareces cansado. (trabajar) *Estaba trabajando.*

    a Pareces medio dormido. (dormir)

    b Te veo muy relajada. (hacer yoga)

    c Antonio se ve muy sereno. (meditar)

    d Elvira tenía la luz encendida. (leer)

    e ¿Qué hacíais en la cocina tú y Esteban? (preparar la cena)

    f ¿Qué hacías en tu habitación a esta hora, Pepe? (ver el fútbol en la tele)

2 Express indirect suggestions and commands.

Ejemplo: No mueva el pie. (Me dijo que . . .) *Me dijo que no moviera el pie.*

    a Vuelva Vd. mañana. (Me dijo que . . .)

    b Descanse Vd. un poco. (Me aconsejó que . . .)

    c No fumen mucho. (Nos recomendó que . . .)

    d Haz más ejercicio. (El doctor quiere que . . .)

    e Por favor, llegad a la hora. (Rosa nos pidió que . . .)

    f No trabajes tanto. (Mi mujer no quiere que . . .)

 3 Role play – While on holiday in Spain you have problems with your stomach and you go to the chemist to buy something. Play the part of the customer.

Farmacéutico	¿Dígame?
Cliente(a)	**(a)** *Say you would like something for a stomach ache.*
Farmacéutico	¿Tiene Vd. diarrea también?
Cliente(a)	**(b)** *Yes, you've also got diarrhoea. You had some fish the night before and later you began to feel unwell.*
Farmacéutico	Mire, le voy a dar estas pastillas que son muy buenas. Tome dos, tres veces al día hasta que se sienta mejor. Y tenga cuidado con la alimentación. No coma nada frito.
Cliente(a)	**(c)** *Thank you. How much is it?*
Farmacéutico	Son seis euros.

4 Your Spanish friend Rocio wants to know what the chemist told you. Refer to the preceding dialogue and tell her.

Notice the construction **hasta que se sienta mejor**, which carries a verb in the subjunctive.

Rocio   ¿Cómo te fue en la farmacia?

Tú   *Tell your friend that the chemist gave you some pills. Say that she told you to take them two to three times daily until you feel better. Also, she advised you to be careful with food and to not eat anything deep fried.*

5 **How would you say the following in Spanish? There are several ways of expressing some of these ideas. Check the Key to the exercises to see how.**

   a He broke his leg while playing football, so he won't be able to play for some time.

   b I'm not feeling well. I have a headache and I'm feverish.

   c She said she wouldn't be able to see me this afternoon. She has an appointment with the doctor at four o'clock.

   d The doctor told me to rest and to come back in a fortnight if I'm still not feeling well.

   e She phoned the office to say she's not coming to work because she's caught flu.

   f He fell and twisted his ankle. It is swollen and he says it hurts him very much.

6 **To be healthy and in good shape we must eat a balanced diet. Here is some information about the kind of food we ought to eat. Complete the sentences with appropriate words from the box. (New vocabulary will be found in the Spanish–English vocabulary.)**

> huevos   músculos   alimenticia   comer   mantenimiento
> leguminosas   proteínas   productos

El hecho de _____ en exceso no quiere decir que se estén consumiendos los _____ más ricos en nutrientes. Entre los _____ que contienen mayor calidad y cantidad _____ se encuentran las carnes, pescados, aves y _____. De igual manera las _____, nueces y alegrías, que son productos sumamente ricos en _____, necesarias para la producción, _____ y reparación de los tejidos, _____, órganos, sangre, piel, cabello, etcétera.

(Diario Excélsior, México D. F.)

7 10.03 **Role play – Have a go at asking and giving responses using language you are already familiar with. Focus on making your conversation fluent. Speak in the pauses and listen to make sure that you said things correctly.**

¡A escuchar!

8 10.04 **La dieta mediterránea. In a radio talk, a specialist on food and diet refers to Spanish people's eating habits and to the changes that are taking place. Look over the key vocabulary and the questions before you listen.**

tierra adentro	*inland*
alimentación (f)	*diet*
grasa (f)	*fat*
fibra (f)	*fibre*
meseta central (f)	*central plateau*
riesgo sanitario (m)	*health risk*
equilibrada/o	*balanced*
saludable	*healthy*
aconsejable	*advisable*
alimentario	*diet* (adjective)

  a Which are the Spanish regions where the Mediterranean diet is most popular?

  b Why is the health risk higher in the central plateau, and in the north and north-west?

  c How does the Madrid diet compare with that of other Spanish regions?

  d What sort of breakfast do people in Madrid tend to have?

  e Why are more and more people eating outside their homes?

  f What sort of diet do people in Catalonia tend to have?

9 10.05 **Dictado. Now for some note taking in Spanish. You are a journalist attending the same talk from the same nutrition expert. Listen again to a short extract as many times as necessary and transcribe what you hear so you can quote it later.**

10 10.06 **Keep practising your note-taking skills with a second extract from the lecture. (Check the Key to the exercises to make sure your text is accurate, especially as regards written accent marks.)**

11 Four readers of a health magazine wrote to the editor seeking help with their problems. What are their problems? Read the letters and find out.

verse imposibilitado/a	*to be unable*
ponerse colorado/a	*to turn red*
ardor (m)	*burning*
verse afectado/a por	*to suffer from*
pecho (m)	*chest*
desmayarse	*to faint*

El sol y la piel blanca

Mi piel es sumamente blanca y cada vez que llega el verano, me veo imposibilitada de tomar el sol con normalidad porque me pongo colorada y se me produce un ardor muy intenso. Además de eso, nunca consigo broncearme. ¿Qué puedo hacer? Rosa Saavedra

Problemas estomacales

Tengo 18 años y soy un gran aficionado al turismo de aventura. Mi problema es que casi siempre me veo afectado por problemas estomacales que más de una vez han arruinado mis vacaciones. Esto suele ocurrir especialmente cuando viajo a zonas donde las condiciones higiénicas son precarias, y donde no siempre es posible encontrar asistencia médica. ¿Qué podría hacer para prevenir estos problemas? Ignacio Carrera

Problemas cardíacos

Desde hace unos meses siento palpitaciones muy fuertes en el pecho que, por lo general, se producen de día y sin una razón aparente. Estoy muy preocupada porque nunca me había pasado y además solo tengo 32 años. ¿Qué me aconseja? Claudia Parra

Desmayo por exceso de trabajo

Desde hace un año tengo un trabajo que me exige mucho esfuerzo físico y psicológico. Llego a casa muy cansado y por la mañana me cuesta mucho levantarme. Hace unos días estaba trabajando en el jardín y me desmayé. Fui al médico y me dijo que no me preocupara, que simplemente tenía que aprender a relajarme. ¿Qué me sugieren ustedes? Alejandro García

(Adapted from Revista Buena Salud)

12 Which of the following suggestions would be appropriate for each person?

a Haz ejercicios de respiración para evitar el estrés.

b Puedes tener algún problema de corazón. Será mejor que pidas consejo a un especialista.

c Utiliza un buen bronceador que te proteja.

d No consumas alimentos crudos.

e Evita la exposición a los rayos ultravioletas, especialmente al mediodía.

f Hierve siempre el agua que vas a beber.

g Tómate unos días de vacaciones e intenta descansar los fines de semana.

h No te alarmes, pero si el problema continúa, pide hora con un cardiólogo.

Test yourself

1 Rephrase the following sentences using other constructions or verbs with the same meaning.

a Tengo dolor de cabeza.

b El niño tiene dolor de estómago.

c No me siento bien.

d ¿Qué decías?

e Ángel dormía plácidamente.

2 Answer the following questions using indirect speech. The direct suggestions or commands are given in brackets.

a ¿Qué le dijo (a Vd.) el especialista? (Deje de fumar.)

b ¿Qué te aconsejó tu novio? (No se lo digas a nadie.)

c ¿Qué os sugirieron? (Aprended español.)

d ¿Qué te pidió tu madre? (No sigas con la dieta.)

e ¿Qué le recomendó (a Vd.) la doctora? (Haga algún deporte.)

Test 1 assesses your ability to express certain key ideas in a different way, while Test 2 focuses on your ability to make the changes that are necessary when changing from direct into indirect speech. Check the Test yourself in the Key to the exercises to see how well you performed. If you are still uncertain about the construction in Test 2, go back to section 2 of the Grammar section before you go on to the next unit.

SELF CHECK	
I CAN . . .	
○	. . . describe minor ailments.
○	. . . refer to an action in progress.
○	. . . express indirect suggestions and commands.

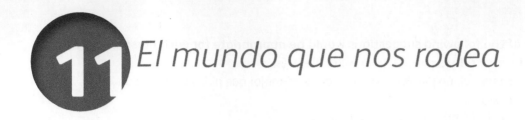

11 El mundo que nos rodea

In this unit you will learn how to:

▶ *ask and give opinions.*

▶ *agree and disagree.*

▶ *express relationships of cause and effect.*

▶ *offer solutions.*

▶ *express unfulfilled conditions.*

CEFR: *Can elaborate a point of view and round off with an appropriate conclusion, e.g. join a debate about smoking; can read in detail about complex and abstract topics, if given the chance to read several times, e.g. an article about environmental issues (C1).*

Conversations

1 ¿A QUÉ SE DEBE? *WHAT IS IT DUE TO?*

En una entrevista con una periodista española, el director gerente de una cadena de hoteles menciona el deterioro del medio ambiente como una de las causas de la disminución del turismo en España.

medio ambiente (m)	environment
cadena (f)	chain
se viene dando un descenso	there has been a decrease
obedecer a . . .	to be due to . . .
atravesar	to go through
esparcimiento (m)	entertainment
con los brazos cruzados (m pl)	twiddling one's thumbs (Lit. with one's arms crossed)
tomar medidas (f pl)	to adopt measures
a mi juicio . . .	in my opinion . . .

1 11.01 **Listen for the following things: four reasons why tourism numbers have been down in Spain, three possible remedial actions the country could take. Try to jot down some notes in Spanish or in English.**

Periodista	Señor Riveros, desde hace un par de años se viene dando en España un cierto descenso del número de turistas que nos visitan. ¿A qué se debe, cree Vd., esta disminución?
Sr. Riveros	Pues, creo que este descenso obedece a varios factores. Por un lado está el deseo natural de la gente de conocer otros lugares. Países como Grecia, México y algunas naciones de Asia, para nombrar solo algunos, están gastando

una buena cantidad de recursos en promover sus atracciones turísticas, con resultados bastante positivos. Por otro lado, la mayor conciencia ecológica de la población europea está haciendo que esta mire hacia lugares más naturales, con menos contaminación, y sin las grandes aglomeraciones y el deterioro que se observa en nuestras costas.

Otra causa, no menos importante, es la económica. La crisis por la que han atravesado algunos países ha hecho que la gente limite más sus gastos de esparcimiento y vaya en busca de lugares que les resulten más favorables económicamente. España es hoy un país caro y al turista que proviene de otros continentes no le favorece pasar sus vacaciones en nuestro país.

Periodista Parece que se trata de una situación irreversible, ¿no cree Vd.?

Sr. Riveros No, en eso no estoy de acuerdo. Pienso que se trata de una situación pasajera. Podría durar todavía uno o dos años más, pero creo que al final se estabilizará. Pero, no nos podemos quedar de brazos cruzados. Habría que tomar medidas para mejorar algunos de los aspectos que he mencionado. Tendríamos que descontaminar nuestras playas y nuestro mar, habría que ajustar los precios de manera que España resulte más atractiva económicamente y, naturalmente, sería necesario mejorar la calidad de nuestros servicios. Si no hacemos nada, la situación difícilmente mejorará.

Periodista Da la impresión de que las autoridades no han tomado muy en serio el problema. ¿No cree Vd.?

Sr. Riveros Sí, en eso estoy absolutamente de acuerdo con Vd. A mi juicio, lo que está sucediendo en el sector turismo es también responsabilidad de las autoridades de gobierno, no solo de los que trabajamos directamente en él.

 2 11.02 **How well did you follow the main points? Return to the audio and listen to make sure you captured the key ideas.**

3 ¿Verdadero o falso?

    a En España ha disminuido el número de visitantes.

    b La gente prefiere pasar sus vacaciones en casa.

    c Otros países están promoviendo fuertemente el turismo.

    d La gente tiene más dinero para viajar.

    e España resulta económica para los visitantes extranjeros.

    f Las costas españolas están contaminadas y deterioradas.

> **CULTURE TIP**
>
> With more than 60 million tourist visits per year, Spain is the third most visited country in the world, behind only France and the USA. The most popular places are Catalonia, the Canary Islands and Andalusia. Most visitors come from other European Union countries, with the United Kingdom in first place, followed by France, Germany and the Nordic countries. As of 2013, the number of foreign visitors to Spain was once again on the rise.

4 Read or listen again. How is the following expressed in the interview?

   a dos años

   b ¿Cuál es la razón/causa?

   c por una parte

   d Están invirtiendo mucho dinero.

   e por otra parte

   f una situación que no es permanente

2 ¿CUÁL ES SU OPINIÓN? *WHAT'S YOUR OPINION?*

Uno de los problemas que preocupa a los españoles, como a otros europeos, es el excesivo aumento del tráfico en las grandes ciudades. Esta es la opinión de una madrileña sobre este tema.

¡qué quiere que le diga!	*what can I say!*
cada vez más	*more and more*
desde luego	*certainly*
si se hubiera hecho	*if it had been done*
preocupar	*to worry*

1 11.03 **Which of these three traffic-calming measures is mentioned in the opinion survey?**

   a Limit access to the city centre for private vehicles.

   b A congestion charge for motorists.

   c Allow private vehicles to circulate only on alternate days.

Entrevistador	Señora, buenos días. Estamos haciendo un estudio sobre los problemas del tráfico en las grandes ciudades españolas. ¿Cuál es su opinión al respecto?
Señora	¿Cómo dice? Con el ruido del tráfico no le oigo nada.
Entrevistador	He dicho que estamos realizando un estudio sobre los problemas del tráfico en las grandes ciudades y me gustaría conocer su opinión.
Señora	Pues, ¡qué quiere que le diga! Que el tráfico en Madrid es insoportable. Aquí ya no se puede vivir. Hay cada vez más coches y más ruido.
Entrevistador	¿Estaría de acuerdo Vd. en que se limitara de alguna manera el acceso de vehículos privados al centro de la ciudad?
Señora	Desde luego. Creo que se debería favorecer más al transporte público. Si se hubiera hecho antes, hoy no tendríamos este problema. Madrid sería una ciudad más limpia y con menos ruido.

2 11.04 **Now listen to a streamlined version of the conversation and answer the following questions in Spanish.**

   a ¿Qué opina la señora sobre el tráfico en Madrid?

   b Según ella, ¿cuál sería la solución para resolver el problema del tráfico?

   c ¿Cómo favorecería a Madrid esta solución?

NEW EXPRESSIONS

Complete the missing English translations, then hide either column and test your memory.

Asking and giving opinions

¿Cuál es su opinión?	*What is your opinion?*
Me gustaría conocer su opinión.	*I'd like _____ your opinion.*
¿No cree Vd.?	*Don't you think so?*
Creo que ...	*I think (that) ...*
Pienso que se trata de ...	*_____ it is about ...*
A mi juicio ...	*In my opinion ...*
¿Qué opina Vd.?	*What do you think?*
¿Qué le parece esto?	*What do you think of this?*
Opino que ...	*I believe that ...*
Me parece que ...	*It seems to me that ...*
Considero que ...	*I consider that ...*
A mi parecer ...	*It appears to me ...*
Que yo sepa ...	*As far as I know ...*
Según mi punto de vista ...	*In my view ...*

Agreeing and disagreeing

¿Estaría Vd. de acuerdo?	*Would you _____?*
Estoy de acuerdo.	*I agree.*
No estoy de acuerdo.	*_____*
¡De acuerdo!	*Right, OK, all right!*
¿Vale? (familiar)	*Is that all right?, OK?*
¡Vale! (familiar)	*All right, OK!*

Expressing relationships of cause and effect

¿A qué se debe ...?	*What is it due to?*
Se debe a ...	*It is due to ...*
Obedece a ...	*It is due to ...*
¿Cuál es la causa/la razón/ el motivo (de) ...?	*What is the reason for ...?*
La causa/razón/el motivo es ...	*The reason is ...*

Offering solutions

Habría que (+ infinitive) ...	*One would have to ...*
Tendríamos que (+ infinitive) ...	*We _____ ...*
Sería necesario (+ infinitive) ...	*It would be necessary to ...*
La solución sería (+ infinitive)	*The solution would be to ...*
Podríamos (+ infinitive) ...	*We could ...*
Se podría (+ infinitive) ...	*One could ...*

Expressing unfulfilled conditions

Si se hubiera hecho antes, hoy no tendríamos este problema.	*If it had been done before, today we wouldn't have this problem.*
Si le hubiéramos/hubiésemos invitado, seguramente habría aceptado.	*If we had invited him, he would surely have accepted.*
Si hubieras/hubieses tenido dinero, ¿lo habrías comprado?	*If you'd had money, would you have bought it?*

Using what you know and some intuition, how would you translate the following? Que yo sepa, muchos problemas del medio ambiente no tienen solución. Habría que reconsiderar por completo nuestro estilo de vida. En mi opinión, los costes serían demasiado altos.

Language discovery

You have seen this language in action. Now can you work out the rules?

1 Complete the verb form in the si (*if*) clauses.

   a Si (yo) _____ (olvidar) nuestro aniversario, nunca me lo habrías perdonado.

   b Si me lo _____ (pedir), te habría solucionado el problema.

   c Si tu amiga _____ (insistir) un rato más, habría terminado en otra pelea.

2 How do you say the following in Spanish?

   a If they'd telephoned me . . .

   b If you had liked his sisters . . .

   c If you had come back earlier . . . (vosotros)

3 What is the meaning of these phrases?

   a ¡Ojala que me lo hubieras/hubieses dicho!

   b Habría sido mejor que me mintieras.

1 EXPRESSING UNFULFILLED CONDITIONS

The sentence **Si se hubiera hecho antes, hoy no tendríamos este problema** *If it had been done before, today we wouldn't have this problem* expresses an unfulfilled condition (it was not done before). The verb in the *if*-clause is in the pluperfect subjunctive (**hubiera hecho**) while the verb in the second clause is in the conditional (**tendríamos**). More often, however, in unfulfilled conditions, the pluperfect subjunctive in the *if*-clause is followed by a clause with a verb in the conditional perfect:

Si yo hubiera/hubiese sabido, no habría venido.	*If I had known, I wouldn't have come.*
Si nos lo hubieras/hubieses dicho, te habríamos ayudado.	*If you had told us, we would have helped you.*
Le habríais visto, si hubierais/hubieseis llegado a la hora.	*You would have seen him, if you had arrived on time.*

2 THE PLUPERFECT SUBJUNCTIVE

The pluperfect subjunctive is formed with the imperfect subjunctive of **haber** (for the formation of the imperfect subjunctive, see Unit 9) followed by a past participle (for past participles, see Unit 8). Remember that the imperfect subjunctive has two alternative endings, **-ra** or **-se**.

Si (yo) hubiera/hubiese llamado . . .	*If I had called . . .*
Si (tú) hubieras/hubieses sabido . . .	*If you had known . . .*
Si (él/ella/Vd.) hubiera/hubiese estado allí . . .	*If (he/she/you) had been there . . .*
Si (nosotros) hubiéramos/hubiésemos viajado . . .	*If we had travelled . . .*
Si (vosotros) hubierais/hubieseis bebido . . .	*If you had drunk . . .*
Si (ellos/ellas/Vds.) hubierais/hubieseis hablado español . . .	*If they/you had spoken Spanish . . .*

Consider now the use of the imperfect subjunctive in non-conditional sentences such as the following ones:

Ojalá hubiesen llegado.	*I wish they had arrived.*
¡Cómo desearía que me hubiese llamado!	*How I wish he/she had called me.*
Habría sido mejor que les hubieras dicho la verdad.	*It would have been better if you had told them the truth.*

In all three examples the action expressed by the pluperfect subjunctive is one that did not take place.

3 THE CONDITIONAL PERFECT

The conditional perfect is formed with the conditional of **haber** followed by a past participle (see Unit 8).

. . . (yo) habría aceptado.	*. . . I would have accepted.*
. . . (tú) habrías regresado.	*. . . you would have come back.*
. . . (él/ella/Vd.) habría comido.	*. . . he/she/you would have eaten.*
. . . (nosotros) habríamos salido.	*. . . we would have gone out.*
. . . (vosotros) habríais ganado.	*. . . you would have won.*
. . . (ellos/ellas/Vds.) habrían perdido.	*. . . they/you would have lost.*

In a sentence like **Si la casa no hubiera/hubiese sido tan cara, la habríamos comprado** *If the house hadn't been so expensive, we would have bought it*, the conditional perfect in the second clause may be replaced by the **-ra** form of the pluperfect subjunctive: **. . . la hubiéramos comprado**, with exactly the same meaning.

 Practice

 1 **Express unfulfilled conditions. To get the right form of the past participle, look up the verbs in your dictionary and check whether they belong to the 1st (-ar), 2nd (-er) or 3rd (-ir) conjugation.**

Ejemplo: Subieron los precios. Disminuyó el turismo. *Si no hubieran subido los precios, no habría disminuido el turismo.*

   a Perdí mi trabajo. No fui a España.

   b No teníamos dinero. No pudimos viajar.

   c Aumentaron los precios. Descendió el turismo.

   d No encontraron plaza en el avión. Tuvieron que esperar otro vuelo.

   e Carlos tuvo un accidente. Cancelamos el viaje.

   f No nos invitaron a la fiesta. No fuimos.

 2 **Rephrase the following sentences using a construction with the words in brackets.**

   a ¿Qué le parece a Vd. el tráfico en Madrid? (opinar)

   b Creo que es demasiado caótico. (parecer)

   c ¿Qué le parece la prohibición de fumar en lugares públicos? (opinión)

   d Pienso que es una muy buena idea. (creer)

   e La menor llegada de turistas obedece a la crisis económica. (deberse)

   f También tendrían que descontaminar las playas. (haber)

   g ¿Cuál es la causa de tanta contaminación acústica? (deberse)

   h En mi opinión este es un problema cultural. (mi parecer) ¿No te parece? (creer)

 3 **More and more people are concerned about issues to do with the environment and their health these days. Take, for example, smoking or the destruction of the ozone layer, to mention just two. Imagine you are being interviewed on the subject of smoking. Write the answers to these questions.**

permitir	to allow
un hecho muy conocido (m)	a well-known fact
muerte (f)	death
tabaquismo (m)	cigarette smoking
prohibir	to ban
evitar	to avoid
empezar a	to take up

Pregunta	¿Qué le parece el hecho de que en España se haya prohibido fumar en lugares públicos? ¿Está usted de acuerdo con esa medida?
Tú	**(a)** *Yes, you agree with that completely. You think people should not be allowed to smoke in public places. People who disagree with this think only of themselves. It is a well-known fact that many deaths are due to cigarette smoking.*
Pregunta	¿Está usted también de acuerdo con la prohibición de la publicidad del tabaco?
Tú	**(b)** *Certainly. Cigarette advertising should have been banned long ago. If it had been done earlier, many deaths would have been avoided. It would also be necessary to educate people, especially the young, so that they don't take up smoking.*

4 As you read this article about the hole in the ozone layer, answer this question: Is it true or false that scientists believe human activity is directly responsible for the depletion of the ozone layer?

calentamiento (m)	*warming*
patrón (m)	*pattern*
cosecha (f)	*crop, harvest*
agujero (m)	*hole*
hueco (m)	*hole*
agrandarse	*to enlarge*
paulatinamente	*little by little, gradually*

EL AGUJERO DE OZONO, MÁS GRANDE

La falta de ozono es también una de las causas del llamado 'efecto invernadero', que está provocando el calentamiento de la Tierra.

'No creo que los seres humanos puedan sobrevivir sin una capa de ozono, y sin ella la cantidad de radiaciones ultravioleta que llegaría del espacio a la Tierra destruiría la mayor parte de las formas de vida tal como las conocemos', explicó el director de la división de ciencias aplicadas para la Tierra de la NASA, Shelby Tilford.

El ozono también influye sobre la temperatura de las capas superiores de la atmósfera. Sin el ozono, los patrones de lluvia cambiarían drásticamente junto a otros aspectos esenciales del clima terrestre, lo que afectaría a las cosechas agrícolas y a la vida acuática.

Los científicos informaron por primera vez acerca de la formación del agujero en la capa de ozono sobre la Antártida en 1985. El hueco ha ido agrandándose paulatinamente. Los científicos opinan que el agujero en el ozono sobre la Antártida, que aparece por esta época del año, es una clara evidencia de que la contaminación causada por el hombre está dañando la atmósfera. Si esta tendencia continúa, se puede prever una alta incidencia de los casos de cáncer en la piel, daños en las cosechas y en las aguas.

5 **What expressions are used in the text to say the following?**
   a the greenhouse effect
   b the Earth's warming
   c ultraviolet radiation
   d the higher layers of the atmosphere
   e rain patterns would change drastically
   f the hole in the ozone layer

6 **What do the following mean?**
   a No creo que los seres humanos puedan sobrevivir.
   b Destruiría la mayor parte de las formas de vida.
   c ... lo que afectaría a las cosechas agrícolas y a la vida acuática.
   d El hueco ha ido agrandándose paulatinamente.
   e El agujero en el ozono sobre la Antártida está dañando la atmósfera.

> **TIP**
> There is more than one correct way to translate the sentences in Exercise 6 and your own translations
> may well differ from the ones given. Once you have checked the answers in the Key go through the text
> again a few times and make a note of or look up other expressions or vocabulary that you think relevant.

¡A escuchar!

Antonio García, leader of an action group which is fighting to reduce noise pollution in Madrid, is interviewed by a journalist.

7 11.05 **First, look at the vocabulary, then practise the key expressions a few times.**

conseguir	to get, achieve
vecinos (m pl)	neighbours, residents
terraza (f)	area outside a bar or café
desconsideración (f)	lack of consideration
insoportable	unbearable
bastar	to be enough
hacer cumplir	to uphold, enforce
mientras tanto	in the meantime

8 11.06 **Now listen to the conversation. Make notes in English or Spanish of the main points until you feel confident with the new material. Then answer the following questions:**
   a What is the main purpose of the organization?
   b What examples of noise pollution does Antonio give?
   c What comparison does he make between Madrid and other European capitals?
   d How does he propose to achieve his objectives?

9 **Can you complete the following phrases with the missing verbs? If necessary, listen to the interview again.**
   a hacer que la gente _____ conciencia
   b que las autoridades _____ normas legales

c que nos _____ una mejor calidad de vida

d no nos _____ dormir por la noche

e la vida _____ insoportable

f seguiremos _____ hasta _____ oír.

10 The following passage looks at air pollution in Mexico City and other places. Look at the key words and phrases and consider the questions which come before the text, then read it through and answer them.

a su vez	*in turn*
superan con creces	*they far exceed*
fallecido/a	*dead*
padecer una afección (f)	*to suffer from an illness*
adoptar medidas (f pl)	*to adopt measures*
rechazo (m)	*rejection*
mejora (f)	*improvement*
placa de matrícula (f)	*number/licence plate*

a ¿Cuáles son las tres causas principales de la contaminación en la Ciudad de México?

b ¿Cuál es el nivel máximo de partículas contaminantes recomendado por la OMS (Organización Mundial de la Salud)? ¿En qué situación se encuentra la capital mexicana?

c ¿Cuántas personas mueren anualmente a causa de la contaminación atmosférica?

d El texto menciona tres razones que impiden que se tomen medidas más estrictas para combatir la contaminación. ¿Cuáles son?

e El texto menciona tres medidas que podrían adoptar las autoridades de gobierno para combatir la contaminación atmosférica. ¿Cuáles son?

Contaminación: 4 millones de autos en México DF

La Ciudad de México, con aproximadamente 20 millones de habitantes, es la más grande de las capitales de Hispanoamérica y una de las más grandes del mundo. Pero, es a su vez una de las que presenta el mayor grado de contaminación atmosférica en todo el planeta. Otras ciudades hispanoamericanas, entre ellas Santiago de Chile, Lima y Bogotá, sufren también un problema similar.

Las causas se encuentran en la gran concentración humana y en la excesiva centralización, que lleva a que la mayor parte de las industrias se establezcan en la capital, y también al aumento constante en el número de automóviles, todo lo cual hace que los esfuerzos que se realizan por mitigar esta situación sean prácticamente estériles. La capital mexicana tiene una de las mayores concentraciones de vehículos del mundo y las emisiones de partículas contaminantes superan con creces las recomendaciones de la Organización Mundial de la Salud (OMS), cuyo índice máximo de tolerancia es de 90 miligramos por metro cuadrado.

En el Distrito Federal mexicano, el IMECA (índice metropolitano de calidad del aire) supera a veces los 300 milígramos. Las cifras para Santiago de Chile, cuya población es de seis millones de habitantes, tres veces menos que la de la capital mexicana, son muy similares, y las causas que motivan la contaminación no son muy diferentes a las de otras ciudades con similar problema. Europa y Norteamérica tampoco escapan a esta grave situación. En España, Barcelona presenta unos de los mayores índices de contaminación. En los Estados Unidos, Los Ángeles es una de las más afectadas. Según estadísticas de la OMS, el número de personas fallecidas por causa de la contaminación atmosférica llega a los dos millones de personas cada año, mientras millones de otras padecen de afecciones respiratorias y cardíacas y otras enfermedades asociadas a la toxicidad del aire.

Las medidas adoptadas por las autoridades políticas y sanitarias no han sido lo suficientemente eficaces para mejorar la calidad del aire. Las restricciones impuestas a los agentes causantes de los gases tóxicos, principalmente a las industrias, son débiles y solo se hacen evidentes durante episodios de alerta ambiental. Intereses económicos, presiones políticas, y el propio rechazo de muchos de los afectados, dificultan la aplicación de medidas más drásticas y permanentes en el tiempo. Las mejoras en el transporte público, la restricción vehícular y el cierre definitivo o temporal de las industrias más contaminantes, son algunas de las medidas que contempla la acción gubernamental.

En la Ciudad de México y Santiago de Chile, por ejemplo, se limita la utilización de vehículos particulares un día a la semana. En la capital chilena, el control de la llamada restricción vehicular se realiza a través del último dígito de la placa de matrícula del coche, cuatro dígitos en períodos de menos contaminación, más dígitos en días de alerta ambiental. En la Ciudad de México la restricción, conocida con el nombre de "Hoy no circula", también se realiza a través del último dígito de la placa de matrícula, afectando regularmente a dos terminaciones y en días de mayor contaminación a cuatro. Los conductores se informan sobre el programa de restricción y cómo les afectará a través de los medios de comunicación y de Internet.

> **LEARNING TIP**
> The language in this text, which you might find in any newspaper, has not been simplified. The idea is that you should develop your reading skills through authentic material. Don't be satisfied with only answering the questions correctly. Go back to the text a few times, consider some of the constructions used and list some of the new words, both general and specific to the topic.

? Test yourself

1 Link the following sentences using the Spanish equivalent of the construction *If (I) had (not) . . ., (I) would have (not) . . .*

  a (Yo) no tenía dinero. No salí de vacaciones.
  b No llegaron a la hora al aeropuerto. Perdieron el vuelo.
  c Bebió en exceso. Tuvo un accidente.
  d No tenían visado. No pudieron viajar.
  e Se acostó tarde. No despertó a tiempo.

2 How would you express the following in Spanish? Use the formal form.

  a What's your opinion? (Give three alternatives.)
  b In my opinion . . . (Give three alternatives.)
  c Don't you think that . . .?
  d Do you agree with me?
  e I agree with you. This is due to . . .

As explained in the Language discovery section, the constructions in Test 1 have alternative verb forms. Generally, in everyday speech, people tend to be consistent with the form they use. Do likewise and try to learn one of them, for example Si hubiera . . ., habría . . . *If I had . . ., I would have . . .*, but it is important that you are aware of and can understand the others. Check your answers for both tests and, if you are satisfied with your performance, go on to the next unit.

SELF CHECK

	I CAN . . .
○	. . . ask and give opinions.
○	. . . agree and disagree.
○	. . . express relationships of cause and effect.
○	. . . offer solutions.
○	. . . express unfulfilled conditions.

12 Ellos y ellas

In this unit you will learn how to:
▸ *express comparisons.*
▸ *express probability.*
▸ *express contrast or opposition.*

CEFR: *Can sustain a monologue with detailed descriptions, e.g. express an opinion about gender issues; can summarize long demanding texts; can give a clear presentation, expanding and supporting viewpoints, e.g. making comparisons (C1).*

Conversations

1 TAN MODERNOS COMO LOS DEMÁS *AS MODERN AS THE REST*

Una periodista entrevista a un hombre español sobre el tema del machismo.

estar superado (superar)	*to be over (to overcome)*
hogar (m)	*home*
machismo (m)	*social attitudes which discriminate against women in favour of men*
labores domésticas (f pl)	*housework*

1 12.01 **Listen to the interview and the language commentary a couple of times. Then answers these questions:**
   a Does Pepe think that machismo is a purely Spanish phenomenon?
   b Does Pepe belong to the older or the younger generation of Spanish men? How can you tell?

Periodista	Pepe, a menudo se oye decir que el hombre español es más machista que los europeos del norte. ¿Estás de acuerdo con esta apreciación?
Pepe	Bueno, del tema del machismo se ha hablado mucho y se han escrito muchas cosas, pero fundamentalmente, creo yo, este es un concepto que en las generaciones jóvenes tiene cada vez menos importancia. Con esto no quiero decir que el problema esté superado. Aún quedan muchas situaciones de desigualdad hombre-mujer que sería necesario resolver. Pero eso también es cierto en otras sociedades europeas.
Periodista	¿Qué pasa dentro del hogar, por ejemplo? ¿Comparte el hombre español las labores domésticas?
Pepe	Hoy en día, creo que sí, aunque no mayoritariamente. Depende mucho de la edad de las personas y del medio social. Pero entre la gente joven, no cabe duda de que ha habido un cambio de actitud. El hombre ayuda a fregar los cacharros, a hacer la compra, a cuidar de los hijos. Es lo que yo he podido observar. En eso creo que somos tan modernos como los demás.

2 The three domestic activities mentioned in the text are: fregar los cacharros; hacer la compra; cuidar de los hijos. Can you guess their meanings?

3 Can you think of other domestic chores people normally do? Complete the expressions with a suitable word from the box.

| la limpieza | al bebé | la aspiradora | el suelo | los cristales | la ropa |

a lavar _____
b pasar _____
c limpiar _____
d hacer _____
e barrer _____
f bañar _____

2 LA MUJER EN LA SOCIEDAD ESPAÑOLA *WOMEN IN SPANISH SOCIETY*

Un periodista entrevista a una dirigente feminista española.

papel (m)	*role*
bachillerato (m)	*secondary school*
desequilibrio (m)	*imbalance*
desempeñarse	*to perform*
de hecho	*in fact*

1 12.02 As you listen to the first part of the interview, focus on identifying the two areas where Spanish women have made the most progress. What are they?

| **Periodista** | En su opinión, ¿cuáles han sido los cambios más importantes en lo que respecta a la situación de la mujer en la sociedad española? |
| **Dirigente** | A nivel general, yo diría que el cambio fundamental ha sido el abandono, por parte de la mujer, del papel netamente pasivo que la sociedad le había asignado, y su incorporación activa a la vida económica y social del país. A nivel más específico, creo que la principal transformación se ha dado dentro |

del área de la educación. La mujer española se ha incorporado masivamente al sistema educativo. Más de la mitad de los estudiantes de bachillerato son de sexo femenino, y en educación superior, el porcentaje de participación femenina llega casi al 50 por ciento. Sin embargo, todavía persisten diferencias en lo que respecta a la elección del tipo de estudios a seguir. La mujer aún se inclina por las profesiones consideradas tradicionalmente femeninas, mientras que en las carreras de carácter técnico se nota un claro predominio del hombre

Periodista	¿Qué posibilidades hay de que este desequilibrio cambie en el futuro?
Dirigente	Bueno, de hecho ya está cambiando, pero es necesario que se dé una orientación profesional más adecuada y que las universidades y otras instituciones de educación superior entreguen más información sobre las carreras técnicas que actualmente ofrecen. De esta manera, es probable que se llegue a un mayor equilibrio, puesto que la mujer es tan capaz como el hombre de desempeñarse en cualquier área de la ciencia o la tecnología. En el campo de la informática, por ejemplo, se viene apreciando un notable aumento del elemento femenino.

2 12.03 **As you listen to the second part of the interview, try to understand what effect women joining the workforce has had on family life?**

consiguiente	*resulting*
paro (m)	*unemployment*
en el ámbito familiar (m)	*within the family*
tasa de natalidad (f)	*birth rate*
número medio (m)	*average number*
abrirse camino (m)	*to force one's way*

Periodista	¿Comó ve Vd. la situación de la mujer en el campo laboral?
Dirigente	A mí me parece que aquí aún existen fuertes desajustes que es necesario rectificar. Por un lado, ha habido un crecimiento de la población activa femenina, frente a una reducción de la masculina. No obstante, el paro ha afectado más a la mujer que al hombre, con las consiguientes frustraciones para aquellas mujeres que desean trabajar, muchas de ellas jóvenes, pues no hay que olvidar que la población activa femenina es más joven que la masculina.
Periodista	¿Qué repercusiones ha tenido en el ámbito familiar este nuevo papel que ha asumido la mujer?
Dirigente	Bueno, el cambio más importante ha sido, sin duda, el descenso de la tasa de natalidad. El número medio de hijos por mujer ha bajado ostensiblemente y probablemente seguirá descendiendo.
Periodista	Se dice que uno de los campos donde la mujer española ha tenido más dificultades para integrarse ha sido el de la política. ¿A qué se debe, cree Vd., esta situación?

Dirigente A mi juicio, los partidos políticos, especialmente los más tradicionales, no se han preocupado lo suficiente de los problemas que afectan a la población femenina. Además, las dificultades con que la mujer se enfrenta para iniciar una carrera política son tales, que muchas desisten de hacerlo. Pero aquí también ha habido cambios trascendentales, y en los últimos años, frente a las presiones del elemento femenino dentro de los partidos, hemos visto cómo la mujer se ha venido abriendo camino y ocupando cargos de gran responsabilidad política. Probablemente, esta situación seguirá mejorando.

LANGUAGE TIP

Notice the use of the gerund after **venir** *to come* to refer to an action which increases gradually with time:

Se viene apreciando un notable aumento del elemento femenino.	*A considerable increase in the number of women is being observed.*
La mujer se ha venido abriendo camino y ocupando cargos de gran responsabilidad política.	*Women are steadily forcing their way and occupying positions of great political responsibility.*

---

3 Answer the following questions in English.

a What percentage of secondary school students are women?

b Which studies do women tend to choose?

c What has happened in computing with regard to the recruitment of new students?

d What contradiction does the feminist leader see when it comes to comparing the female and male working populations?

e How does the female working population compare with the male one in terms of age?

f What effect has the increase in the female workforce had on the family?

4 Scan both parts of the interview and find sentences with the same meaning as:

a Yo creo que todavía hay grandes desequilibrios que hay que cambiar.

b La población activa femenina ha crecido y la masculina se ha reducido.

c Sin embargo, la tasa de desempleo es más alta entre mujeres que entre hombres.

d El número medio de hijos posiblemente continuará bajando.

e No ha habido suficiente preocupación por los problemas que se relacionan con la mujer.

 5 12.04 **Listen to a summary of the complete interview's main points. For writing practice, try taking a few of the sentences as dictation. For speaking practice, try to repeat whole sentences, imitating the intonation of the native speaker.**

El cambio fundamental ha sido . . .
A nivel más específico, creo que
. . . mientras que en las carreras . . .
Es necesario que . . .
De esta manera, es probable que . . .

NEW EXPRESSIONS

1 **Which is the correct phrase to use in these comparisons: menos que, en comparación con, or mientras que?**

   a Cada año hay más gente viviendo en mi pueblo, _____ el número de tiendas va disminuyendo.

   b _____ la generación de sus padres, las parejas de hoy son más iguales.

   c En EEUU, se fuma mucho _____ en España.

2 **Which is the most suitable expression to complete these contrastive statements: aunque, poco probable, or sin embargo?**

   a Es la pura verdad, _____ no lo creas.

   b Es _____ que aumente la tasa de natalidad en España. La gente tiene cada vez menos hijos.

   c Según los expertos, va disminuyendo la contaminación, _____ no lo veo así. Solo hay que observar la cantidad de basura que tiramos.

Expressing comparisons

La población activa femenina es más joven que la masculina.	The female working population is younger than the male one.
La mujer es tan capaz como el hombre.	Women are as capable as men.
menos que	less than
en comparación con	in comparison with, compared with
frente a	in comparison with, compared with
mientras que	whilst

Expressing probability

Es probable/posible que se llegue a un mayor equilibrio.	It is possible that a greater balance may be reached.
Probablemente/posiblemente seguirá descendiendo.	It will probably continue to fall.
es improbable	it is improbable, unlikely
es poco probable	it is not very likely
quizá(s), tal vez, a lo mejor	perhaps

Expressing contrast or opposition

El porcentaje de participación femenina llega casi al 50%. Sin embargo, todavía persisten diferencias . . .	The percentage of women's participation has reached almost 50%. However, there are still differences . . .
Ha habido un crecimiento de la población activa femenina, frente a una reducción de la masculina. No obstante, el paro ha afectado más a la mujer que al hombre.	There has been an increase in the female working population as opposed to a decrease in the male one. Nevertheless, unemployment has affected women more than men.
Me han aumentado el sueldo, aunque no lo merecía.	They've given me a pay rise, even though I didn't deserve one.

Language discovery

You have seen this language in action. Now can you work out the rules?

1 What is the opposite of these phrases?

   a el más conocido
   b las peores condiciones
   c la hija mayor
   d el mejor trato

2 Which is the correct word to use in these sentences, pero or sino?

   a A ellos les gusta el flamenco, _____ no a nosotros.
   b No dijo que no podía, _____ que no quería.
   c No te pongas la corbata roja _____ la amarilla.
   d No viajáis muy a menudo _____ siempre viajáis muy lejos.

3 In the following sentences replace the infinitive with the correct verb form – either indicative or subjunctive.

   a Aunque él (estar) en paro, piensan comprar un coche nuevo.
   b Aunque (ser) tarde, llámanos cuando llegues a casa.
   c A pesar de que no (sentirme) bien, no quiero perderme la fiesta.

1 THE PLUPERFECT TENSE

The Spanish pluperfect tense (e.g. **La sociedad le había asignado . . .**) is equivalent to the English pluperfect (e.g. *Society had assigned to her . . .*). It is formed with the imperfect form of **haber** (**había, habías, había, habíamos, habíais, habían**) followed by a past participle which does not change (for the formation of past participles, see Unit 8).

La sociedad le *había asignado* un papel netamente pasivo.

Society had assigned to her a purely passive role.

Él y su mujer *habían trabajado* casi toda la vida.

He and his wife had worked almost all their life.

El sitio nos resulta familiar, aunque nunca *habíamos estado* aquí.

The place looks familiar, although we had never been here.

2 COMPARISONS

a Positive comparison

La población activa femenina es más joven que la masculina.

The female working population is younger than the male one.

b Negative comparison

La mujer hispanoamericana es menos liberal que la española.

Latin American women are less liberal than Spanish women.

c Comparison of equality

La mujer es tan capaz como el hombre.

Women are as capable as men.

d Irregular forms

bueno	*good*	**mejor**	*better*
malo	*bad*	**peor**	*worse*
grande	*big*	**mayor**	*bigger, greater, older* (also **más grande** for size)
pequeño	*small*	**menor**	*smaller, younger* (also **más pequeño**)

e Superlative forms

To say *the youngest, the most capable*, use the construction **el/la/los/las** followed by **más** or **menos**:

el/la más joven or **el/la menor**	*the youngest*
los/las más capaces	*the most capable*

With irregular forms use **el/la/los/las** followed by the appropriate word.

el/la menor/mayor	*the youngest/oldest*
el/la mejor/peor	*the best/worst*

3 EXPRESSING CONTRAST OR OPPOSITION

The word most commonly used for expressing contrast or opposition is **pero** *but*, but there are a number of others:

a Sino, **sino que** *but*. **Sino** is normally used instead of pero after a negative statement, while **sino que** is used before a verb phrase.

No hoy, sino mañana.	*Not today, but tomorrow.*
No le envié un email, sino que le llamé por teléfono.	*I didn't send him an email, but I phoned him.*

b Sin embargo *however*. This functions like **pero**, but its use is restricted to more formal spoken and written language.

No se llevan bien, sin embargo siguen juntos.	*They don't get on well, however they continue together.*

c Aunque *although, even though, even if*. If what follows is a fact, use an indicative verb, otherwise use the subjunctive verb, in which case **aunque** translates *even if*.

Aunque ella trabaja fuera de casa, él no ayuda con las tareas domésticas.	*Although/Even though she goes out to work, he doesn't help her with the domestic chores.* (a fact)
Aunque mañana llueva iremos a verte.	*Even if it rains tomorrow we'll come and see you.* (not yet a fact)

d A pesar de *in spite, despite*. You can use this with a noun, a pronoun or an infinitive.

A pesar de la lluvia/eso saldremos a cenar.	*In spite of/Despite the rain/that we'll go out for dinner.*
No nos ha olvidado a pesar de estar lejos.	*He/She hasn't forgotten us in spite of/despite being far away.*

e A pesar de que *in spite of/despite the fact that, even though, even if.* Use this with an indicative verb if what follows is a fact, otherwise use the subjunctive.

A pesar de que estoy ocupado, te ayudaré.	*Despite the fact that/Even though I'm busy, I'll help you.*
No volveré con él, a pesar de que me lo pida.	*I won't go back to him, despite the fact that he may ask me to. (. . . even if he asks me to.)*

f No obstante *nevertheless, despite, in spite of.* This is more formal than the other phrases and is restricted to writing or very formal speech.

El país ha progresado, no obstante todavía queda mucho por hacer.	*The country has progressed; nevertheless there is still a lot to do. (Despite the fact that the country has progressed, there is . . .)*

 ## Practice

1 **Translate the following sentences into Spanish.**
  a She was better than him, and in spite of that she didn't get the job.
  b Although Carlos is older than Sofía, they get on very well together.
  c María had lived in the United States for several years, however her English wasn't as good as her brother's.
  d They hadn't lived in Madrid but in Barcelona, although they had been here more than once.
  e Despite being younger, he is not as active as the others.
  f We'll go on holiday, even if we have to borrow money (**pedir dinero prestado**).

2 **Match the words and phrases (a–j) with one of similar meaning (1–10). Look back at Conversations 1 and 2 if you need to refresh your memory.**

a	por un lado	**1**	con frecuencia
b	no cabe duda	**2**	indudablemente
c	de esta manera	**3**	en relación con
d	a mi juicio	**4**	por otra parte
e	a menudo	**5**	en realidad
f	además	**6**	ya que
g	puesto que	**7**	a mi parecer
h	hoy en día	**8**	por una parte
i	en lo que respecta a	**9**	así
j	de hecho	**10**	en la actualidad

¡A escuchar!

Teresa Morales talks to a journalist from a Spanish magazine about her life with Paco, her husband.

  3 12.05 **First, study the key words and phrases, then listen to Teresa.**

¿cómo os arregláis?	*how do you manage?*
tareas del hogar (f pl)	*housework*
eludir	*to avoid*

asistenta (f)	*charwoman*
planchar	*to iron*
camino de casa	*on the way home*
guisar	*to cook*
labores compartidas (f pl)	*shared work*
ajuste(s) (m)	*adjustment(s)*

How well have you understood? Read and decide: ¿Verdadero o falso?

　a Teresa y Paco llevan pocos años de casados.

　b La limpieza del piso la hace Teresa.

　c La comida la prepara Paco.

　d La asistenta friega los platos.

　e Teresa y Paco no funcionan bien como pareja.

　f Según Teresa, cuando vengan los hijos no habrá mayores cambios.

 12.06 By now you are probably familiar enough with the interview to answer some further questions in Spanish. Speak in the pauses and listen to confirm your answers. This exercise is meant to give you practice in listening and speaking without the text to read along. Try it several times if necessary.

 4 Carla wrote to a magazine seeking advice with a personal matter. What is Carla's problem? Read the letter and find out.

> ## Mi marido no quiere que trabaje
>
> Estimada Eli:
>
> El problema por el que te escribo es que, en siete años de matrimonio, aún no logro convencer a mi marido de que quiero trabajar. Él dice que tenemos una situación económica muy buena y que no es necesario que salga de casa. Tenemos una hija de seis años que ya va al colegio y creo que yo podría conseguir una ocupación, al menos, de media jornada. Se trata de sentirme útil, ya que terminé mi carrera de ingeniería comercial y siempre soñé con realizarme en ella. Ahora no es eso lo que persigo, pero al menos hacer algo relacionado con el tema que estudié. Mi marido dice que podría hacer talleres, tomar cursos, pero creo que el problema es que él teme que yo me desarrolle profesionalmente, por miedo o celos. No sé qué hacer. ¿Cómo hacerlo entender?
>
> Carla

A response was printed in a Letters to the editor column:

de media jornada (f)	*part-time*
ingeniería comercial (f)	*economics* (L. Am.)
perseguir	*to pursue*
taller (m)	*workshop*

Now complete the reply with an appropriate word from the box:

> inseguridad   cambio   actividad   sensación   horizontes razones
> apoyo   estatus   necesidad   seria

Carla:

Da la _____ de que a tu marido le incomodaría que tú salieras a trabajar por muchas _____: posiblemente por machismo, por _____ o por celos, pero también es probable que sea por _____ social o porque piense que tu hija estará más protegida contigo en casa.

Creo que debieras hablar en forma muy _____ con tu marido. Dile que has decidido realizar una _____ de acuerdo a lo que estudiaste y que le estás pidiendo su _____ porque es una _____ concreta que tienes. Explícale que este _____ te producirá felicidad, satisfacción, que tus _____ van a cambiar y que van a poder conversar de otros temas.

Why do you think Carla's husband is acting the way he is? And what advice would you give her? Compare your ideas with those of the newspaper editor.

5 **The article which follows looks at the birth rate in Spain and explains why it has one of the lowest birth rates in Europe.**
Which of the following reasons for the decrease in the birth rate are mentioned in the text? Read the article and find out.
   a El Estado sanciona a las familias que tienen numerosos hijos.
   b La incorporación de la mujer al trabajo.
   c Los españoles confían más en la ayuda estatal.
   d Las viviendas son demasiado pequeñas como para una familia numerosa.
   e La transformación de las costumbres que se produjo después de la desaparición de Franco.
   f El tener hijos implica obligaciones que las parejas no quieren asumir.
   g La adopción de medidas para el control de la natalidad.

cifra (f)	figure
caída (f)	fall
estado de bienestar (m)	welfare state
esconderse	to hide
criar	to bring up
asignación familiar (f)	child benefit
relevo (m)	relay, replacement

Cuando los hijos son caros

A sus 34 años, Mariló Corral tiene un hijo de seis y duda al pensar en tener otro. Periodista de profesión, actualmente está desempleada, lo que condiciona su deseo de dar a luz de nuevo. Sin embargo, dice que la mayoría de sus amigas tienen solo un hijo, 'pues tener un niño es muy caro'.

Este testimonio refleja algunos de los motivos del bajo índice de natalidad que se registra en España, y que en 2012 solo llegó a 1,32 hijos por mujer, según cifras del Instituto Nacional de Estadística Español, mientras que la media europea es de 1,6 hijos. Esta tasa no alcanza el 2,1 necesario para asegurar el relevo generacional, y es una de las más bajas de Europa.

Sin embargo, la caída de la natalidad en España preocupa, pero no alarma. De hecho constituye una tendencia desde 1984.

Según el sociólogo Salvador Giner, este fenómeno se debe al cambio cultural sufrido por España tras la muerte de Franco. Destaca la mayor confianza de los españoles en el Estado de bienestar, la revolución que significó el control de la natalidad y el ingreso de la mujer a la vida laboral.

Pensárselo dos veces

Inquieto y gracioso, Marc es el primer hijo de Rosalía Pallarés, una administrativa de 35 años. Casada hace cinco y medio, asegura que siempre quiso tener hijos, pero bajo una planificación familiar. 'Para traer niños al mundo es mejor pensárselo dos veces. No poder mantenerlos es una pena', dice.

Sin embargo, a juicio del investigador Diego Levis, detrás de las excusas económicas se esconde la incapacidad de las parejas para asumir la responsabilidad que representa criar y educar un hijo.

6 **Read the text again and find another word or phrase meaning the following:**
  a Está sin trabajo/en paro.
  b Tener un hijo.
  c Otra vez.
  d Las razones.
  e A juicio de . . .
  f Oficinista.
  g Pensarlo muy bien.
  h Es una lástima.

Young Europeans as a whole base the decision of having children on a range of other reasons. Do you agree with them? Look at the chart and compare these with the ones mentioned by the people in the article.

seguro/a	secure
vivienda (f)	housing
disponer de	to have
cuidado infantil (m)	childcare
asignación (f)	allowance

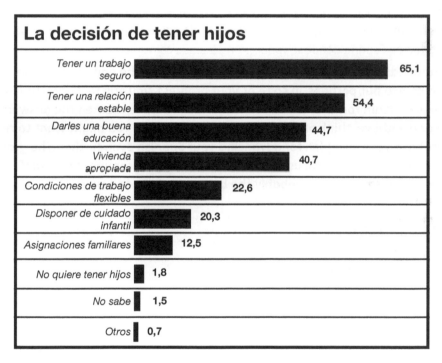

La decisión de tener hijos

Tener un trabajo seguro	65,1
Tener una relación estable	54,4
Darles una buena educación	44,7
Vivienda apropiada	40,7
Condiciones de trabajo flexibles	22,6
Disponer de cuidado infantil	20,3
Asignaciones familiares	12,5
No quiere tener hijos	1,8
No sabe	1,5
Otros	0,7

Test yourself

1 Complete the sentences with a suitable word.

   a Antes de casarse, Daniel y Marité _____ vivido en Santander.

   b Perdona, (yo) no te _____ visto. ¿Dónde estabas?

   c Ya (nosotros) _____ terminado de cenar cuando llegó Ricardo y su mujer.

   d El español no es tan difícil _____ el alemán.

   e Elena es _____ que su hermana. Elena tiene veintitrés años y su hermana dieciocho.

2 Complete the sentences with the correct word from the box.

a pesar de   sino que   aunque   sin embargo   sino

   a No, no es ese el que quiero, _____ el otro.

   b _____ nos inviten, creo que no aceptaremos la invitación.

   c _____ las dificultades, logró terminar sus estudios universitarios.

   d Eran muy buenos amigos, _____ después de aquel incidente nunca más se vieron.

   e No fue en España donde se conocieron _____ coincidieron en unas vacaciones.

¡Enhorabuena! *Congratulations!* **You have now reached the end of your** *Enjoy Spanish* **course but perhaps, in spite of your progress, you still feel uncertain about how to use certain forms or constructions. Once you have checked the answers to Tests 1 and 2 above, think of what areas of the language you might want to revise and establish your own plan for advancing your Spanish even further. The grammar notes in the units may serve as a guideline, but using a grammar book, preferably one containing exercises, is probably the best option. ¡Buena suerte!**

SELF CHECK

I CAN ...
... express comparisons.
... express probability.
... express contrast or opposition.

Key to the exercises

Conversation 1

1 Yes, at the end of the conversation he says he wouldn't change his life for another.
2 a No tiene que perder el tiempo yendo de un punto a otro de la ciudad en el coche, y no tiene un horario fijo. **b** Se considera bastante disciplinado. **c** Se sienta frente al ordenador. **d** Su familia y sus amigos conocen sus hábitos y no lo llaman por la mañana, a no ser que sea para algo importante. **e** Recibe a sus amigos, escuchan música, toman unas copas y charlan. A veces van al cine o a cenar fuera.
3 a 3. **b** 1. **c** 2.

Conversation 2

1 Alicia works long hours on average: llego a la fábrica sobre las nueve de la mañana; nunca (vuelvo a casa) antes de las nueve o las diez de la noche.
2 a Difícilmente puedo hablar. **b** Ya que . . . **c** A eso de . . . **d** Tardaría mucho tiempo. **e** No está nada mal. **f** Lo que pasa es que . . . **g** Tomar una copa. **h** De vez en cuando.
3 a whether they like it or not. **b** whenever it may be. **c** whatever he/she may say. **d** if we like it or not.

Conversation 3

1 Teresa es ama de casa.
2 In **lo que haga falta** whatever we may need the verb form (subjunctive) expresses an unreal situation; in **hace falta . . .** *we need* . . . it is a fact: there is no more rice!
3 a Se levanta a eso de la siete y media para preparar el desayuno para su familia. **b** Sus chicos salen para el colegio sobre las nueve menos cuarto. **c** Después, se arregla y sale a hacer las compras. **d** Luego, vuelve a casa para preparar el almuerzo. **e** Mira un rato la tele, a veces duerme una siesta, pero no acostumbra a hacerlo. **f** Siempre hay algo que hacer en casa. Teresa tiene muchas tareas domésticas como lavar la ropa o planchar.

New expressions

a coffee; eat much (a lot); in the morning; generally, normally, usually; finally.

Language discovery

1 They mean the same thing: he /she usually eats at home with the children. **2** Sentence **a** is a certain fact (I have time); sentence **b** is not certain and may or may not happen (I don't think I'll have time). **3 a** I'll call you when I can (meaning: when I'm free, not now), **b** When(ever) I can, I call you on the phone.

Practice

1 me despierto / me levanto / me ducho / desayuno / salgo / voy / cojo / vuelvo / almuerzo / me marcho / voy / juego / doy / me acuesto.

2 trabaja / se despierta / se levanta / se ducha / desayuna / sale / va / coge / vuelve / almuerza / se marcha / va / juega / da / se acuesta.

3 a 6. **b** 3. **c** 5. **d** 1. **e** 4. **f** 2.

4 a ¿A qué hora sales de casa? Normalmente salgo a las ocho y media. **b** ¿Y cómo vas al trabajo? Voy en el metro. **c** ¿A qué hora llegas a la oficina? Generalmente llego entre las nueve menos diez y las nueve. **d** ¿Y qué haces por la mañana? Pues, reviso el correo electrónico, abro la correspondencia, la leo y la clasifico, escribo las cartas que me dicta mi jefe, recibo a los clientes de la empresa y fijo citas con el gerente, contesto el teléfono, asisto a reuniones . . . **e** ¿A qué hora y dónde almuerzas normalmente? Normalmente almuerzo a la una y media con algunos compañeros de trabajo en el bar de la esquina. **f** ¿A qué hora sales de la oficina? Salgo a las siete de la tarde. **g** ¿Y qué haces normalmente por la noche? Ceno, veo la televisión, escucho música, doy un paseo con mi novio.

5 a V. **b** F. **c** F. **d** F. **e** V.

6 a ¿Qué haces? **b** ¿Vuelves a casa a comer? **c** Y por la tarde, ¿qué sueles hacer? **d** Yo también veo la televisión por la noche, pero solo un rato. Siempre hay algo que hacer en casa.

7 a Two: one in the morning, one in the afternoon. **b** Cristóbal goes home to take a half-hour nap. **c** He dedicates a couple of hours a day to studying.

8 a sobre, hacia. **b** nuevamente, otra vez, de nuevo, una vez más. **c** tal vez, quizá, a lo mejor. **d** se ducha, toma una ducha. **e** frugal, ligero. **f** se pone el bañador, para seguir entrenando, de vuelta en casa. **g** normalmente, casi siempre, nunca. **h** consiga – conseguir, sea – ser.

9 a lleguen. **b** sale. **c** regrese. **d** llame. **e** invite. **f** se levantan. **g** conozcas. **h** está. **i** digas. **j** trabaja.

Test yourself

1 a I don't usually eat much at night unless I have to go out. **b** It bothers Julia to be interrupted but it doesn't happen very often. **c** We are tied to a certain routine which, whether we like it or not, we have to keep to. **d** We go to the supermarket once or twice a week, depending on what is needed. **e** I don't want you to call me unless it's absolutely necessary. **f** It would be impossible to come back home for lunch, as I'd waste a lot of time going in the car, the bus or whatever.

2 a estés. **b** sé. **c** recuerdo, envíes. **d** pueda, sea. **e** vienes, quieras. **f** escribas, des.

UNIT 2

Conversation 1

1 They agree to go to the cinema tomorrow because Ana is feeling too tired today.

2 a No la ha visto, pero le gustaría verla. **b** Los fines de semana suele ir a la sierra. **c** Se va el viernes por la tarde y regresa el domingo por la noche. **d** Pablo invita a Ana a bajar a la playa.

Conversation 2

1 Manuel, he prefers artistic and cultural pursuits.

2 a Porque no había piscina en su barrio. **b** Porque trabaja y está casada y tiene dos hijos pequeños. **c** Cogen el coche y se van con los chicos de paseo. **d** Le gusta pintar y visitar exposiciones de arte.

Language discovery

1 ¿Te gustan las películas de Almodóvar?; He visto su última película, pero me encantaría verla otra vez. **2** gustar (to like) < encantar (to thoroughly enjoy) < fascinar (to love/adore) **3** They have different meanings: question **a** inquires about a person's attitude towards eating out, whereas questions **b** and **c** are invitations to dine out. **4** con regularidad *regularly*, and con más frecuencia *more frequently*.

Practice

1 a haces. **b** Me/Te/Le. **c** gustan. **d** Prefiero, gusta, ti. **e** gustan, no. **f** prefieres. **g** más. **h** A/te. **i** Me.

2 Follow Dialogue 1.

3 Tengo muy poco tiempo. Trabajo en una oficina de 9.00 a 5.00 y estoy casado(a) y tengo tres hijos. Pero cuando puedo, me gusta trabajar en el jardín y también me gusta leer. Ahora estoy leyendo una novela de García Márquez, que me gusta mucho. Ah, también estudio español, por supuesto. Me gusta mucho el español. / No siempre. Aunque me gusta mucho España, es caro viajar al extranjero, así que prefiero pasar mis vacaciones en otros lugares más cerca de casa. / ¡Fantástico! Muchas gracias.

4 a One is a documentary and the other a comedy. **b** The documentary is about the Spanish Civil War and the events that took place in Catalonia during the Republic. The comedy is about a school teacher who uses his hypnotic powers to impose order in his classroom.

5 a He recibido tu email y me alegro mucho de que vengas a mi ciudad. **b** Estoy seguro(a) de que te gustará mucho. **c** ¿Por qué no te quedas en mi casa unos días? Me gustaría mucho. **d** Puedes llamarme por teléfono para confirmar tu llegada.

6 a More than 80 works. **b** At the Museo Español de Arte Contemporáneo. **c** Mexico, Colombia, Argentina and Chile. **d** se está realizando / podrán apreciar / fue inaugurada por.

7 a Festival de otoño de Madrid. **b** It will include theatre, classical and contemporary dance, etc. **c** Eastern European countries.

8 a F. **b** F. **c** V. **d** F. **e** V. **f** F.

Test yourself

1 a (A él) le gusta el teatro, pero a ella no. **b** Lo que más nos gusta de este lugar/sitio es la gente. **c** ¿Te gusta? Pues, a mí no. Prefiero a Pablo. **d** ¿Qué te parece si vamos a tomar una copa, Silvia? **e** Me parece bien. **f** Les encanta/fascina ver este programa. Pues, a mí no me gusta nada.

2 a de manera muy lenta. **b** con frecuencia. **c** de forma muy descortés. **d** con mucha amabilidad. **e** de manera muy clara. **f** con cuidado.

UNIT 3

Conversation 1

1 It is the man who flies more often. He says: Viajo constantemente. The woman, although she enjoys it, flies less. She says: No lo hago muy a menudo.

2 c, e, f.

3 a 3. b 4. c 1. d 2.

4 a de, por. b de, de. c de, por. d en, desde. e por, a (or para). f de.

Conversation 2

1 Paloma is a little bored because she has been doing the same job for a long time. Mercedes loves her job, but the salary isn't great.

2 a No está nada mal. b Casi cinco años. c El contacto con el público. d Enseña español a extranjeros en un instituto de idiomas. e Sí, le gusta enseñar.

3 a I can't complain either. b The salary is not bad at all. c At the beginning I used to like it a lot. d The relationship is rather impersonal. e I do like teaching. f Come on, things are not so easy!

New expressions

What (The thing) I like least about my job is the salary. She works as a driver for a coach company.

Language discovery

1 c This question here is how long they will be looking for an apartment, not how long they have been looking. **2** a ¿Cuánto tiempo hace que no llueve?, b ¿Cuánto tiempo llevas jugando ajedrez? **3** a The focus is on walking the dog. b The focus is on who walks the dog.

Practice

1 a ¿Cuánto tiempo llevas viviendo en Londres? Llevo tres años viviendo aquí. b ¿Cuánto tiempo llevas estudiando inglés? Llevo dos años y medio (estudiándolo). c ¿Cuánto tiempo llevas jugando al fútbol? Llevo cinco años (jugando). d ¿Cuánto tiempo llevas tocando el piano? Llevo cuatro años (tocando). e ¿Cuánto tiempo llevas trabajando como camarero? Llevo seis meses (trabajando como camarero). f ¿Cuánto tiempo llevas haciendo yoga? Llevo tres semanas (haciendo yoga).

2 a Hace tres años que vive . . . b Hace dos años y medio que estudia . . . c Hace cinco años que juega . . . d Hace cuatro años que toca . . . e Hace seis meses que trabaja . . . f Hace tres semanas que hace . . .

3 desde / como / de / trabajo / él / posibilidad / diferente / busca / lo; horario / empiezo / la / los / son; sueldo / gano / espero / viene; gusta / trabajo / donde / irme.

4 Buenos días. Llamo por el anuncio en el periódico y quisiera hablar con la señorita Toñi. / Sí, ¿Hablo con la señorita Toñi?. / Está bien. Esperaré. / Buenos días, soy (name), he visto el anuncio en el periódico y quisiera más información acerca del puesto. / Sí, trabajé como vendedor(a) durante algún tiempo, aunque nunca he vendido libros. Pero estoy dispuesto(a) a aprender. Ahora vivo en España y necesito ganar algo de dinero y este es el tipo de trabajo que busco. Me interesa mucho. / Sí, ¿cuál es su página web?

5 Follow the model letter and change the relevant information.

 Going further – **a** Muy señores míos: is more impersonal. Estimado señor: signals that the recipient is male. If the writer knew more, he or she would probably include the surname. **b** Nos es muy grato . . . is more formal and much less common in spoken Spanish than Me alegro de decirle que . . .

6 Check the ¡A escuchar! transcript to complete the form about María del Carmen Salas.

7 a ¿Podrías decirme a qué te dedicas? **b** Estoy a cargo de . . . **c** ¿Qué es lo que más te agrada de tu profesión? **d** El trabajo en terreno. **e** Eso es lo que más me agrada. **f** ¿Hay algo que no te guste de tu trabajo? **g** Son muy exigentes. **h** Hay que renovarse constantemente.

8 a Hace cinco años. **b** Trabajaba en Madrid en una empresa privada. **c** Porque no ganaba lo suficiente. **d** Es un puesto seguro y para toda la vida. **e** Principalmente en dar información al público. **f** La mayoría pide información sobre hoteles y sobre sitios de interés en la región.

9 a A Madrid llegó el viernes por la tarde./El viernes por la tarde llegó a Madrid. **b** A las cinco de la mañana le llamó por teléfono su madre./Le llamó por teléfono su madre a las cinco de la mañana. **c** En el restaurante donde comimos dejé el teléfono móvil./Dejé el teléfono movil en el restaurante donde comimos. **d** Por Pepe, que nos llamó, supimos la noticia./Supimos la noticia por Pepe, que nos llamó. **e** El email de César lo recibió Antonia el sábado./El sábado recibió Antonia el email de César.

10 a Translation and interpreting. **b** She's selling books door-to-door. **c** She's living with her parents and two of her brothers (or brothers and sisters) because her income, which is low and fluctuating, doesn't allow her to rent a flat and live independently. **d** She looks up advertisements in the newspaper and sends her CV in the hope of being called for an interview.

11 a Domina perfectamente el inglés y el francés. **b** Trabaja vendiendo libros a domicilio. **c** El haber hecho estudios universitarios . . . **d** . . . con la esperanza de que la llamen al menos para una entrevista. **e** una universidad madrileña **f** puesto que **g** conseguir un empleo/encontrar trabajo **h** bien remunerado **i** el día que ello suceda.

Test yourself

1 a Soy ingeniero. Construyo . . . **b** Soy enfermera. Cuido . . . **c** Soy bombero. Apago . . . **d** Soy carpintero. Fabrico . . . **e** Soy conductora. Conduzco . . . **f** Soy director. Dirijo . . . **g** Soy profesora/catedrática. Enseño . . . **h** Soy cartera. Reparto . . .

2 a Llevan cinco años viviendo en la Costa del Sol. **b** ¿Cuánto tiempo hace que trabajas en/para esta empresa? **c** Victoria va a Nueva York por negocios, pero yo voy de vacaciones. También voy de compras. **d** Lo que más le gusta de enseñar es el contacto con la gente. Lleva mucho tiempo enseñando español. **e** Normalmente las compras las hace mi jefe, pero hoy me toca a mí. (or) Normalmente es mi jefe quien/el que hace las compras, pero hoy . . . **f** Lo que no me gusta de mi trabajo es el sueldo, aunque viajar sí me gusta/sí me gusta viajar.

UNIT 4

Conversation 1

1 Francisca's, his mother is French and he lived in the USA before getting married.
2 a F. **b** V. **c** F. **d** V. **e** F. **f** F.

Conversation 2

1 advanced
2 a Porque para profesores extranjeros de español tienen cursos especiales. **b** Cuatro semanas y dos semanas respectivamente. **c** Porque no dispone de mucho tiempo. **d** Le da un folleto informativo.
3 a ¿Podría darme . . .? **b** Allí le darán . . . **c** . . . en caso de que lo necesite **d** Se lo pregunto . . .

New expressions

at school; advanced-level; a couple of years ago; to the USA.

Language discovery

1 a Jugué al baloncesto. **b** Asistí a un congreso. **c** Hice un curso de baile. **2 a** hace unos/varios días **b** hace un mes/el mes pasado **c** hace un par de/dos años **3 a** ¿Ya le/lo conoces? **b** No lo recordaron. **c** Me da vergüenza contártela. **d** Sandra me lo explicó. **e** Sí, puedo dársela. / Sí, se la puedo dar.

Practice

1 a Me/Te, la. **b** Lo. **c** le. **d** le, me, le, se, lo. **e** me, se, la, le.
2 a Me alegré. **b** fue. **c** hiciste. **d** estudié. **e** conseguí. **f** tuve. **g** asistí. **h** abrió. **i** aprendí. **j** Tuve que. **k** mereció.
3 a Gracias. Es Vd. muy amable. **b** Lo aprendí en la escuela, pero también pasé seis meses en España. ¿Habla Vd. inglés? **c** ¿Dónde estudió francés? **d** Sí, hice varios años de francés en la escuela y tuve una excelente profesora. Y también voy a Francia todos los veranos. El año pasado estuve en Cannes. Me gustó mucho.
4 a ¿Podría decirme si tienen Vds. cursos de español de verano? **b** ¿Cuándo empiezan? **c** ¿Qué niveles ofrecen? **d** ¿Cuánto cuestan? **e** ¿Y cuál es el horario? **f** ¿Pueden ayudarme a encontrar alojamiento?
5 a She asks about Spanish courses for foreign students: dates, levels, class times, and cost of registration. **b** No, she only asks for general information about course levels. **c** She is looking for a family stay.

Dear Sir, This is to request information about the Spanish courses for foreigners which the University of Málaga is running this summer. Please send me detailed information about the dates on which they will take place, the levels which are offered, the timetable and the registration fees. I would be grateful too if you could tell me whether it would be possible to get accommodation through you with a Spanish family. I look forward to hearing from you.
Yours sincerely,

6 a By sending the registration form, two photographs and a photocopy of the document showing that payment has been sent. **b** Certificate in Spanish Language, Diploma in Hispanic Studies. **c** With families or in apartments. **d** They are grouped according to their knowledge of the language: beginners, intermediate and advanced levels. **e** 20 hours. **f** Concerts, shows, films, visits to the main monuments in the city and excursions to other cities.

7 Muy señores míos: He visto el anuncio sobre los cursos que ofrece el Centro de Estudios Eva y estoy interesado/a en el curso de . . . Les ruego que me envíen toda la información referente al curso, incluyendo la fecha en que se realiza, el importe de la inscripción, el horario y la forma de inscripción. Les agradeceré que me hagan llegar la información lo antes posible. Les saluda muy atentamente.

8 a F. **b** V. **c** F. **d** F. **e** V. **f** F.

9 Hace más de 10 años. / Los hice en Santiago. / Sí, tengo muchos recuerdos agradables del colegio. Fue una época muy feliz de mi vida. / Era un buen colegio. Los profesores nos hacían trabajar mucho. / Ni bueno, ni malo. México nos gustó muchísimo.

10 a She used to read and write a lot. When she returned to school she discovered that the rest of the girls did not play her games (reading and writing). **b** She felt ugly, although she was in fact pretty, and she was also lonely, quiet and shy. **c** She had an unhappy childhood, full of fears and questions without answers. She was extremely sensitive and proud, which derived from a low self-esteem and feeling very threatened and vulnerable. **d** His father bought a chemist's and went bankrupt. **e** He describes the relationship with his father as dreadful, and that with his mother's family as the Golden Age.

Test yourself

1 a hizo, hicieron, hice. **b** estuvo, estuvimos. **c** dije, dijo. **d** pusiste, puse. **e** fue, fueron, fuimos. **f** vino, vinieron, vine.

2 a ¿Podría darme/Me podría dar información sobre los cursos de español de verano, por favor? **b** ¿Nos envía/Nos puede enviar información sobre alojamiento también? Le daremos nuestros emails. **c** Me da vergüenza decirlo, pero mi español no es tan bueno como mi francés, aunque lo estudié durante un año. **d** Mi hijo domina perfectamente el francés y el español. Los aprendió en la escuela/el colegio y también pasó algún tiempo en Francia y en España.

3 a The purpose of this letter is to request an information brochure . . . **b** Please/Kindly let me know what the registration fees are . . . **c** I'd be grateful if you would get me accommodation with a Spanish family . . . **d** I look forward to hearing from you.

UNIT 5

Conversation 1

1 They went with a tour group to get the lowest costs.

2 a El año pasado fui a Cuba (the preterite is used for the actions that took place at some point in the past). **b** El hotel donde nos quedamos era excelente (the imperfect provides the background description for the actions expressed by the preterite). **c** a través de una agencia de viajes. **d** de otra manera. **e** mereció la pena.

3 a Las pasó en Cuba. **b** Estuvo allí diez días en total. **c** El hotel era excelente y estaba a cinco minutos de la playa. Tenía piscina, discoteca . . . **d** No, fue a través de una agencia de viajes, porque de otra manera les habría resultado muy caro. **e** Era muy maja. **f** Los viajes organizados no le gustan nada.

4 No, el año pasado fui a México con unos amigos. / México nos gustó muchísimo. Es un lugar muy bonito. Y el hotel donde nos quedamos era excelente. / La gente del grupo era muy maja.

Conversation 2

1 About a month and a half, starting in late July and lasting through August

2 My birthday is still a long way off; There are two months to go to Christmas.

3 a México. **b** un amigo mexicano. **c** en julio. **d** agosto. **e** su amigo. **f** al Oriente.

4 No, el año que viene espero ir a Brasil. / Pienso irme hacia finales de julio. / Me quedaré allí todo el mes de agosto. / Iré con mi familia.

Conversation 3

1 He was going to go out for a walk, but now it's raining heavily.

2 a No ha parado de llover. **b** Está lloviendo a cántaros. **c** ¡Qué lástima! **d** ¡Es una pena! **e** ¡Ojalá!

New expressions

1 Hace sol hoy, pero mañana hará mal tiempo.

2 Sigue/Continúa nevando.

3 La mayoria de la gente viaja acompañada.

Language discovery

1 a, c, d. 2 (nosotros) pasaremos. **3 a** Sus padres eran muy simpáticos. **b** Estaban listos para salir. **4 a** expresses the speaker's hope for him or herself: I hope to have a good time. **b** expresses the speaker's wish for someone else: I hope you have a good time (note the pronoun relative que and the use of the subjunctive).

Practice

1 viajaremos / Saldremos / llegaremos / nos quedaremos / Podrás / Estaremos / daré / harás.

2 a fueron, Estuvieron. **b** Era, iban, estaban. **c** resultó, llegó, esperaba, vivía. **d** pasaron, conocía, llevó. **e** tomaron, pareció, Era. **f** fueron, soñaban.

3 Las pasé en San Sebastián, en el norte de España. / Me gustó mucho San Sebastián. Es una ciudad muy bonita, y el hotel donde me quedé era excelente. Estaba enfrente de la playa, tenía piscina y un restaurante excelente. Y tuve mucha suerte con el tiempo. No hacía mucho calor. / Fui con unos amigos. Nos llevamos muy bien, eran gente muy maja. / No estuvimos mucho tiempo. Desgraciadamente, todos tuvimos que volver a trabajar. / Me encantaría volver, pero el próximo año espero ir a Sudamérica. Pienso viajar a Argentina y Chile. Si tengo dinero me quedaré allí un par de meses. Pienso tomar otro trabajo para pagar mis vacaciones. Y tú ¿fuiste de vacaciones a algún lugar? / ¡Qué lástima!

4 a We're flying with Spanair. **b** No. it's a direct flight. **c** On a private bus. **d** By airplane. **e** Six days. **f** No, from Cancún.

5 a Iré a Cancún y Ciudad de México / al D. F. **b** Primero visitaré Cancún. **c** Me quedaré dos semanas. **d** No, me quedaré en hoteles.

6 a No, the weather will be clear. **b** It will be misty and later on it will be hazy. **c** It will be misty and in the afternoon it will be cloudy. **d** Pollution will be relatively low. **e** 8.36 p.m.

7 a Estará nublado y habrá lloviznas. **b** La mínima probable será de 11 grados y la máxima de 23. **c** La mínima fue de 13,1 a las 8.00 de la mañana y la máxima de 26,8 a las 15.30. **d** Habrá nubosidad parcial, variando a despejado. **e** 14,7 grados.

8 a La mayoría prefiere el viaje organizado, pero con cierto grado de flexibilidad. **b** Prefieren visitar monumentos, museos y parques naturales.

Test yourself

1 a pasará, pasarán, pasaré. **b** hará, haremos. **c** tendrá, tendré. **d** pondréis, pondremos. **e** dirás, diré, dirá. **f** vendrán, vendrá, vendrás.

2 a El hotel donde se quedaron era excelente. No estaba lejos de la playa y también tenía una piscina, pero lamentablemente llovió a cántaros la mayor parte del tiempo. **b** Pero mereció la pena ir. La ciudad era interesante, aunque era un poco ruidosa. **c** Pensamos viajar a Brasil el año que viene/próximo. Patricia estuvo allí hace dos años y habló/me contó maravillas de Río. **d** No, no tomaremos/vamos a tomar un viaje organizado. Preferimos viajar por nuestra cuenta/de forma independiente/independientemente, de otra manera resultará/será demasiado caro. Reservaremos nuestros billetes a través de una agencia de viajes. **e** Pues/Bien, espero ir de vacaciones a/hacia finales de agosto. Hay unas vacaciones en el Caribe que no son nada caras. Ya veremos. Aún/Todavía falta mucho tiempo. **f** – ¿Sigue lloviendo? – Lamentablemente sí, no ha parado de llover desde que nos levantamos. – ¡Qué lástima/pena! Pensaba jugar al tenis.

UNIT 6

Conversation 1

1 Four: Martin, his wife, and their two children; one large room.

2 a Una habitación con una cama de matrimonio y dos camas individuales. **b** Para el 24 de agosto y para siete noches. **c** 80 euros. **d** Está incluido. **e** Sí, hay uno para los clientes.

3 a no se oye bien. **b** tengo entendido que. **c** se paga aparte. **d** en caso de que Vd. prefiera. **e** a partir del 24 de agosto. **f** para uso exclusivo de los clientes.

4 ¿Podría decirme si tiene alguna habitación disponible para la última semana de abril? / Individual. / A partir del 23 de abril. / Para una semana, hasta el treinta de abril inclusive.

Conversation 2

1 She is looking for a small, furnished flat.

2 a F. **b** F. **c** F. **d** V. **e** V.

3 a Llamo por el anuncio. **b** ¿. . . está disponible . . .? / ¿Estará disponible . . .? **c** Ahora le pongo . . . **d** Está muy bien de precio. **e** Es justamente lo que busco. **f** Lo acaban de pintar.

New expressions

a ¿Podría decirme si es un piso de dos habitaciones? ¿Está en la planta alta / el último piso? **b** Busco un piso en un edificio que tenga aparcamiento.

Language discovery

1 a ser. **b** estar. **c** ser. **d** ser. **e** estar. **2** Aquí se habla inglés (an impersonal se where English would use a passive). **3 a** para. **b** por, por. **c** por, por. **d** para.

Practice

1 a está. **b** es. **c** está. **d** es. **e** son. **f** será. **g** Está.

2 para, para, para, para, para, por, para, por, por, por.

3 Follow the model email.

4 a Buenos días. Llamo por el anuncio. **b** Sí, el apartamento que se alquila en la avenida La Marina. **c** ¿Cuántas habitaciones tiene? **d** Es justamente lo que busco. Necesito algo que no sea demasiado grande. **e** ¿Sería posible verlo esta misma tarde?

5 a Vive con sus padres y sus dos hermanos menores. **b** Es grande y muy antiguo. **c** Es muy bonito, es de principios del siglo pasado y está muy bien conservado. **d** Tiene siete habitaciones en total. **e** No, tiene su propia habitación. **f** Es una calle muy ruidosa, pero con una arquitectura interesante. **g** En la esquina. **h** Porque alquilar un piso cuesta una fortuna.

6 Pablo se va a mudar este fin de semana a un piso estupendo a solo quince minutos de la Plaza Mayor. Es un piso de tres habitaciones y tiene vistas al río. Va a compartirlo con dos amigos y van a pagar setecientos ochenta euros mensuales en total.

7 a V. **b** F. **c** F. **d** V.

8 The economic situation and unemployment prevents them from leaving their homes.

9 a 1 Vive con su madre. **2** Dejan el hogar cuando aún son muy jóvenes. **3** Nos llevamos perfectamente. **4** No tienes que hacer nada. **5** La casa donde nació. **6** Todavía viven con sus padres. **7** El deseo de independencia se ha obstaculizado. **b 1** No suelen quedarse. **2** Más allá de los 20 años. **3** Normalmente suele matricularse en una universidad. **4** Para siempre. **5** Si acaso regresan a su ciudad. **6** No se trata, por supuesto, . . . sino.

Test yourself

1 a por, para, para, para. **b** para, para. **c** por. **d** por, por. **e** para, por. **f** por, por, por.

2 a El apartamento que se alquila en la calle Pelayo, ¿está disponible todavía? **b** Es un apartamento amueblado. **c** Está en muy buen estado y es muy bonito. Lo acaban de pintar. **d** Es exterior. **e** Es justamente lo que busco. **f** – ¿En qué piso está? – No estoy seguro, pero ahora le pongo con la persona encargada.

3 a Llamo por el anuncio en el periódico. **b** Eso es. Busco algo para alquilar. ¿Podría darme más información sobre el apartamento? **c** Necesito algo que esté disponible inmediatamente. **d** Pues, también busco algo que no sea demasiado caro. ¿Cuánto es el alquiler mensual? **e** Gracias. Eso es demasiado para mí.

UNIT 7

Conversation 1

1 Just one, at Plaza de Castilla.

2 a V. **b** F. **c** F.

3 a Coja la línea uno. **b** Hasta . . . **c** Cambie a la línea . . .

Conversation 2

1 The train's arrival time and the platform where it comes in.

2 a 2.30. **b** 20 minutos. **c** 2.50.

3 a la hora de llegada. **b** ¿A qué andén llega? **c** el tablero de llegadas.

4 ¿A qué hora llega el Talgo de Barcelona? / ¿Sabe Vd. a qué hora llegará? / ¿A qué andén llega?

Conversation 3

1 . . . right and go as far as Plaza Antón Martín which is 100 metres from here. There we take calle de León on the left and continue as far as calle Lope de Vega. We have to go straight on along Lope de Vega until we reach Paseo del Prado. The museum is on the other side of the Paseo.

2 a Dígame. **b** ¿Nos puede decir . . .? **c** Al salir . . . **d** Tuerzan a la derecha. **e** Sigan todo recto. **f** . . . hasta llegar . . .

3 Vaya hasta la Plaza España que está a cien metros de aquí. / Allí coja la calle Mayor que está a la derecha. / Siga todo recto por la calle Mayor hasta llegar a la estación.

Conversation 4

1 No, trains leave from Atocha and coaches from South Station.

2 a en tren o en autocar. **b** la estación de Atocha. **c** la estación Sur. **d** cada hora, a la hora. **e** siete de la mañana. **f** veintitrés horas.

3 a ¿Podría decirnos . . .? **b** el horario de (los) trenes. **c** cada hora a la hora (exacta). **d** a partir de las siete de la mañana. **e** No nos queda ninguno.

4 a The station on Paseo de Gracia. **b** every 20 minutes. **c** on the underground.

New expressions

Can you tell us; this street; What line do I have to take?; the express train; arrival time.

Language discovery

1 b doblad (vosotros). **2** No habléis entre vosotros. **3** The vowel changes are: **a** e > a (tú) comas, **b** o > a (nosotros) leamos, and **c** o > a (yo) venga. (Note that irregular verbs form the subjunctive on the pattern of the present tense for yo.)

Practice

1 coge / bájate / cruza / sube / sigue

2 *Model answers*: **a** Bien, gracias, ¿y Vd.? **b** Coja la línea 2 en dirección a Ventas. **c** Sí, va directo. **d** Coja la línea 4 en dirección a Esperanza y bájese en América. Allí cambie a la línea 1 en dirección a Castilla. Esa línea le llevará a Colombia. **e** Voy a ir al Museo del Prado y después almorzaré con un amigo español. **f** ¡Por qué no! Volveré al hotel sobre las 7.00.

3 *Model conversation*: **a** – ¿Podría decirme por dónde se va al Banco Central? – Sí, mire, siga Vd. todo recto por la calle Juan Bravo hasta General Pardiñas y allí doble a la derecha. El Banco Central está a una calle de allí, en la esquina de Ortega y Gasset, al lado de la Oficina de Turismo. **b** – Perdone, ¿puede decirme dónde está el Hotel Plaza? – Sí, siga Vd. por la calle de Serrano hasta Ortega y Gasset y allí doble a la izquierda. Suba por Ortega y Gasset. El Hotel Plaza está en la Plaza del Marqués de Salamanca, entre Velázquez y Príncipe de Vergara.

4 salir / doble / vaya / más / tome (*or* coge) / dirección / bájese / está / cuadras / dirección / doble (*or* tuerza) / siga / hasta / esquina.

5 Le envío / decirle / tiene que buscar / coja / bájese / cruce / siga / verá / su derecha / siga / tuerza / no se pierda.

6 a ¿De qué estación sale el Eurocity a París? **b** ¿A qué hora sale de Madrid? **c** ¿Cuántas paradas hace? **d** ¿Cuánto tarda (el viaje)? **e** ¿A qué hora llega a París? **f** ¿A qué estación llega? **g** ¿Se puede reservar/hacer una reserva por teléfono?

7 To go to the airport, you must go straight on as far as the second traffic light, there you have to turn left and continue along that street till the end. There you'll find the main road. To go to the airport you have to turn right. / Siga Vd. todo recto hasta el segundo semáforo y allí doble Vd. a la izquierda y continúe por esa calle hasta el final. Allí encontrará Vd. la carretera. Para ir al aeropuerto tiene que torcer a la derecha.

8 No, está lejos. / Se puede ir en el metro. / Hay que coger la línea uno. / No. Está detrás del museo

9 a viaja – viajar / elige – elegir / pide – pedir / no dudes – dudar / haz – hacer / contrata – contratar / aprovecha – aprovechar / ten – tener. **b** acceder, planear, listado, por separado, la tarifa global, con soltura. **c** alta temporada, un paquete turístico, Te puede salir mucho más económico, No dudes en . . ., un seguro de cancelación, Aprovecha las ofertas de última hora, Pero ten en cuenta que . . .

Test yourself

1 a coja. **b** mire. **c** gire. **d** siga. **e** bájese. **f** cruce. **2 a** No se los des. **b** No se lo digas. **c** No la pongáis aquí. **d** Por favor, no lo hagas. **e** No se la envíes por email. **f** No te bajes aquí.

UNIT 8

Conversation 1

1 No, the problem seems to be on the other side of the transfer, with the English bank.

2 a He pedido una transferencia. **b** Quisiera saber si ha llegado. **c** Aún no ha llegado. **d** He revisado todas las transferencias. **e** Mañana sobre el mediodía **f** Es mejor que llame Vd. por teléfono o escriba a su banco.

3 Buenos días. He pedido una transferencia de dinero a mi banco en Gran Bretaña y quisiera saber si ha llegado. / Mi nombre es (your name) / La pedí hace una semana y me dijeron que la enviarían inmediatamente. / Volveré mañana.

Conversation 2

1 Four, consisting of the international access code and the country code.

2 a ¿Qué prefijo tengo que marcar . . .? **b** Luego marque. . . **c** el número del abonado.

Conversation 3

1 a home address.

2 Correos / muestras / recomienda / postal / urgencia / ventaja / certificado / entrega / caro / conviene.

Conversation 4

1 There has been a mix-up in the dates: the Browns had booked for the 14th but the agency has their reservation starting on the 15th.

2 a Exijo que me entreguen el coche. **b** Les aconsejo que hablen con el encargado.

3 a Lo alquilaron en Manchester. **b** La hizo el Sr. Brown. **c** Porque no tienen ningún coche disponible. **d** Les aconseja que hablen con el encargado.

New expressions

a 2. **b** 3. **c** 2.

Language discovery

1 a Ya hemos cenado. **b** He pedido la cuenta. **c** ¡Pero esto ya me lo has dicho! **2 a** llegarían. **b** llamaría. **3** (tú) tienes, tengas (tú).

Practice

1 a ha llamado / han llegado / han reservado / he ido / he dejado / ha invitado.

2 a . . . el envío llegaría mañana. **b** . . . tardaría dos días en llegar. **c** . . . el paquete estaría allí el lunes. **d** . . . nos entregarían el coche esta tarde. **e** . . . me repararía el coche ahora mismo. **f** . . . me llamaría por teléfono esta noche.

3 a Yo mismo/a he hecho la reserva. **b** No me cabe duda de que era para hoy. **c** ¿Está seguro/a de que no hay ninguna reserva a mi nombre? **d** ¡Es el colmo de la incompetencia! **e** ¡Es increíble! **f** Exijo que nos den una habitación inmediatamente. **g** Pues, quisiera hacer una reclamación. **h** Es la primera vez que nos sucede algo así.

4 a 5. **b** 3. **c** 1. **d** 6. **e** 4. **f** 2.

5 *Model answer*: Primero, introduce tu tarjeta en la ranura y selecciona un idioma. Puedes retirar dinero en español o en inglés si quieres. Después ingresa tu PIN (clave secreta) y sigue las instrucciones que aparecen en pantalla. Escoge un monto y el cajero te lo entregará en libras. No olvides tomar tu recibo. La transacción se descontará automáticamente de tu cuenta corriente.

6 a A service for you to express your opinions and complaints. **b** You have to dial 31 45 45. It is an automatic answer-phone which operates 24 hours a day.

7 a In a hotel: a guest complains about the delay in bringing clean towels to her room. **b** In a garage: a customer complains about the state of his car to the person in charge. **c** In a restaurant: a customer complains about the delay in bringing their order.

8 *Model answers*: **1** El primer lector se queja de las molestias que le causó una línea aérea por la sobreventa de billetes, la que le impidió a él y su mujer realizar el viaje que tenían planeado. **2** La segunda persona se queja sobre la utilización del inglés en lugar del español en las indicaciones en un hotel en Ibiza, donde pasó sus vacaciones.

9 a ya que. **b** insólito. **c** nos quejamos. **d** iniciar. **e** indignación. **f** descortés. **g** nunca lo había experimentado. **h** una suerte de.

Test yourself

1 a ha vuelto/vuelve – vendría. **b** escrito – aconsejado – haga. **c** recomendado – contrate – hecho. **d** diga – dicho. **e** entreguen – harían. **f** marque /Vd. marca – entendido.

2 a código. **b** cajero automático. **c** seguro, entrega, ventaja. **d** anular. **e** reclamación, encargado. **f** colmo.

UNIT 9

Conversation 1

1 a She doesn't think her daughter will like a brown handbag; she would prefer another colour. **b** Within, she budgeted some 100€ and spends 15% less (85€).

2 a Es para regalo. **b** Está de cumpleaños. **c** Están de oferta. **d** Puede cambiarlo. **e** Me lo quedo. **f** Pagar en efectivo. **g** Pagar con tarjeta de crédito. **h** ¿Me lo puede envolver?

3 Unos treinta y cinco euros. / No creo que a mi padre le guste, ¿tiene otras? / Me la quedo. / ¿Puedo pagar con tarjeta de crédito?

Conversation 2

2 a F. **b** F. **c** V. **d** F.

Conversation 3

2 a La imagen no se ve muy bien. **b** Tendrá que revisarlo primero y después, dar un presupuesto por la reparación. **c** El cliente tiene que estar conforme con el presupuesto para que empiece el trabajo.

New expressions

efectivo, dinero; –¡Quién hubiera creído que este restaurante no acepta tarjetas de crédito! –¡No me digas! Por suerte llevo suficiente dinero, no te preocupes.

Language discovery

1 perdieran, tuviera, quisieras (tuvimos is the simple past tense of tener, querremos is the future tense of querer, and perdieron is the simple past tense of perder). **2 a** Si (Vd.) está conforme, podemos empezar ahora mismo. **b** Si estuviera/estuviese conforme, podríamos empezar ahora mismo. **3 a** Me gustaría que pasaras/pasases por mí. **b** Te pido que lo hagas, por favor. **4** Similar, all three refer to the obligation to bring the till receipt. Note that **c** is more impersonal and denotes an imposition from the outside, but that is a very fine nuance.

Practice

1 a Si tuviera vacaciones, viajaría a España. **b** Si el coche no estuviera en mal estado, lo compraría. **c** Si mereciera la pena, lo haríamos reparar. **d** Si no tuvieran que volver al trabajo, se quedarían. **e** Si no estuviera ocupado, los recibiría. **f** Si él hablara bien español, ella le entendería.

2 a Tuve que vender el piso. **b** Tenía que decirte algo importante. **c** No hay nada que hacer. **d** Debo llevar el pasaporte. **e** Necesitaba comprar una maleta. **f** Habrá que traer algo para beber.

3 a Quisiera comprar unos pantalones. ¿Tiene algunos de oferta? No quiero gastar demasiado. **b** Sí, son para mí. Busco algo (que sea) de buena calidad. **c** Sí, son muy bonitos. Me gustan mucho. ¿Los tiene en negro? **d** Tengo la talla 46. ¿Tiene algunos en esa talla? **e** Quisiera probármelos. ¿Dónde está el probador? **f** Me quedan muy bien. ¿Cuánto cuestan? **g** Son un poco caros, pero me gustan. Me los quedo. ¿Aceptan tarjetas de crédito? No llevo dinero.

4 Dear Pat, How nice to get another email from you! I'm glad you're well and I hope you do very well in your final exams. Thank you very much for your invitation for this summer, but unfortunately I don't have enough money to travel. If I could, I would certainly come and see you. You don't know how much I'd like that! Maybe next year, but I'll have to work very hard in order to save money as the trip is very expensive. You will have to come to Venezuela too, some day. There's no need to wait for a formal invitation. I'll be waiting for you. Love, Raúl.

5 a Luis. **b** Raquel. **c** Ana. **d** Raquel. **e** Ana. **f** Luis.

6 a Luis. **b** Ana. **c** Luis. **d** Raquel. **e** Ana.

7 a Cuando necesita algo con urgencia. **b** Cuando necesita varias cosas, porque pierde menos tiempo, hay más variedad, y no resulta más caro. **c** En el supermercado.

8 1 F. **2** V. **3** F.

9 a que / tienda / trato / personal / puedo / semana / trabajo / por / salgo / cerradas / veces / al / hora / comprar. **b** No, his wife does that. Sometimes he accompanies her, but normally he hasn't got time. They have a small supermarket in the area where they buy almost everything. Except for fruit and vegetables, which they buy at the market: it is cheaper and fresher.

10 Tourist apartments – The following services are included in the price of accommodation: water, electricity and gas, rubbish collection and service charges. / When making your reservation, you may be asked to pay a deposit of 15 to 40% of the total price agreed. / If you decide to cancel your reservation, you are entitled to a refund of the deposit, minus a deduction of 5 to 50%, depending on how much notice is given. If the cancellation is made less than seven days in advance, there is no refund.

11 a lista. **b** vacío. **c** tentación. **d** precio. **e** estantes. **f** vergüenza. **g** bolsillo. **h** gastos.

12 a presupuesto. **b** alimentos. **c** gran almacén. **d** de oferta. **e** cajero/a. **f** dependiente/a. **g** la pareja.

Test yourself
1 a 6. **b** 3. **c** 5. **d** 1. **e** 2. **f** 4.
2 a 3. **b** 5. **c** 6. **d** 1. **e** 2. **f** 4.

UNIT 10

Conversation 1
1 Up to two weeks. She asks to see him again in a fortnight if there is no improvement.
2 a Tengo hora. **b** Me caí y me torcí un tobillo. **c** ¿Le duele aquí? **d** La pierna derecha. **e** Me duele mucho. **f** Lo tengo hinchado. **g** Vuelva a verme. **h** No creo que sea necesario.

Conversation 2

1 They won't be able to play tennis together.
2 a 3. **b** 4. **c** 5. **d** 6. **e** 1. **f** 7. **g** 2.

New expressions

Me duele la espalda. Me duelen los brazos. Tengo dolor de/Me duele el estómago. Estoy constipado/a.

Language discovery

1 a The doctor helped her patients (that's what she always did). **b** The doctor was helping her patients (that's what she was doing at that precise time). **c** I work as a nurse in a clinic (that's my permanent job). **d** I work as a male nurse in a clinic (perhaps just for the time being). **2** No, it's the speaker's choice. In conversation native speakers will often choose the option that is quickest to say. **3 a** trayendo. **b** yendo. **c** viniendo. **d** pudiendo. **4 a** Me pidió que fuera a la farmacia. **b** Me pidió que le comprara unas pastillas para la tos.

Practice

1 a Estaba durmiendo. **b** Estaba haciendo yoga. **c** Estaba meditando. **d** Estaba leyendo. **e** Estábamos preparando la cena. **f** Estaba viendo el fútbol en la tele.
2 a Me dijo que volviera mañana. **b** Me aconsejó que descansara un poco. **c** Nos recomendó que no fumáramos mucho. **d** El doctor quiere que haga más ejercicio. **e** Rosa nos pidió que llegáramos/llegásemos a la hora. **f** Mi mujer no quiere que trabaje tanto.
3 a Quisiera algo para el dolor de estómago. **b** Sí, también tengo diarrea. Comí pescado anoche y después empecé a sentirme mal. **c** Gracias. ¿Cuánto es?
4 Me dio unas pastillas. Me dijo que tomara dos, tres veces al día hasta que me sintiera mejor. También me aconsejó que tuviera cuidado con la alimentación y que no comiera nada frito.
5 a Se quebró la pierna mientras jugaba / estaba jugando al fútbol, así que / de manera que no podrá jugar durante algún tiempo. **b** No me siento / encuentro bien. Tengo dolor de cabeza / Me duele la cabeza y tengo fiebre. **c** Dijo que no podría verme esta tarde. Tiene hora con el doctor a las cuatro. **d** El doctor me dijo que descansara y que volviera de aquí a / dentro de quince días si aún / todavía no me siento bien. **e** Llamó por teléfono a la oficina para decir que no va a venir a trabajar porque ha cogido una / tiene (la) gripe. **f** Se cayó y se torció el tobillo. Está hinchado y dice que le duele mucho.
6 comer / alimentos / productos / alimenticia / huevos / leguminosas / proteínas / mantenimiento / músculos.
7 Hola, ¿cómo te has sentido? / ¿Y qué te dijo? / ¡Hombre! Lo siento. / No muy bien, aún no se me pasa el dolor. Ayer por la tarde fui al médico. / Me dijo que no está roto el tobillo. Me puso una venda y me dijo que tratara de no mover mucho el pie.
8 a In Andalusia and Levante. **b** Because the diet in these regions includes an excessive amount of proteins, animal fats and sugar. **c** In Madrid, the diet is balanced and healthy, better than in the capitals of other Spanish communities. **d** Breakfasts are light. **e** Because of their work. **f** The diet in Catalonia includes an excessive amount of proteins, fats and not many carbohydrates.

9 Por el contrario, es en la meseta central, norte y noroeste, donde el riesgo sanitario es más alto, pues se consume un exceso de proteínas, grasas animales y azúcares. La preocupación de los científicos es que España se contamine de la dieta continental, en vez de que los demás se contagien de la dieta mediterránea.

10 El comer cada vez con más frecuencia fuera de casa por razones laborales, sobre todo, es otra de las características de los cambios alimentarios de los madrileños. Madrid está siguiendo la tendencia de la Comunidad Europea, donde casi el 4 por ciento de la población activa realiza cinco almuerzos semanales fuera de casa.

11 Rosa's skin is too white and she easily gets sunburnt. Ignacio suffers from stomach upsets when on holiday. Claudia suffers from palpitations. Alejandro is working too hard and he fainted while working in the garden.

12 Rosa: **c** and **e**. Ignacio: **d** and **f**. Claudia: **b** and **h**. Alejandro: **a** and **g**.

Test yourself

1 a Me duele la cabeza. **b** Al niño le duele el estómago. **c** No me encuentro bien. **d** ¿Qué estabas diciendo? **e** Ángel estaba durmiendo plácidamente.

2 a Me dijo que dejara/dejase de fumar. **b** Me aconsejó que no se lo dijera/dijese a nadie. **c** Nos sugirieron que aprendiéramos/aprendiésemos español. **d** Me pidió que no siguiera/siguiese con la dieta. **e** Me recomendó que hiciera/hiciese algún deporte.

UNIT 11

Conversation 1

1 *Reasons*: People are always inclined to discover new places; Other countries have successfully promoted tourism to their shores; Many people want to travel to 'green ' places; The economic crisis has forced people to cut back on their leisure budget. *Remedies*: The beaches and the coastal waters would have to be cleaned up; There would need to be cost adjustments to make it cheaper for tourists to come to Spain; The level of services would have to improve too. (Note that these answers are in shorthand and not a literal translation of Sr. Riveros' replies.)

3 a V. **b** F. **c** V. **d** F. **e** F. **f** V.

4 a un par de años. **b** ¿A qué se debe? **c** por un lado. **d** Están gastando una buena cantidad de recursos. **e** por otro lado. **f** una situación pasajera.

Conversation 2

1 a Limit access to the city centre for private vehicles.

2 a Piensa que el tráfico en Madrid es insoportable. **b** Ella cree que se debería favorecer más al transporte público. **c** Madrid sería una ciudad más limpia y con menos ruido.

New expressions

Missing words: to know; I think; agree; I don't agree; would have to.

Translation: As far as I know, there is no solution to many environmental problems. One would have to rethink one's/It would take rethinking our way of life completely. In my opinion, the costs would be too high.

Language discovery

1 a Si (yo) hubiera/hubiese olvidado . . . **b** Si me lo hubieras/hubieses pedido . . . **c** Si tu amiga hubiera/hubiese insistido . . . **2 a** Si me hubieran/hubiesen llamado . . . **b** Si te hubieran/hubiesen gustado sus hermanas . . . **c** Si hubierais/hubieseis vuelto más temprano . . . **3 a** If only you'd told me! **b** It would have been better if you had lied to me.

Practice

1 a Si no hubiera perdido mi trabajo, habría / hubiera ido a España. **b** Si hubiéramos tenido dinero, habríamos / hubiéramos podido viajar. **c** Si no hubieran aumentado los precios, no habría / hubiera descendido el turismo. **d** Si hubieran encontrado plaza en el avión, no habrían / hubieran tenido que esperar otro vuelo. **e** Si Carlos no hubiera tenido un accidente, no habríamos/hubiéramos cancelado el viaje. **f** Si nos hubieran invitado a la fiesta, habríamos/hubiéramos ido.

2 a ¿Qué opina Vd. sobre/acerca de . . .? **b** Me parece que es . . . **c** ¿Cuál es su opinión sobre/acerca de . . .? **d** Creo que es . . . **e** La menor llegada de turistas se debe a . . . **f** También habría que . . . **g** ¿A qué se debe tanta . . .? **h** A mi parecer, este es . . . ¿No crees tú?

3 a Sí, estoy totalmente de acuerdo con eso. No debe permitirse que la gente fume en lugares públicos. Es un hecho muy conocido que muchas muertes se deben al tabaquismo. **b** Por supuesto. La publicidad del tabaco debería haberse prohibido hace mucho tiempo. Si se hubiera hecho antes se habrían evitado muchas muertes. También sería necesario educar a la gente, especialmente a los jóvenes para que no empiecen a fumar.

4 a True, human activity causes pollution which, in turn, damages the atmosphere.

5 a el efecto invernadero. **b** el calentamiento de la Tierra. **c** radiaciones ultravioleta. **d** las capas superiores de la atmósfera. **e** los patrones de lluvia cambiarían drásticamente. **f** el agujero en la capa de ozono.

6 a I do not believe that the human species can survive. **b** It would destroy the majority of life forms. **c** . . . which would affect crops and sea life. **d** The hole has been gradually growing. **e** The hole in the ozone layer over Antarctica is damaging the atmosphere.

8 a Its main purpose is to make people aware of the problems caused by noise pollution, and to get the authorities to establish legal rules which can give us a better quality of life. **b** Other than traffic noise, he mentions problems caused by neighbours who, with their radio and television too loud, bother other people. And bar and disco owners who, with their music at full volume, disturb people's sleep. **c** He says there is a lack of consideration which is not seen in other European capitals. **d** By establishing prohibitions and enforcing them by means of legislation.

9 a tome. **b** establezcan. **c** den. **d** dejan. **e** se ha hecho. **f** protestando, hacernos.

10 a La gran concentración humana; la excesiva centralización; el aumento constante en el número de automóviles. **b** OMS: 90 milígramos por metro cuadrado; Ciudad de México supera a veces los 300 milígramos. **c** 2 millones. **d** Intereses económicos; presiones políticas; el propio rechazo de muchos de los afectados. **e** Mejoras en el transporte público; restricción vehicular; cierre definitivo o temporal de las industrias más contaminantes.

Test yourself

1 a Si hubiera/hubiese tenido dinero, habría/hubiera salido . . . **b** Si hubieran/hubiesen llegado a la hora al aeropuerto, no habrían/hubieran perdido . . . **c** Si no hubiera/hubiese bebido en exceso, no habría/hubiera tenido . . . **d** Si hubieran/hubiesen tenido visado, habrían/hubieran podido . . . **e** Si no se hubiera/hubiese acostado tarde, habría/hubiera despertado a tiempo.

2 a ¿Cuál es su opinión? / ¿Qué opina/piensa usted? **b** En mi opinión . . . / A mi parecer . . . / A mi juicio . . . **c** ¿No cree usted que . . .? **d** ¿Está (usted) de acuerdo conmigo? **e** Estoy de acuerdo con usted. Esto se debe/obedece a . . .

UNIT 12

Conversation 1

1 a No, Pepe says that other European countries have gender equality issues, too. **b** He's probably older himself. When he talks about younger men helping around the house, Pepe says that is what he has observed.

2 to wash the dishes/do the washing up; to do the shopping; to look after the children.

3 a lavar la ropa. **b** pasar la aspiradora. **c** limpiar los cristales. **d** hacer la limpieza. **e** barrer el suelo. **f** bañar al bebé.

Conversation 2

1 They have become active members of the Spanish economy through work, and they have increased their access to education.

2 With more women in work, there has been a decrease in the national birth rate.

3 a More than half of secondary school pupils are women. **b** Women tend to choose studies which traditionally have been considered as appropriate for women. **c** There has been a notorious increase in the number of women. **d** On the one hand, there has been an increase in the female work force and a decrease in the male work force. However, unemployment has affected women more than men. **e** The female working population is younger than the male one. **f** The average number of children per woman has gone down.

4 a A mí me parece que aquí aún existen fuertes desajustes que es necesario rectificar. **b** Ha habido un crecimiento de la población activa femenina, frente a una reducción de la masculina. **c** No obstante, el paro ha afectado más a la mujer que al hombre. **d** Probablemente seguirá descendiendo. **e** No se han preocupado lo suficiente de los problemas que afectan a la población femenina.

New expressions

1 a mientras que. **b** En comparación con. **c** menos que. **2 a** aunque. **b** poco probable. **c** sin embargo.

Language discovery

1 a el menos conocido. **b** las mejores condiciones. **c** la hija menor. **d** el peor trato. **2 a** pero. **b** sino. **c** sino. **d** pero. **3 a** está. **b** sea. **c** me siento.

Practice

1 a Ella era mejor que él, y a pesar de/pese a eso no consiguió/obtuvo el trabajo. **b** Aunque Carlos es mayor que Sofía, se llevan muy bien. **c** María había vivido en los Estados Unidos durante varios años, sin embargo su inglés no era tan bueno como el de su hermano.
d No habían vivido en Madrid, sino en Barcelona, aunque habían estado aquí más de una vez. **e** A pesar de/Pese a ser más joven, no es tan activo como los demás/otros. **f** Iremos de vacaciones, aunque tengamos que pedir dinero prestado.

2 a 8. **b** 2. **c** 9. **d** 7. **e** 1. **f** 4. **g** 6. **h** 10. **i** 3. **j** 5.

3 a F. **b** F. **c** V. **d** F. **e** F. **f** V.

4 Carla's husband does not want her to go out to work. / sensación, razones, inseguridad, estatus, seria, actividad, apoyo, necesidad, cambio, horizontes.

5 b, c, e, f, g.

6 a Está desempleada. **b** Dar a luz. **c** De nuevo. **d** Los motivos. **e** Según. **f** Administrativa. **g** Pensárselo dos veces. **h** Es una pena.

Test yourself

1 a habían. **b** había. **c** habíamos. **d** como. **e** menor.
2 a sino. **b** aunque. **c** a pesar de. **d** sin embargo. **e** sino que.

¡A escuchar! transcripts

UNIT 1

01.05

Antonio	Hola, Pilar. ¿Cómo estás?
Pilar	Muy bien, ¿y tú?
Antonio	Bien, gracias. Ayer vi a María y me dijo que ya habías encontrado trabajo. Me alegro mucho. Estarás muy contenta, ¿no?
Pilar	Por supuesto. Estoy trabajando en un colegio cerca de casa. Es un colegio muy bueno, pero hay que trabajar muchísimo. Empiezo a las ocho de la mañana y no salgo hasta la una.
Antonio	Te levantas muy temprano, entonces.
Pilar	A las siete de la mañana. Por suerte está muy cerca de casa, y en quince minutos estoy allí.
Antonio	¿Y por la tarde no trabajas?
Pilar	Por ahora no, pero con lo del colegio tengo bastante que hacer. Por la tarde preparo las clases, a veces tengo reuniones con los padres o con otros profesores. ¡En fin! Me falta tiempo para hacer todo lo que quisiera. Pero tenemos que vernos uno de estos días.
Antonio	Sí, por supuesto. No trabajas los sábados, ¿verdad?
Pilar	No, los sábados estoy libre.
Antonio	Bueno, ¿por qué no me acompañas a comprar un regalo el sábado por la mañana? Mi hermana está de cumpleaños y no sé qué regalarle.
Pilar	De acuerdo. ¿A qué hora?
Antonio	¿A las once te parece bien?
Pilar	Sí, está bien.
Antonio	Bueno, pasaré a buscarte a esa hora. Hasta el sábado, entonces.
Pilar	¡Chao!

UNIT 2

02.04

Gran asistencia de público ha tenido la exposición de arte latinoamericano que se está realizando en Madrid, en el Museo Español de Arte Contemporáneo. Los asistentes podrán apreciar más de ochenta obras de los más connotados pintores iberoamericanos, provenientes de los principales países de la región, entre ellos México, Colombia, Argentina y Chile. La exposición, que fue inaugurada por la Reina Sofía, ha contado también con la presencia de importantes personajes del mundo artístico, tanto español como iberoamericano.

02.05

El viernes 25 se dará comienzo a un nuevo ciclo del Festival de Otoño de Madrid, que incluirá teatro, danza clásica y contemporánea, música clásica, y otras actividades, tales como cine, conferencias, coloquios y exposiciones. El Festival de este año dedicará una especial atención a los países de Europa del Este, en cada uno de los campos artísticos, en especial la danza y la música.

Este acontecimiento cultural servirá para mostrar aquellos espectáculos y creaciones que no se pueden contemplar habitualmente en los escenarios madrileños.

UNIT 3

María del Carmen Salas

03.04

Periodista	¿Cómo te llamas?
M. del Carmen	Me llamo María del Carmen Salas.
Periodista	¿Cuántos años tienes?
M. del Carmen	Tengo 38 años.
Periodista	¿Podrías decirme a qué te dedicas?
M. del Carmen	Soy periodista. Trabajo en la revista Claudia. Es una revista femenina que se publica en Madrid una vez por semana.
Periodista	¿Tienes alguna responsabilidad especial dentro de la revista?
M. del Carmen	Bueno, la revista tiene varias secciones especializadas y yo estoy a cargo de la sección Salud. Escribo artículos relacionados con el tema de la salud, que sean de especial interés para la mujer. Además, realizo entrevistas con médicos y otros profesionales que tengan que ver con el tema.
Periodista	¿Qué es lo que más te agrada de tu profesión?
M. del Carmen	Pues, principalmente el contacto con la gente, el trabajo en terreno, salir a hacer entrevistas, también el contacto con las lectoras a través de correspondencia. Creo que eso es lo que más me agrada. Además, esta es una actividad muy creativa, hay que saber usar la imaginación y hacer cosas diferentes para satisfacer a la mayoría de las lectoras.
Periodista	¿Hay algo que no te guste de tu trabajo?
M. del Carmen	Que no me guste, no, pero debo confesar que es una profesión que exige mucha dedicación, hay que estar dispuesta a aceptar críticas, ya que las lectoras son muy exigentes, y hay que renovarse constantemente. Y eso no es nada fácil.

Javier Molina

03.05

Periodista	¿Cómo te llamas?
J. Molina	Me llamo Javier Molina Sánchez.
Periodista	¿Qué edad tienes, Javier?
J. Molina	Tengo 29 años.
Periodista	¿En qué trabajas?
J. Molina	Soy funcionario de la Oficina de Turismo de Alicante.
Periodista	¿Llevas mucho tiempo trabajando allí?
J. Molina	Trabajo allí desde hace cinco años.
Periodista	¿Dónde trabajabas antes?
J. Molina	En Madrid. Trabajaba en una empresa privada, pero no ganaba lo suficiente y decidí cambiarme. Tuve suerte al encontrar un puesto aquí. Ahora tengo un trabajo seguro y para toda la vida. Al menos así lo espero. Y el sueldo no está nada mal. Por otra parte, Alicante es una ciudad muy agradable para vivir, es un lugar tranquilo. Y la propiedad aquí está más barata que en Madrid. Así he podido comprarme un pequeño piso. En Madrid ahora es imposible. ¡Con esos precios!
Periodista	¿En qué consiste tu trabajo específicamente?
J. Molina	Pues, principalmente en dar información al público. A Alicante vienen muchísimos turistas, muchos ingleses, alemanes . . . Muchos no hablan castellano y yo sé inglés y algo de alemán también. La mayoría viene a pedir información sobre hoteles y sobre sitios de interés en la región. Es una región muy bonita y el clima es estupendo.

UNIT 4

04.04

Pregunta	Gloria, me gustaría que hablásemos un poco acerca del tema de la educación y de tu propia experiencia como estudiante. Seguramente tendrás muchos recuerdos de aquella época. Después de todo eres muy joven y no te habrás olvidado aún, ¿verdad? ¿Cuándo dejaste el colegio?
Respuesta	Hace casi dos años. Tengo muchos recuerdos agradables del colegio. Fue una época muy feliz de mi vida.
Pregunta	¿Dónde hiciste tus estudios?
Respuesta	En un colegio religioso de La Coruña. Era un colegio solo para chicas. La verdad es que me habría gustado ir a un colegio donde hubiese habido chicos, pero vamos, mis padres quisieron que fuese allí y no estuvo nada mal. Por el contrario, disfruté muchísimo e hice excelentes amigas allí.
Pregunta	En pocas palabras, ¿cómo describirías el colegio donde fuiste?
Respuesta	Pues, era bastante bueno. Los profesores eran muy estrictos y nos hacían trabajar mucho. En general, guardo un buen recuerdo de ellos. Había

excepciones, claro, como es normal. La profesora de matemáticas, por ejemplo, no me gustaba nada. No tenía sentido del humor y nos llevábamos muy mal. En cambio, con otros no. La profesora de historia era una persona simpatiquísima y mis relaciones con ella fueron siempre estupendas.

Pregunta ¿Fuiste una buena estudiante?

Respuesta Ni buena ni mala. Dependía de la asignatura. Había asignaturas que me gustaban mucho y otras que simplemente no me gustaban. En historia y en inglés, por ejemplo, nunca tuve problemas. Eran mis asignaturas favoritas y estudiaba muchísimo. En cambio, en matemáticas y ciencias me iba bastante mal y más de una vez suspendí.

Pregunta ¿Y a qué te dedicas ahora?

Respuesta Estudio en una escuela de traductores e intérpretes.

UNIT 5

El tiempo

05.06

Nublado con lloviznas y temperaturas extremas probables de once la mínima y veintitrés grados la máxima anunció para hoy en Santiago la Dirección Meteorológica de Chile. Las temperaturas extremas de ayer en la capital fueron trece grados, una décima (13,1), la mínima, a las ocho de la mañana y veintiséis grados, ocho décimas (26,8), la máxima, a las quince horas y treinta minutos (15,30). Perspectivas para mañana viernes veintiuno de febrero en el área metropolitana, nubosidad parcial variando a despejado. Temperatura del momento, catorce grados, siete décimas (14,7) con una humedad relativa de un ochenta y siete por ciento (87 %).

Ocho de la mañana, dieciséis minutos (8,16). Hasta aquí las informaciones. Por su atención muchas gracias y buenos días.

UNIT 6

Un nuevo piso

06.05

Soledad	Hola, ¿qué hay?
Pablo	Hola.
Soledad	¿Y cómo os ha ido con la búsqueda de piso? ¿Habéis encontrado algo?
Pablo	Pues sí, por fin hemos encontrado lo que buscábamos. No sabes lo difícil que ha sido.
Soledad	¡Hombre!, me alegro. ¿Y qué tal está?
Pablo	Pues, no está nada mal. Está a unos quince minutos en autobús de la Plaza Mayor, en la calle Conde de Villaseca. ¿La conoces?
Soledad	Sí, sí, por allí vive mi hermana. Es un barrio bastante bueno y muy tranquilo.

Pablo	Y el piso es bastante grande. Tiene tres habitaciones, mucho sol y una vista estupenda. Desde allí se puede ver el río.
Soledad	¡Qué maravilla! Y de precio, ¿qué tal?
Pablo	Un poco caro, setecientos ochenta euros al mes, pero vamos . . ., somos tres, doscientos sesenta cada uno, que tampoco es demasiado. ¿No te parece?
Soledad	Está bien. Yo estoy pagando sobre quinientos. ¿Os habéis mudado ya?
Pablo	No, todavía no, pero lo haremos este fin de semana. Tendrás que venir a vernos.
Soledad	Por supuesto.

Hotel O'Higgins

06.06

Hotel O'Higgins de Viña del Mar le ofrece un fin de semana grande con precios para chicos. Dos noches, tres días, para dos adultos y hasta dos niños menores de doce años sin costo en la misma habitación por solo treinta y cinco mil pesos. Incluye desayuno e impuesto. Además, sus niños disfrutarán del plan familiar del Hotel O'Higgins donde personal especializado realiza actividades y entretenciones para que usted pueda tomar un merecido descanso. Reservas en Santiago, teléfonos 713165 y 696 6826.

UNIT 7

En viaje al aeropuerto

07.08

Conductor	Perdone, ¿la carretera para el aeropuerto, por favor?
Guardia	Sí, mire, siga Vd. todo recto hasta el segundo semáforo y allí doble Vd. a la izquierda y continúe por esa calle hasta el final. Allí encontrará Vd. la carretera. Para ir al aeropuerto tiene que torcer a la derecha.
Conductor	Muchas gracias.
Guardia	De nada.

Buscando la oficina de turismo

07.09

Turista	Por favor, ¿sabe Vd. dónde está la oficina de turismo
Transeúnte	Pues, está un poco lejos de aquí, pero puede ir en el metro. Coja Vd. la línea 1 hasta la estación de La Unión. Al salir de la estación verá Vd. el Museo de Arte Moderno. La oficina de turismo está detrás del museo, en la calle Libertad.
Turista	Gracias.

UNIT 8

a ¡Dígalo por la PR!

08.07

¡Dígalo por la PR!. Un espacio que hemos dedicado para que usted exponga sus comentarios y sus quejas. ¡Dígalo por la PR: el sistema de contestación automático que opera durante las 24 horas para que Vd. pueda ser escuchado. Llame ahora mismo al 31 45 45 y ¡dígalo por la PR! La Romántica, XHPR 101.3 MHz, transmitiendo las 24 horas del día desde Veracruz.

b ¡Quejas y más quejas!

08.07

1 ¿Oiga? ¿Quiere Vd. enviar a la camarera a la habitación 320, por favor? Le he pedido que me traiga toallas limpias. Esto fue hace más de una hora y todavía estoy esperando. Las necesito ahora mismo.

2 Vd. es el jefe, ¿verdad? Mire, he traído el coche a reparar y vea Vd. el estado en que lo han dejado. Está peor que antes. El trabajo que han hecho no vale nada. Esta es la última vez que traigo el coche aquí.

3 Perdone Vd., pero ¿a qué hora nos trae lo nuestro? Hemos pedido hace casi media hora. Tráiganos al menos el vino.

UNIT 9

a Rosario Santos

09.05

Periodista	¿Compra Vd. normalmente en grandes almacenes como éstos o prefiere comprar en una tienda pequeña?
Rosario	Bueno . . ., la verdad es que eso depende . . . Hombre, si se trata de una cosa que necesito con urgencia, la compro en cualquier tienda de mi barrio, pero cuando tengo que comprar varias cosas, prefiero venir aquí. Así no tengo que andar de un lado para otro. Vamos, que a veces se pierde mucho tiempo. Además, mire Vd., aquí hay más variedad y si va Vd. a una tienda pequeña del barrio muchas veces no encuentra lo que busca o es más caro.
Periodista	¿Y los comestibles dónde los suele comprar?
Rosario	Pues, normalmente voy al supermercado. Hay uno cerca de casa y allí hago la compra para toda la semana. Así me resulta más barato y más cómodo. Vamos, yo sé que hay gente que va todos los días a comprar una o dos cosas, luego se ponen a charlar con las vecinas, a cotillear y qué sé yo. Yo no, señor, eso no, que en casa hay muchísimo que hacer.

b Ana Belmar

09.06

Periodista	Ana, ¿tú compras normalmente en grandes tiendas como esta o en tiendas más pequeñas?
Ana	Bueno, hoy he venido aquí porque están de rebajas y, claro, hay que aprovechar. Pero, por lo general, prefiero ir a alguna tienda pequeña donde haya más cosas exclusivas, sobre todo tratándose de ropa. A veces pagas un poco más, pero te llevas algo que realmente te gusta.
Periodista	¿Te gusta vestir a la moda?
Ana	Vaya, sí, aunque no siempre puedo comprar lo que quisiera. Si trabajara, quizá sí, podría hacerlo, pero soy estudiante y el dinero me lo da mi padre.

c Andrés Calle

09.07

Periodista	Vd., señor, ¿suele comprar aquí, en una gran tienda o prefiere hacerlo en una tienda pequeña?
Andrés	Pues, lo cierto es que prefiero ir a una tienda más pequeña donde el trato sea más directo, más personal. Pero eso solo lo puedo hacer el fin de semana. Yo soy administrativo y trabajo por la mañana y por la tarde y cuando salgo, las tiendas ya están cerradas. Por eso vengo a veces aquí, pues está abierto al mediodía. Aprovecho la hora de la comida para comprar lo que necesito.
Periodista	¿Y la compra de comestibles la hace Vd. también?
Andrés	Pues no, de eso se encarga mi mujer. A veces la acompaño, pero normalmente no tengo tiempo. Pero, tenemos un pequeño supermercado en el barrio donde compramos casi todo. Excepto la fruta y las verduras, claro, eso se compra en el mercado. Es más barato, más fresco . . .

UNIT 10

a La dieta mediterránea

10.04

Presentador	Buenos días. Damos comienzo a un nuevo programa de la serie La buena mesa. En la primera parte del programa de hoy tenemos una invitada especial, la experta en nutrición Angélica Muñoz quien se referirá a los cambios que ha experimentado la dieta de los españoles.
Invitada	Buenos días. En primer lugar quisiera referirme a la llamada dieta mediterránea. Pues bien, la dieta mediterránea está de moda, aunque hasta hace poco no gozaba de muy buena reputación. Los médicos y nutriólogos han descubierto que en los países mediterráneos la incidencia de enfermedades cardiovasculares es mucho menor que en tierra adentro.

En España, las características de este tipo de alimentación se dan, sobre todo, en Andalucía y en el Levante. Allí, la base de la dieta es el pescado, las grasas vegetales y los vegetales que contienen gran cantidad de fibra.

Por el contrario, es en la meseta central, norte y noroeste, donde el riesgo sanitario es más alto, pues se consume un exceso de proteínas, grasas animales y azúcares. La preocupación de los científicos es que España se contamine de la dieta continental, en vez de que los demás se contagien de la dieta mediterránea.

Ahora, veamos lo que pasa en Madrid. La dieta de los madrileños es equilibrada y saludable, mejor que la del resto de capitales comunitarias.

No obstante, los madrileños toman menos verduras de las necesarias y demasiadas proteínas y sal. Como complemento, hay que decir que en Madrid se come poco pan y patatas y mucha fruta, leche y pescado.

¿Y qué hay de los desayunos? Pues, los desayunos que se toman los madrileños son ligeros y se advierte una tendencia a no cocinar por la noche en casa. Uno de cada cinco escolares no desayuna y muchos de los que lo hacen, consumen menos calorías de las aconsejables.

El comer cada vez con más frecuencia fuera de casa por razones laborales, sobre todo, es otra de las características de los cambios alimentarios de los madrileños. Madrid está siguiendo la tendencia de la Comunidad Europea, donde casi el 4 por ciento de la población activa realiza cinco almuerzos semanales fuera de casa.

Algo similar sucede en Cataluña. Los catalanes ingieren demasiadas proteínas y grasas y pocos hidratos de carbono . . .

b Dictado note taking (1)

10.05

Por el contrario, es en la meseta central, norte y noroeste, donde el riesgo sanitario es más alto, pues se consume un exceso de proteínas, grasas animales y azúcares. La preocupación de los científicos es que España se contamine de la dieta continental, en vez de que los demás se contagien de la dieta mediterránea.

b Dictado note taking (2)

10.06

El comer cada vez con más frecuencia fuera de casa por razones laborales, sobre todo, es otra de las características de los cambios alimentarios de los madrileños. Madrid está siguiendo la tendencia de la Comunidad Europea, donde casi el 4 por ciento de la población activa, realiza cinco almuerzos semanales fuera de casa.

UNIT 11

11.06

Periodista	¡Ya era hora! Este verano, un gran número de madrileños ha comenzado a protestar por el ruido que hacen otros españoles. En una entrevista, preguntamos la opinión de Antonio García, quien dirige el grupo 'Por una ciudad más tranquila'.
Antonio	Pues, el propósito principal es hacer que la gente tome conciencia sobre los problemas causados por la contaminación acústica, y conseguir que las autoridades establezcan normas legales que nos den una mejor calidad de vida. Y no me refiero solo al ruido causado por el tráfico. También están los propios vecinos, que con su radio o televisión demasiado altos molestan a los demás, así como los propietarios de terrazas y discos, que con su música a todo volumen y a toda hora no nos dejan dormir por la noche. En fin, existe una desconsideración hacia el resto de las personas que no se observa en otras capitales europeas. En ciertos barrios de Madrid la vida se ha hecho insoportable y el nivel de estrés va en aumento.
Periodista	¿Crees tú que la acción de este grupo pueda conseguir su objetivo?
Antonio	Vamos . . . sabemos que no será fácil y que no basta con hacer una campaña al respecto. Simplemente hay que establecer prohibiciones y hacerlas cumplir mediante una legislación. Mientras tanto seguiremos protestando hasta hacernos oír.

UNIT 12

12.05

Pregunta	Teresa, tú y Paco os habéis casado hace muy poco tiempo, ¿verdad?
Teresa	Sí, hace poco más de un año.
Pregunta	Y ambos sois profesionales, ¿no es así?
Teresa	Sí, Paco es arquitecto y yo soy psicóloga.
Pregunta	¿Y cómo os arregláis con las tareas del hogar? Con la limpieza, la cocina, la compra, y todas aquellas tareas que hay en toda casa y que no se pueden eludir. ¿Quién las hace? ¿Tenéis a alguien que os ayude?
Teresa	Pues, tenemos una asistenta que viene dos veces por semana a limpiar el piso y a planchar, pero todo lo demás lo hacemos Paco y yo. La compra la hago yo, pues salgo antes del trabajo y camino de casa, paso por el supermercado. En cambio, Paco, que cocina mucho mejor que yo, se encarga de guisar. Los fines de semana lo hacemos juntos, pero vamos, a él le encanta la cocina y a mí no. Pero yo soy la que friega los platos.
Pregunta	¿Son labores compartidas, entonces?
Teresa	Totalmente. De otra manera, quizá no funcionaríamos bien como pareja. Me molestaría tener que encargarme yo de todo. En cambio así, las cosas marchan muy bien y no hay ningún tipo de resentimiento. Por el contrario, Paco y yo tenemos una excelente relación.
Pregunta	¿Y cuando vengan los hijos?
Teresa	Pues, probablemente tendremos que hacer ciertos ajustes, pero fundamentalmente, no creo que las cosas vayan a cambiar.
Pregunta	¿Sois una pareja feliz, entonces?
Teresa	Sin duda.

Irregular verbs

The following list includes only the most common irregular verbs. Only irregular forms are given (verbs marked with an asterisk* are also stem- or radical-changing).

Pluperfect subjunctive forms, which are derived from the third person plural of the preterite tense, are not included.

abrir to open

past participle: abierto

andar to walk

preterite: anduve, anduviste, anduvo, anduvimos, anduvisteis, anduvieron

conducir to drive

present indicative: (yo) conduzco

present subjunctive: conduzca, conduzcas, conduzca, conduzcamos, conduzcáis, conduzcan

preterite: conduje, condujiste, condujo, condujimos, condujisteis, condujeron

dar to give

present indicative: (yo) doy

preterite: di, diste, dio, dimos, disteis, dieron

present subjunctive: dé, des, dé, demos, deis, den

decir* to say

present indicative: (yo) digo
present subjunctive: diga, digas, diga, digamos, digáis, digan

preterite: dije, dijiste, dijo, dijimos, dijisteis, dijeron

future: diré, dirás, dirá, diremos, diréis, dirán

conditional: diría, dirías, diría, diríamos, diríais, dirían

imperative (familiar, singular): di (formal, singular): diga

gerund: diciendo

past participle: dicho

escribir to write

past participle: escrito

estar to be

present indicative: estoy, estás, está, estamos, estáis, están

present subjunctive: esté, estés, esté, estemos, estéis, estén

preterite: estuve, estuviste, estuvo, estuvimos, estuvisteis, estuvieron

imperative (familiar, singular): está

hacer to do, make

present indicative: (yo) hago present subjunctive: haga, hagas, haga, hagamos, hagáis, hagan

preterite: hice, hiciste, hizo, hicimos, hicisteis, hicieron

future: haré, harás, hará, haremos, haréis, harán

conditional: haría, harías, haría, haríamos, haríais, harían

imperative: (Vd.) haga, (tú) haz

past participle: hecho

ir to go

present indicative: voy, vas, va, vamos, vais, van

present subjunctive: vaya, vayas, vaya, vayamos, vayáis, vayan

imperfect: iba, ibas, iba, íbamos, ibais, iban

preterite: fui, fuiste, fue, fuimos, fuisteis, fueron

imperative: (Vd.) vaya, (tú) ve

gerund: yendo

leer to read

preterite: (él, ella, Vd.) leyó, (ellos, ellas, Vds.) leyeron

gerund: leyendo

oír to hear

present indicative: oigo, oyes, oye, oímos, oís, oyen

present subjunctive: oiga, oigas, oiga, oigamos, oigáis, oigan

preterite: (él, ella, Vd.) oyó, (ellos, ellas, Vds.) oyeron

imperative: (Vd.) oiga, (tú) oye

gerund: oyendo

poder* to be able to, can

preterite: pude, pudiste, pudo, pudimos, pudisteis, pudieron

future: podré, podrás, podrá, podremos, podréis, podrán

conditional: podría, podrías, podría, podríamos, podríais, podrían

poner to put

present indicative: (yo) pongo

present subjunctive: ponga, pongas, ponga, pongamos, pongáis, pongan

preterite: puse, pusiste, puso, pusimos, pusisteis, pusieron

future: pondré, pondrás, pondrá, pondremos, pondréis, pondrán

conditional: pondría, pondrías, pondría, pondríamos, pondríais, pondrían *imperative:* (Vd.) ponga, (tú) pon

past participle: puesto

querer* to want, love

preterite: quise, quisiste, quiso, quisimos, quisisteis, quisieron

future: querré, querrás, querrá, querremos, querréis, querrán

conditional: querría, querrías, querría, querríamos, querríais, querrían

saber to know

present indicative: (yo) sé

present subjunctive: sepa, sepas, sepa, sepamos, sepáis, sepan

preterite: supe, supiste, supo, supimos, supisteis, supieron

future: sabré, sabrás, sabrá, sabremos, sabréis, sabrán

conditional: sabría, sabrías, sabría, sabríamos, sabríais, sabrían

imperative: (Vd.) sepa

salir to go out

present indicative: (yo) salgo

present subjunctive: salga, salgas, salga, salgamos, salgáis, salgan

future: saldré, saldrás, saldrá, saldremos, saldréis, saldrán

conditional: saldría, saldrías, saldría, saldríamos, saldríais, saldrían

imperative: (Vd.) salga, (tú) sal

ser to be

present indicative: soy, eres, es, somos, sois, son

present subjunctive: sea, seas, sea, seamos, seáis, sean

preterite: fui, fuiste, fue, fuimos, fuisteis, fueron

imperfect indicative: era, eras, era, éramos, erais, eran

imperative: (Vd.) sea, (tú) sé

tener* to have

present indicative: (yo) tengo

present subjunctive: tenga, tengas, tenga, tengamos, tengáis, tengan

preterite: tuve, tuviste, tuvo, tuvimos, tuvisteis, tuvieron

future: tendré, tendrás, tendrá, tendremos, tendréis, tendrán

conditional: tendría, tendrías, tendría, tendríamos, tendríais, tendrían

imperative: (Vd.) tenga, (tú) ten

traer to bring

present indicative: (yo) traigo

present subjunctive: traiga, traigas, traiga, traigamos, traigáis, traigan

preterite: traje, trajiste, trajo, trajimos, trajisteis, trajeron

imperative: (Vd.) traiga

gerund: trayendo

venir* to come

present indicative: (yo) vengo

present subjunctive: venga, vengas, venga, vengamos, vengáis, vengan

preterite: vine, viniste, vino, vinimos, vinisteis, vinieron

future: vendré, vendrás, vendrá, vendremos, vendréis, vendrán

conditional: vendría, vendrías, vendría, vendríamos, vendríais, vendrían

imperative: (Vd.) venga, (tú) ven

gerund: viniendo

ver to see

present indicative: (yo) veo

present subjunctive: vea, veas, vea, veamos, veáis, vean

imperfect indicative: veía, veías, veía, veíamos, veíais, veían

imperative: (Vd.) vea

past participle: visto

volver* to come back

past participle: vuelto

Spanish–English vocabulary

Words already listed in each unit have not been included in this vocabulary. Basic vocabulary and grammatical words have also been omitted.

a lo mejor *perhaps*
abierto/a *open*
abogado/a *lawyer*
abrirse *to open up*
aburrido *boring*
aburrido/a *bored*
acabar de (v) *to have just finished*
acceder *to have access*
acerca de *about*
además *besides*
administrativo/a *office worker*
adquirir *to acquire, obtain*
afección (f) *illness*
aficionado/a a *fond of*
agencia de empleos (f) *employment agency*
agenda (f) *diary*
agradar *to please*
agradecer *to be grateful*
ahorrar *to save*
ajedrez (m) *chess*
ajustar *to adjust*
alcanzar *to reach*
alegrarse *to rejoice*
alegría (f) *joy*
algodón (m) *cotton*
alimentación (f) *food*
almacén (m) *supermarket*
alojamiento (m) *accommodation*
alquilar *to rent, hire*
alumno/a *student*
amenaza (f) *threat*
amistades (f pl) *friends*
ampliamente *fully*
ampliar *to expand*

amplio/a *varied, wide*
antecedentes (m pl) *background*
anuncio (m) *advertisement, announcement*
apagar *to turn off*
aparcamiento (m) *car park*
apartado postal (m) *P. O. box*
apestar *to stink*
aplicar *to apply*
aplicarse una ducha *to take a shower*
aprender *to learn*
aprovechar *to take advantage of*
apuntar *to point to; jot down*
arreglarse *to get ready, dress up*
arruinarse *to ruin, go bankrupt*
artículos electrodomésticos (m pl) *electrical household appliances*
ascensor (m) *lift*
asegurar *to assure*
asépticamente *aseptically*
así *so, thus*
asignar *to allocate (funds), assign*
asimismo *likewise*
asistencia (f) *attendance*
asistir *to attend*
asombro (m) *surprise*
asumir *to assume, take on*
atajar *to stop from spreading*
atender *to look after*
atraer *to attract*
aumento (m) *increase*
aunque *although*
ausencia (f) *absence*
avance (m) *progress*
ayudar *to help*

bajarse *to get off*
bañador (m) *swimming costume*
barrio (m) *area, neighbourhood*
barroco/a *baroque*
basura (f) *rubbish*
boletín (m) *form*
bonificado/a *subsidized*
brevemente *briefly*
bronceador (m) *sun cream*
bruto/a *gross*
buscador/ra *hunter (treasure)*
buscar *to look for*
búsqueda (f) *search*
buzón de vacaciones *P. O. box (during holidays)*
cabe: no – duda *there is no doubt*
cabello (m) *hair*
cajero automático (m) *cash point*
calidad (f) *quality*
callarse *to be quiet, to hush*
camino (m) *road*
campo (m) *field*
campo de fútbol (m) *football pitch*
cansado/a *tired*
capa de ozono (f) *ozone layer*
capaz *capable*
cargamento (m) *cargo*
cargo (m) *post, charge*
carrera (f) *career*
carretera (f) *main road*
carta (f) *letter*
casamiento (m) *marriage*
caseta (f) *kiosk*
casi *almost*
cayo (m) *cay (geography)*
celos (m pl) *jealousy*
cercano *nearby*
certificado (m) *registered*
charlar *to chat*
chófer (m) *driver*
ciencias aplicadas (f pl) *applied sciences*
cifra (f) *figure*
ciudadano/a *citizen*
clave (f) *user password, PIN number*
cobrar *to charge*
cocina (f) *cuisine*
código (m) *access code*
coger *to take (transport)*
colega (m/f) *colleague*
colocado/a *placed*
comienzo (m) *beginning*
comodidad (f) *comfort*
compartir *to share*
concepto: en – de *by way of*

conducir *to drive*
conductor/a *driver*
confección (f) *preparation*
conseguir *to get*
consignado/a *recorded*
construir *to build*
consultorio (m) *clinic*
consumidor (m) *consumer*
contabilidad (f) *accountancy*
contagiarse *to contaminate, infect*
contaminación (f) *pollution*
contar *to tell*
contestación (f) *answer*
contratado/a *agreed*
contribuyente (m/f) *contributor*
convenir *to be convenient*
convivir *to live together*
corroborar *to corroborate*
correo (m) *email address*
criar *to raise, bring up*
cuenta corriente (f) *checking account*
cuidar *to look after*
culpable (m/f) *guilty*
cumplir (años/meses) *to be (years/months) old*
cumplir un horario *to comply with a timetable*
dañar *to damage*
dañino/a *damaging*
dar un paseo *to go for a walk*
dato (m) *information*
de hecho *in fact*
de igual modo *likewise*
deber (m) *duty*
deberse *to be due to*
decir: es – *that is to say*
dedicarse a *to do*
dejar *to let*
dejar claro *to reveal*
demasiado (adv) *too much*
deporte (m) *sport*
deportivo/a (adj) *sporty*
desafío (m) *challenge*
desajuste (m) *imbalance*
desarrollar *to develop*
descanso (m) *rest*
descrito/a *described*
descubrir *to discover*
descontar *to deduct*
desgraciadamente *unfortunately*
desigual *unequal*
desocupado/a *free, unoccupied*
despacho (m) *office, study, dispatch, sending*
despejado/a *clear, cloudless*
desplazarse *to travel*

destinatario/a *addressee*
detallado/a *detailed*
deterioro (m) *deterioration*
devolución (f) *refund*
devolver *to return (merchandise)*
diario/a (adj) *daily*
dibujos animados (m pl) *cartoons*
dictar *to dictate*
dirigir *to lead*
dirigirse *to go, address*
disfrutar *to enjoy*
disminución (f) *decrease*
dispensario (m) *clinic*
disponible *available*
domiciliario/a (adj) *home*
dominar *to master*
dotado/a *equipped*
duda (f) *doubt*
dudar *to doubt, hesitate*
duplicarse *to double*
edad (f) *age*
edad escolar (f) *school age*
edificio (m) *building*
efectivo/a *cash;* en – *in cash*
efecto invernadero (m) *greenhouse effect*
efectuar *to do, carry out*
elegir *to choose*
embarcarse *to board*
empresa (f) *company, firm*
empresario/a *entrepreneur*
en línea *online*
enseguida *immediately*
encargarse de *to be responsible for*
encuesta (f) *survey*
enfermarse *to fall ill*
enfermedad (f) *illness*
enfrentar *to face*
enfrentarse a *to confront*
enhorabuena (f) *congratulations!*
enseñar *to show, teach*
entender *to understand*
entorno (m) *environment*
entregar *to give, hand in*
entrevistar *to interview*
envío (m) *correspondence, despatch*
envolver *to wrap up*
escoger *to choose*
escolares (m pl) *school children*
esconder *to hide*
escritor/a *writer*
escritura (f) *writing*
espalda (f) *back*
espantoso/a *dreadful*
especialista (m/f) *specialist*

esperanza (f) *hope*
esquina (f) *corner*
estacionario/a *stable*
estar de moda *to be in fashion*
estricto/a *strict*
estudio (n, m) *study*
estudios superiores (m pl) *higher education*
estupendo/a *wonderful*
etapa (f) *stage*
étnico/a *ethnic*
evitar *to avoid*
exigente *demanding*
éxito (m) *success*
expedito *quick, speedy*
exponer *to put forward*
extranjero (n, m) *foreigner, abroad*
extranjero/a (adj) *foreign*
extraño/a *stranger*
fabricante (m/f) *manufacturer*
fabricar *to manufacture*
facilitar *to provide*
factura (f) *receipt, invoice*
facultativo/a *optional*
falta (f) *lack*
faltar *to lack*
fallecer *to pass away, to die*
fallecido/a *the departed; the dead*
famoso/a *famous*
fatal *terrible*
favorecer *to favour*
ficha de inscripción (f) *registration form*
figurar *to appear*
fijar citas *fix appointments*
finalizar *to end*
folleto informativo (m) *information brochure*
formación (f) *training*
forzado/a *forced*
fregar los platos/los cacharros *to wash up, do the washing up*
frito/a *fried*
funcionar *to function, work*
gabinete (m) *section*
ganar *to earn, win*
gasto (m) *expense*
golpe (m) *coup*
graduado/a *graduate*
hacer falta *to be necessary*
hasta tal punto *to such a point*
hecho (m) *fact*
hogar (m) *home*
hora (f) *time, hour;* tener – *to have an appointment (with doctor, etc.)*
horario (m) *timetable, working hours*
hueco (m) *hole*

hundido/a *sunk*
idioma (m) *language*
impartir *to teach*
impedir *to prevent*
imponerse *to prevail*
importe (m) *cost, value*
impuesto (m) *tax*
inclinarse *to be inclined*
incluso *even*
índice (m) *rate*
infeliz *unhappy*
informática (f) *computing, computer science*
ingeniero/a *engineer*
ingresar *to insert, to key in*
inquietante *disturbing*
insoportable *unbearable*
intimidad (f) *privacy*
investigación (f) *research*
jefe/a *boss*
jet (f) *jet set* (Spain)
joyería (f) *jewellery*
jugador/a *player*
juguete (m) *toy*
juventud (f) *youth*
lamentablemente *regrettably*
lástima: ¡qué – ! *what a pity!*
leguminosa (f) *pulse*
lento/a *slow*
líder (m/f) *leading*
limpio/a *clean*
listado (m) *listing*
litoral (m) *coast*
llamada (f) *(telephone) call*
llevar a cabo *to carry out*
llevar *to bear, deliver*
llevarse bien/mal *to get on well/badly*
llover *to rain;* **– a cántaros** *to rain cats and dogs, pour (down)*
locutorio (m) *telephone exchange*
lograr *to achieve*
lucha (f) *struggle*
lugar (m) *place*
lujo *luxury*
malestar (m) *illness*
maleta (f) *suitcase*
malgastar *to misspend*
manera: de otra_ (f) *otherwise*
mano de obra (f) *labour*
maravilla (f) *wonder*
marcado/a *marked*
marchar *to go, leave*
marea (f) *tide*
mariachi (m) *band that plays popular Mexican music*

más bien *rather*
matricularse *to register, enrol*
matrimonio (m) *marriage*
mediante *through*
medida (f) *measure*
mejora (f) *improvement*
mejorar *to improve*
mentir *to lie*
mentira (f) *lie*
merecer la pena *to be worth it*
merecer *to deserve*
mesa (f) *table (food)*
método (m) *method*
microbús (m) *small bus*
miembro (m/f) *member*
mientras *whilst*
mismo: ahora – *right now*
modalidades (f pl) *facilities*
módico/a *moderate, reasonable*
modo: de igual – *likewise*
molestia (f) *trouble, inconvenience*
monto (m) *amount, sum*
mudarse *to move house*
mundo (m) *world*
músculo (m) *muscle*
muy señor mío *dear sir*
muy señora mía *dear madam*
nacimiento (m) *birth*
nada mal *not bad at all*
nadar *to swim*
natación (f) *swimming*
netamente *purely*
nevera (f) *fridge*
nivel (m) *level*
novio/a *boyfriend, girlfriend*
nuez (f) *nut*
nutriente (m) *nourishing food*
nutriólogo/a *dietitian*
obstante: no – *nevertheless*
obtención (f) *obtaining, securing*
ocio (m) *leisure*
ocurrir *to take place; to happen*
oferta (f) *offer;* **de –** *on offer*
ojalá *I hope so, let's hope so*
operador/a postal *postal worker*
ordenador (m) *computer*
orgullo (m) *pride*
padecer *to suffer*
página web (f) *website*
pantalla (f) *screen*
papel (m) *role*
paquetería (f) *parcel service*
paradero (m) *stop*
pareja (f) *couple*

paro (m) *unemployment*
particular *private*
partido político (m) *political party*
partir: a – de *from, starting*
pasajero/a *passing, temporary*
pasar a buscar *to pick up*
pasillo (m) *corridor*
paso subterráneo (m) *subway*
pastas (f pl) *small cakes*
pastilla (f) *pill*
paulatinamente *gradually*
pelea (f) *argument*
peletería (f) *furs*
película (f) *film*
pena: es una – *it's a pity*
pensión (f) *board, boarding house;* –
  completa *full board;* media – *half board*
peor: en el – de los casos *at worst*
perder el tiempo *to waste time*
perderse *to get lost*
pérdida (f) *loss*
periodista (m/f) *journalist*
permanencia (f) *stay*
permitido/a *allowed*
peruano/a *Peruvian*
pesar: a – de *in spite of*
petición: a – de *at the request of*
piel (f) *skin, leather*
piscina (f) *swimming pool*
piso (m) *floor, flat*
planear *to plan*
planta (f) *floor,* – baja/alta *ground/top floor*
plaza (f) *seat*
pleno *full*
pleno: en – centro *right in the centre*
población activa (f) *working population*
poner en conocimiento *to let know*
poner en marcha *to start up, move*
por el contrario *on the contrary*
por suerte *luckily*
por supuesto *of course*
potencia (f) *power*
precisar *to need*
predominio (m) *predominance*
prejuicio (m) *prejudice*
prever *to forsee*
probador (m) *fitting room*
promover *to promote*
propensión (f) *tendency*
propietario/a *owner*
proporcionar *to provide*
proteger *to protect*
proveniente *coming from*

puesto (m) *post*
puesto que *as*
quedar *to be left*
quedar: me lo/la quedo *I'll take it* (m/f)
queja (f) *complaint*
quejarse *to complain*
rastreado/a *tracked, traced*
rato (m) *moment; while*
recibir *to receive*
recibo (m) *receipt*
recogida (f) *from* recoger *(to pick up)*
recordar *to remember*
rectificar *to rectify*
recursos (m pl) *resources*
regalar *· to give a present*
reinstaurar *to restore, re-establish*
rellenar un impreso *to fill in a form*
remitente (m/f) *sender*
renovarse *to renew oneself*
repartir *to distribute*
reparto (m) *delivery*
resentimiento (m) *resentment*
respirar *to breathe*
restante *remaining*
resultar *to be*
retroceder *to go back*
revelar *to reveal*
revisar *to check*
revista (f) *magazine*
rivalizar *to rival*
rodeado/a *surrounded*
rogar *to pray; to beg*
roto/a *broken*
ruego: le – *kindly, please*
ruido (m) *noise*
ruidoso/a *noisy*
salud (f) *health*
salvaje *wild*
seco/a *dry*
seguir *to carry on*
seguidamente *then*
seguro (m) *insurance*
semáforo (m) *traffic light*
sencillo/a *simple*
sentido del humor (m) *sense of humour*
sentimiento (m) *feeling*
ser *to be;* a no – *unless;* o lo que sea *or
  whatever*
ser humano (m) *human being*
sesión (f) *show (film)*
sierra (f) *mountain*
siglo (m) *century*
sitio (m) *place*

sobre (m)   *envelope*
sobrevivir   *to survive*
solfeo (m)   *music theory*
solicitar   *to request*
solucionar   *to solve*
sometido/a   *subjected*
subir   *to go up*
suceder   *to happen*
sueldo (m)   *salary;* **– bruto**   *gross salary*
suelo (m)   *floor, ground*
suerte (f)   *luck*
superar   *to be over, to overcome*
talla (f)   *size (clothes)*
tampoco   *neither*
tardar   *to take (time)*
tarea (f)   *work, labour*
tarjeta (f)   *card*
techo (m)   *roof*
tejido (m)   *tissue*
temer   *to fear*
temporada (f)   *season;* **– alta**   *high season*
temprano   *early*
tener en cuenta   *to take into account*
teniente (m)   *lieutenant*
tesoro (m)   *treasure*
tienda (f)   *shop*
Tierra (f)   *Earth*
tirar   *to throw out*
título (m)   *degree, certificate*
título académico (m)   *university degree*
título universitario (m)   *university degree*
toalla (f)   *towel*
tomar una copa   *to have a drink*
tono (m)   *dialling tone*
tono: a –   *in harmony, in tune*

torcer   *to turn*
tos (f)   *cough*
traductor/a   *translator*
traer   *to bring*
tranquilo/a   *quiet*
transbordar   *to change* (transport)
trasladar   *to transfer*
traslado (m)   *transfer*
tratamiento (m)   *treatment*
través: a – de   *through*
usuario (m)   *user*
utilizar   *to use*
vale   *OK*
validez (f)   *validity*
valle (m)   *valley*
varón (m)   *man, male*
vecino/a   *neighbour, resident*
venda (f)   *bandage*
ventaja (f)   *advantage*
vergüenza (f)   *shame*
viaje (m)   *journey, trip*
viajero/a   *travelling;* **(m)** *traveller*
vías respiratorias (f pl)   *respiratory tract*
vidrio (m)   *glass*
vista (f)   *view*
vivienda (f)   *house, housing*
volver   *to go back*
vuelo (m)   *flight*
vuelta (f)   *return*
ya   *already*
ya no   *no longer*
ya que   *as, since, for*
yate (m)   *yacht*
zapatería (f)   *shoe shop*
zapato (m)   *shoe*

English–Spanish vocabulary

Abbreviations	
adj	adjective
adv	adverb
f	feminine
m	masculine
n	noun
pl	plural

about   **acerca de; sobre, a eso de** (time)
abroad   **extranjero** (m)
achieve: to –   **lograr**
access code   **código** (m)
accommodation   **alojamiento** (m)
accompany: to –   **acompañar**
account   **cuenta** (f)
accountancy   **contabilidad** (f)
address: to –   **dirigirse**
addressee   **destinatario/a**
advantage   **ventaja** (f)
advantage: to take –   **aprovechar**
advertisement   **anuncio** (m)
agree: to –   **estar de acuerdo, acordar; contratar**
agreement   **acuerdo** (m)
almost   **casi**
already   **ya**
although   **aunque**
amount   **monto** (m)
ankle   **tobillo** (m)
answer   **respuesta, contestación** (f)
appear: to –   **aparecer, figurar**
apply: to –   **aplicar; solicitar** (e.g. a job)
appointment   **cita** (f)
argument   **pelea** (f)
arrival   **llegada** (f)
article   **artículo** (m)
as   **como, puesto que, dado que**
as . . . as   **tan/tanto como**
ashamed: to be –   **tener vergüenza**
assign: to –   **asignar**
assume: to –   **asumir**
assure: to –   **asegurar**
attendance   **asistencia** (f)
attract: to –   **atraer**
available   **disponible**
avoid: to –   **evitar**

back   **espalda** (f)
background   **antecedentes** (m pl)
baker's   **panadería** (f)
bear: to –   **llevar, soportar**
bed   **cama** (f)
beginning   **comienzo, principio** (m)
besides   **además**
birth   **nacimiento** (m)
bored   **aburrido/a**
boring   **aburrido**
boss   **jefe/a**
boyfriend   **novio**
breathe   **respirar**
brief   **breve**
bring: to –   **traer**
brochure   **folleto** (m)
broken   **roto/a**
build: to –   **construir**
building   **edificio** (m)
bus   **autobús, microbús** (small bus), **camión** (m) (Mexico)
business   **negocio** (m)
cake   **pastel** (m), **tarta** (f), **pastas** (f pl) (small cakes)
car park (m)   **aparcamiento, estacionamiento** (Latin Am.)
card   **tarjeta** (f)
cargo   **cargamento** (m)
carry on: to –   **seguir**
carry out: to –   **efectuar, realizar, llevar a cabo**
cartoons   **dibujos animados** (m pl)
cash: to pay –   **pagar en efectivo**; – point **cajero automático** (m)
century   **siglo** (m)
certain   **seguro/a**
challenge   **desafío** (m)
change: to –   **cambiar; transbordar** (transport)
charge: to –   **cobrar**

chat: to – **charlar, conversar, platicar** (Latin Am.)

check: to – **revisar, checar** (Mexico)

citizen **ciudadano/a**

clean **limpio/a**

clear **claro/a; despejado** (sky)

clerk **administrativo**/a

clinic **consultorio** (m)

clothes **ropa** (f)

cloudless **despejado/a**

coach **autocar, autobús, camión** (m) (Mexico)

coast **costa** (f), **litoral** (m)

code (telephone) **prefijo, código** (m)

colleague **colega** (m/f)

comfort **comodidad** (f)

company (firm) **empresa, compañía, firma** (f)

complain: to – **quejarse**

complaint **queja** (f)

computer **ordenador, computador** (m), **computadora** (f)

confront: to – **enfrentarse a**

congratulations! **enhorabuena** (f)

consumer **consumidor/a**

contaminate: to – **contaminar; contagiar, infectar**

contrary: on the – **por el contrario**

cook: to – **cocinar, guisar**

corner **esquina** (f)

correspondence **correspondencia** (f), **envío** (m)

corridor **pasillo** (m)

cost **valor** (m), **coste** (m), **costo** (m) (Latin Am.), **importe** (m)

cotton **algodón** (m)

cough (n) **tos** (f)

couple **pareja** (f)

course **curso** (m)

course: of – **por supuesto, desde luego, claro**

cover: to – **cubrir**

credit card **tarjeta de crédito** (f)

cuisine **cocina** (f)

daily **diario/a** (adj)

damage **daño** (m)

damage: to – **dañar**

damaging **dañino/a**

dead (n) **fallecido/a**

decrease **disminución** (f)

degree **título** (m) (university)

delay **retraso** (m)

delivery **reparto** (m), **despacho** (m)

demand: to – **exigir**

demanding **exigente**

describe: to – **describir**

deserve: to – **merecer**

despatch (n) **envío** (m)

despatch: to – **enviar, despachar**

despite **pese a**

deterioration **deterioro** (m)

develop: to – **desarrollar**

development **desarrollo** (m)

devote: to – **dedicar**

diary **agenda** (f)

dictate: to – **dictar**

die: to – **morir, fallecer**

discount **descuento** (m)

distribute: to – **repartir**

double room **habitación doble/con cama de matrimonio** (f)

doubt **duda** (f)

doubt: to – **dudar**

drink **copa** (f)

drink: to have a – **tomar una copa**

drive: to – **conducir**

driver **conductor/a, chófer** (m/f)

dry **seco/a**

dry: to – **secar**

duty **deber** (m)

earn: to – **ganar**

electrical household appliances **electrodomésticos** (m, pl)

email **correo electrónico** (m)

email address **correo, (e)mail** (m)

employment **empleo** (m)

engineer **ingeniero/a**

enjoy: to – **disfrutar**

enrol: to – **inscribirse, matricularse**

entrepreneur **empresario/a**

environment **medio ambiente** (m), **entorno** (m)

equipped **dotado/a**

even **incluso**

even though **aunque, a pesar de que**

executive **ejecutivo/a**

exhibition **exposición** (f)

expand: to – **ampliar**

expense **gasto** (m)

face: to – **enfrentar**

facilities **equipamiento** (m); **modalidades** (f pl)

fact **hecho** (m)

fact: in – **de hecho, efectivamente**

factory **fábrica** (f)

famous **famoso/a**

fashion **moda** (f)

favour: to – **favorecer**

fear: to – **temer**

field **campo** (m)

figure **cifra** (f), **número** (m)

film **película** (f), **film** (m)

finish (to have just –ed) **acabar de**

fitting room   **probador** (m)

flat   **piso** (m), **apartamento, departamento** (m)
   (Latin Am.)

flight   **vuelo** (m)

floor   **planta** (f), **piso** (m); **suelo** (m)

fond of   **aficionado/a a**

food   **alimento** (m), **alimentación** (f)

foot   **pie** (m)

football field   **campo de fútbol** (m)

forced   **forzado/a**

foreign, foreigner   **extranjero/a**

foresee: to –   **prever**

form   **boletín** (m), **impreso** (m), **formulario** (m)

free   **libre, desocupado/a**

fridge   **nevera** (f), **frigorífico** (m)

fried   **frito/a**

friends   **amistades** (f pl)

full   **lleno/a, pleno/a**

full board   **pensión completa** (f)

fully   **ampliamente, totalmente,
completamente**

function: to –   **funcionar**

fur   **piel** (f)

get: to –   **conseguir, obtener**

get: to – on well/badly   **llevarse bien/mal**

get off: to –   **bajarse**

gift   **regalo** (m)

girlfriend   **novia** (f)

give: to –   **dar, entregar**

glass   **vaso** (m); **vidrio** (m) (material)

go: to – bankrupt   **arruinarse**

go: to – down   **bajar**

go: to – up   **subir**

graduate   **graduado/a**

grateful: to be –   **agradecer**

greenhouse effect   **efecto invernadero** (m)

gross   **bruto/a**

ground   **suelo** (m)

guest   **invitado/a**

guilty   **culpable** (m f)

habit: to be in the – of **acostumbrar, soler**

hair   **cabello, pelo** (m)

half board   **media pensión** (f)

hand: to – in   **entregar**

happen: to –   **pasar, suceder, ocurrir**

have: to –   **tener, disponer de, contar con**

heal: to –   **sanar**

health   **salud** (f)

help   **ayuda** (f)

hesitate: to –   **dudar**

hide: to –   **esconder**

higher   **superior**

higher education   **estudios superiores** (m pl)

highway   **carretera** (f)

hire: to – a car   **alquilar un coche**

hole   **hueco** (m)

home   **hogar** (m)

hope   **esperanza** (f)

hope: to –   **esperar**

housing   **vivienda** (f)

however   **sin embargo**

human being   **ser humano** (m)

humour: sense of –   **sentido del humor** (m)

hurt: to –   **doler**

hush: to –   **callarse**

ill: to be –   **estar enfermo/a**

ill: to fall –   **enfermarse**

illness   **enfermedad** (f), **afección** (f), **malestar** (m)

impose: to –   **imponer**

improve: to –   **mejorar**

improvement   **mejora** (f)

include: to –   **incluir**

increase   **aumento** (m)

increase: to –   **aumentar**

information brochure   **folleto informativo** (m)

information   **información** (f), **dato** (m)

insurance   **seguro** (m)

interpreter   **intérprete** (m/f)

interview: to –   **entrevistar**

invoice   **factura** (f)

iron: to –   **planchar**

jealousy   **celos** (f pl)

jewellery   **joyas** (f pl); **joyería**

journey   **viaje** (m)

keep: to – fit   **mantenerse en forma**

key   **llave** (f); **clave** (f); **cayo** (m) (geography)

key in: to –   **ingresar**

kiosk   **cabina, caseta** (f), **quiosco** (m)

kitchen: open-plan –   **cocina americana** (f)

labour   **mano de obra** (f)

lack: to –   **faltar**

language   **idioma** (m), **lengua** (f)

last   **último/a**

lawyer   **abogado/a**

lead: to –   **dirigir**

learn: to –   **aprender**

leave: to –   **irse, dejar, abandonar**

leg   **pierna** (f)

leisure   **ocio** (m)

level   **nivel** (m)

lie (n)   **mentira** (f)

lie: to –   **mentir**

lift   **ascensor** (m), **elevador** (Mexico)

likewise   **asimismo, de igual, del mismo modo,
   de la misma manera**

listing   **listado** (m)

longer: no – **ya no**
look after: to – **cuidar, atender**
look for: to – **buscar**
loss **pérdida** (f)
luck **suerte** (f)
luckily **por suerte**
luxury **lujo** (m)
magazine **revista** (f)
main road **carretera** (f)
male **varón** (m)
manufacture: to – **fabricar**
manufacturer **fabricante** (m/f)
marriage **casamiento** (m), **matrimonio** (m)
marry: to – **casarse**
master: to – **dominar**
measure (n) **medida** (f)
member **miembro** (m/f)
misspend: to – **malgastar**
mobile phone **teléfono móvil/portátil** (m),
    celular (Latin Am.) (m)
mountain **sierra** (f), **montaña** (f)
move: to – house **mudarse**
muscle **músculo** (m)
nearby **cercano/a**
necessary: to be – **ser necesario, hacer falta**
neighbour **vecino/a**
neighbourhood **barrio** (m)
neither **tampoco**
nevertheless **no obstante**
nut **nuez** (f)
OK **vale, de acuerdo**
often **a menudo**
oil **petróleo** (m); **aceite** (m) (cooking and
    car oil)
online **en línea**
optional **facultativo/a**
owner **propietario/a**
ozone layer **capa de ozono** (f)
pain **dolor** (m)
paint: to – **pintar**
painting **pintura** (f)
parcel service **paquetería** (f)
party **fiesta** (f); **partido** (m) (politics)
pass away: to – **fallecer**
pay: to – **pagar**
performance **función** (f)
perhaps **a lo mejor, tal vez, quizá(s)**
pick up: to – **pasar a buscar, recoger**
pill **pastilla** (f), **tableta** (f), **píldora** (f)
plan: to – **planear, programar**
platform **andén** (m)
player **jugador/a**
please: to find pleasant **agradrar**

point to: to – **apuntar**
political party **partido político** (m)
pollution **contaminación** (f)
post office **(oficina de) correos** (f)
P. O. box **apartado postal** (m)
post **puesto** (job) (m); **correo** (mail) (m)
power **potencia** (f)
pray: to – **regar**
prejudice **prejuicio** (m)
present: to give a – **regalar, hacer un regalo**
prevail: to – **imponerse**
private **privado/a**
progress **progreso** (m), **avance** (m)
promote: to – **promover**
protect: to – **proteger**
provide: to – **proporcionar, proveer**
pulse **leguminosa** (f)
purely **netamente, puramente**
quality **calidad** (f)
quick **rápido/a, expedito/a**
quiet **tranquilo/a**
raise: to – **criar**
rate **índice** (m)
rather **más bien**
reach: to – **alcanzar**
realize: to – **darse cuenta**
reasonable **razonable; módico/a** (e.g. price)
receipt **factura** (f), **recibo** (m)
refund **devolución** (f)
register: to – **inscribirse, matricularse**
registered **certificado/a**
regrettably **lamentablemente,
    desgraciadamente**
rejoice: to – **alegrarse**
relax: to – **relajarse**
remain: to – **quedar**
remember: to –' **recordar**
rent: to – **alquilar, rentar** (Mexico)
representative **representante** (m/f)
request: to – **solicitar, pedir**
research **investigación** (f)
resident **vecino/a; residente** (m/f)
responsible: to be – for **encargarse de**
rest **descanso** (m)
return **regreso** (m), **vuelta** (f)
return: to – **volver, regresar; devolver** (to give
    back)
right now **ahora mismo, inmediatamente,
    enseguida**
road **camino** (m)
roof **techo** (m)
rubbish **basura** (f)
ruin: to – **arruinar**

salary **sueldo, salario** (m)

save: to – **ahorrar**

school age **edad escolar** (f)

school children **escolares** (m pl)

school **colegio** (m), **escuela** (f)

science **ciencia** (f)

screen **pantalla** (f)

search **búsqueda** (f)

season **estación** (f); **temporada** (f) (period)

seat **asiento** (m); **plaza** (f) (e.g. on a plane)

send: to – **enviar, mandar**

sender **remitente** (m f)

sew: to – **coser**

shame **vergüenza** (f)

share: to – **compartir**

shoe shop **zapatería** (f)

shoe **zapato** (m)

shop **tienda** (f)

shopping: to do the – **hacer la compra/las compras**

show **sesión** (f) (cinema), **función** (f)

show: to – **mostrar, enseñar**; (film) **poner, dar** (Latin Am.)

shower: to – **ducharse**

since **ya que, puesto que; desde** (from)

single room **habitación individual/sencilla** (f)

sink: to – **hundir**

size **tamaño** (m); **talla** (f) (clothing)

slow **lento/a**

so **entonces; tan**

solve: to – **solucionar**

specialist **especialista** (m/f)

speedy **expedito/a, rápido/a**

spite: in – of **a pesar de, pese a**

sport **deporte** (m); **deportivo/a** (adj)

sports centre **polideportivo** (m)

stable **estacionario/a**

stamp **sello** (m), **estampilla** (f) (Latin Am.)

start: to – **empezar, comenzar, poner en marcha**

stay: to – **quedarse**

stink: to – **apestar**

stop **parada** (f), **paradero** (m) (Latin Am.)

stop: to – **parar, detener, atajar**

strict **estricto/a**

struggle **lucha** (f)

study (n) **estudio**

subway **paso subterráneo** (m)

success **éxito** (m)

suitcase **maleta, valija** (Argentina) (f)

sun cream **bronceador** (m)

supermarket **almacén** (m)

survey **encuesta** (f)

survive: to – **sobrevivir**

swim: to – **nadar**

swimming pool **piscina** (f), **alberca** (f) (Mexico); **pileta** (Argentina) (f)

swimming **natación** (f)

swimming costume **bañador** (m)

swollen **hinchado/a**

table **mesa** (f)

take: to – time **tardar**

tissue **tejido** (m)

tax **impuesto** (m)

tell: to – **contar, decir**

tendency **tendencia, propensión** (f)

then **entonces, después, seguidamente**

though **aunque**

threat **amenaza** (f)

through **mediante; a través de, por**

throw out: to – **tirar**

thus **así, de esta manera/este modo**

tide **marea** (f)

time: spare – **tiempo libre** (m)

timetable **horario** (m)

tired **cansado/a**

tissue **tejido** (m)

toast **tostadas** (f pl), **pan tostado** (m) (Mexico)

too much **demasiado** (adv)

towel **toalla** (f)

traffic light **semáforo** (m)

training **formación** (f)

transfer **traslado** (m)

translator **traductor/a**

traveller **viajero/a**

traveller's cheque **cheque** (m) **de viaje/de viajero**

treasure **tesoro** (m)

treatment **tratamiento** (m)

trip **viaje** (m)

trouble **molestia** (f)

turn: to – **torcer, girar, doblar**

turn: to be one's – **tocar a uno/a**

understand: to – **comprender, entender**

unequal **desigual**

unfortunately **desgraciadamente, desafortunadamente**

use: to – **usar, utilizar**

user **usuario/a**

validity **validez** (f)

valley **valle** (m)

varied **variado/a, amplio/a**

view **vista** (f)

walk: to go for a – **dar un paseo**

wash: to – **lavar, lavarse**

waste: to – **perder**

wear: to – **llevar, usar**
website **página web** (f)
while **rato, momento** (m)
whilst **mientras**
wild **salvaje** (m f)
win: to – **ganar**
wonder **maravilla** (f)
wonder: to – **preguntarse**
wonderful **maravilloso/a; estupendo/a**
work **trabajo** (m), **tarea** (f)

work: to – **trabajar; funcionar**
worker **trabajador/a**
working hours **horario de trabajo** (m)
working population **población activa** (f)
world **mundo** (m)
worth: to be – it **merecer/valer la pena**
writer **escritor/a**
yacht **yate** (m)
young **joven**

Grammar index

A reference like 11.2 indicates where a grammar point is presented. The first number points to the Unit and the second number to the Language discovery subsection within that unit.

Letters point to the relevant unit section, i.e. 1.C3 refers to Unit 1, Conversation 3, 5.NE refers to Unit 5, New expressions, 7.P3 refers to Unit 7, Practice, exercise 3.

"Global scale" of the Common European Framework of Reference for Languages: learning, teaching, assessment (CEFR)

Advanced	**CEFR LEVEL C2**	Can understand with ease virtually everything heard or read. Can summarise information from different spoken and written sources, reconstructing arguments and accounts in a coherent presentation. Can express him/herself spontaneously, very fluently and precisely, differentiating finer shades of meaning even in more complex situations.
Advanced	**CEFR LEVEL C1**	Can understand a wide range of demanding, longer texts, and recognise implicit meaning. Can express him/herself fluently and spontaneously without much obvious searching for expressions. Can use language flexibly and effectively for social, academic and professional purposes. Can produce clear, well-structured, detailed text on complex subjects, showing controlled use of organisational patterns, connectors and cohesive devices.
Intermediate	**CEFR LEVEL B2 (A Level)**	Can understand the main ideas of complex text on both concrete and abstract topics, including technical discussions in his/her field of specialisation. Can interact with a degree of fluency and spontaneity that makes regular interaction with native speakers quite possible without strain for either party. Can produce clear, detailed text on a wide range of subjects and explain a viewpoint on a topical issue giving the advantages and disadvantages of various options.
Intermediate	**CEFR LEVEL B1 (Higher GCSE)**	Can understand the main points of clear standard input on familiar matters regularly encountered in work, school, leisure, etc. Can deal with most situations likely to arise whilst travelling in an area where the language is spoken. Can produce simple connected text on topics which are familiar or of personal interest. Can describe experiences and events, dreams, hopes and ambitions and briefly give reasons and explanations for opinions and plans.
Beginner	**CEFR LEVEL A2: (Foundation GCSE)**	Can understand sentences and frequently used expressions related to areas of most immediate relevance (e.g. very basic personal and family information, shopping, local geography, employment). Can communicate in simple and routine tasks requiring a simple and direct exchange of information on familiar and routine matters. Can describe in simple terms aspects of his/her background, immediate environment and matters in areas of immediate need.
Beginner	**CEFR LEVEL A1**	Can understand and use familiar everyday expressions and very basic phrases aimed at the satisfaction of needs of a concrete type. Can introduce him/herself and others and can ask and answer questions about personal details such as where he/she lives, people he/she knows and things he/she has. Can interact in a simple way provided the other person talks slowly and clearly and is prepared to help.